MOTORWAY SERVICES ARE BORING —

motorways are boring – but they're a necessary and convenient evil when you need to break the journey.

However, we think there's a lot more to good pit stops than strong coffee and the loo. The nation's highways and byways take us through some beautiful countryside. They skim fabulous towns and villages unseen through the crash barrier, and equally wonderful eateries.

Between us, we've hunted out original, quirky and soothing places to stop within easy reach of arterial routes. Places that we – aged thirty-something and seventy-something – think will appeal to like-minded people, whether you're travelling with friends, meeting family or riding solo.

For us, that means good-quality, preferably local food from makers and growers, space for children and pets to let off steam, fascinating attractions and knockout views, no more than 15 minutes' drive from a junction. It's places with conscience that care about the provenance of their ingredients and their impact on the environment. It's eating and resting better and supporting local businesses without adding much to overall journey time. It may even mean transforming your journey.

The notion of 'special' has long been at the heart of Alastair Sawday's guides, but we know that it's highly subjective. We recognise that one person's idea of special is not necessarily another's, so do expect variety.

These venues have been included simply because we like them and we do our best in the text to highlight why. Our opinions and tastes are ours alone and we hope you will share them. Do remember that the information in this book is a snapshot in time and things may have changed since we published it (we hope for the better).

You'll find a 'how to' guide at the back of the book which will guide you through the maps, symbols and information provided.

Third edition
Copyright © 2019
Printslinger Co. Ltd
Published in November 2019
ISBN-13: 978-1-906136-96-3

Printslinger Ltd,
c/o Alastair Sawday Publishing Ltd
Merchants House, Wapping Road,
Bristol BS1 4RW

SERIES EDITOR:
Alastair Sawday

EDITOR:
Laura Collacott

PAGE LAYOUT & PRINT PRODUCTION:
Jules Richardson

SUB-EDITOR:
Emily Walmsley

DESIGN:
Ryan Thomas

RESEARCHERS:
Ross Bryant, Rachel Williams, Helena Kaill

PRINTING:
Printed in England by Pureprint

SALES:
Signature Book Representation (UK) Ltd
+44 (0)845 862 1730
sales@signaturebooksuk.com

DISTRIBUTION:
Central Books Ltd
+44 (0)20 8525 8800
orders@centralbooks.com

Photo credits:
Cover © Iris Thorsteinsdottir iristhors.com
p.6 © Iris Thorsteinsdottir iristhors.com
p.14 © Derek Beattie Images/Shutterstock.com
p.70 © Steve Silver Smith/Shutterstock.com
p. 116 © Alexander Glen/Shutterstock.com
p.130 © DaBrick/Shutterstock.com
p.154 © Richard Bowden/Shutterstock.com
p.206 © Theo Duijkers/Shutterstock.com

p.228 © Aleksey Dushutin/Shutterstock.com
p.262 © Steven Musgrove/Shutterstock.com
p.295 © Paul Nash/Shutterstock.com
p.328 © Konstantin Tronin/Shutterstock.com
p.364 © Paul Cowan/Shutterstock.com
p.404 © Richard O'Donoghue/Shutterstock.com
p.434 © Shaiith/Shutterstock.com

Sawday's

The EXTRA M1LE

Delicious Alternatives to Motorway Services

The CONTENTS

Travelling well
with the Extra Mile

I spent a week in France with a colleague a while ago; she didn't trust my map reading so brought her Sat Nav along. The two systems clashed time and again. I would slip off the main road to enjoy a view, a quiet village or a dip in a river. The Sat Nav was having none of it. It was a fun-killer hectoring me - without humour. Worse still: I occasionally made a mistake; it didn't! When we returned home my colleague had little idea where she had been or the shape of her journey, while I had been exploring a new landscape, allowing Normandy to take a new and exhilarating shape in my brain. It is a region of unending surprises, as most are, and my maps allowed me to explore and enjoy them.

This wonderful guide reveals delights typically discovered by map users, but mobile phones definitely help to find our places. We encourage you to make a risk-free escape from the beaten track – all in the name of fun, variety and infinitely better food. Not to mention peace of mind, support for local food producers and independent businesses, and – of course – that strange uplift you feel when you have escaped the clutches of those dreadful service stations.

I am happy to rail against them. They are useful, but they are also expensive, soulless, vulgar, commercial and heartless. They peddle trash to a desperate public disorientated by long journeys, traffic jams, delays and diversions. They lower the spirits where The Extra Mile raises them, depress visitors with rapid-and-vapid plastic 'consumer experiences' rather than human contact and warmth. The food is predictable (another cup of weak coffee anyone, with a production line flapjack?), their lavatories process you rather than satisfy you, the crinkling sound of the unwrapping of biscuits dulls the ear. In fact you, the customer, are often processed and ejected by the pressure of numbers.

Why the modern obsession with getting from A to B as quickly as possible, as if the country between them is null and void, a mere filling between the places that matter? Look at a map and you see that you will be passing countless opportunities to lift your day, turn the journey into something memorable and delightful. We have done much of the work for you, finding cafés that feed both body and soul, farm shops where you can stock up with home-grown (even organic) produce, pubs whose landlords are genuinely pleased to see you. There are houses of ravishing beauty, garden centres, charitable projects keen to earn a few quid by feeding and watering you and your children – and even your pets.

These special places, typically 'Sawday' in their variety and capacity to delight, have been seen and chosen just to make your journeys special – rather than a chore. Ignore them at your peril, for without them your journey may be pure tedium, a functional act, time-spending rather than pleasure-seeking. It could be so much more. You could, for example, enjoy a recently re-opened private garden and then settle for a tea and cake in the unusual and delightful café – run by volunteers from the village. Or you might find yourself in the heart of a working farm, the lunch just emerged from the farm kitchen and the farm cats lurking hungrily at your feet.

This is the beginning of a new age, an age of quickening awareness of the state of the planet and our role in its threatened demise. Food production contributes at least 10% of the harm our crazy system does to our own environment. So it is with real delight that we offer you these places and the wonderful people who run them. Your food miles will be lower, the production less harmful – even beneficial – and you will be part of a solution rather than part of the problem. Strong stuff, I know, but we all now understand the state we are in. The Extra Mile wants to be part of the change we want to see.

Alastair Sawday
GOES THE EXTRA MILE

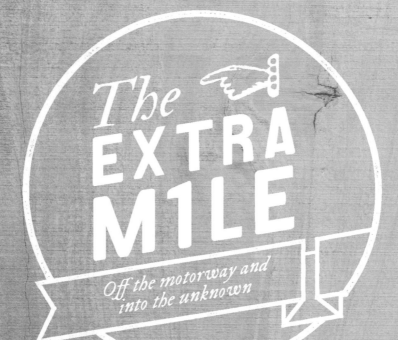

The EXTRA M1LE

Off the motorway and into the unknown

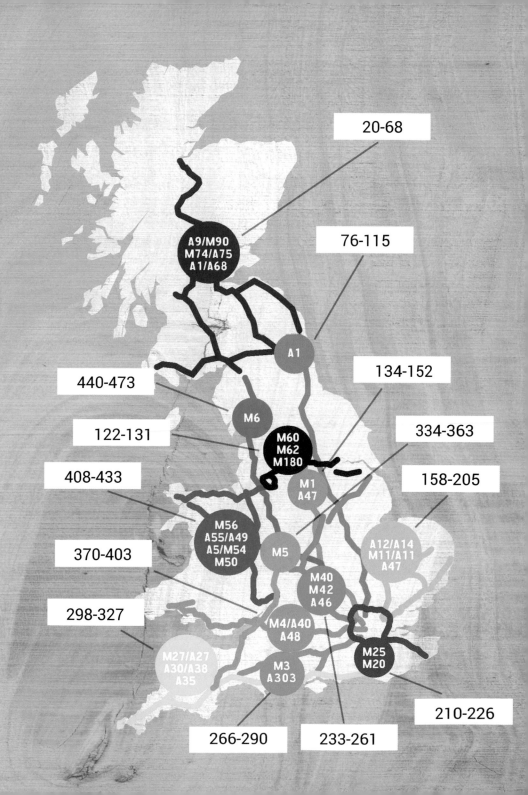

Pip's Railway Carriage

Vegetarian and vegan

Good for your health and good for the planet, more and more people have turned to a plant-based diet and restaurants have stepped up to the mark with creative and delicious options. Here are our favourites if you're shunning meat.

1. THE WALNUT TREE

Jan Wise, way ahead of the curve, has been impressing vegetarians and carnivores alike with her creative plant-based dishes for a decade. Chefs know their flavours inside out and aren't afraid to experiment with ingredients from around the world.

PAGE 188

2. PIP'S RAILWAY CARRIAGE

Many of the dishes here are led by what can be harvested from the fields, which means abundant organic salads in summer, and warming comfort food with a twist in the colder months, much of it vegetarian.

PAGE 287

3. THRIVE

Owner Amanda set up Thrive to offer both a space for well-being classes (she's a yoga teacher) and a place to share her love of vegan and vegetarian food. Toasted mozzarella and pesto sandwiches are served alongside tempting pancake stacks, slices of cake (try the vegan carrot) and bowls of imaginative salads.

PAGE 271

4. CROSS LANES ORGANIC FARM

A beacon of sustainability, Cross Lanes Organic Farm serves a wide range of delicious meals using organic, fresh, wild, local and home-grown ingredients, and that respect for Mother Earth translates into some sterling vegetarian options.

PAGE 84

5. THE FOLD

The eco-conscious will adore The Fold, a community enterprise on a rambling organic farm in the Worcestershire countryside with the gentle mission of encouraging sustainable living and escaping the commercial norm. Herbivores are well catered for with an excellent range of vegan and vegetarian soups, tarts,salads and freshly baked traybakes and scones.

PAGE 335

6. THE MORINGA TREE

As is fitting for a place that celebrates coffee and plants, the Moringa Tree serves some excellent vegetarian dishes despite its dinky size, including excellent Sri Lankan curries.

PAGE 167

Speyside Centre

For a leg stretch

The Extra Mile is not just for escaping mediocre services and limp pasties, but also for helping you explore more and get the most out of your journey. Unfurl yourself from the car and glimpse some of the UK's beautiful scenery by combining a walk with a stop at one of these spots.

1. DARSHAM NURSERIES

Step out of the car after a long journey and you'll instantly be revived by the scents of roses and other shrubs sold at Darsham Nurseries. Refuel in the stylish café then stretch your legs at the Darsham Marshes nature reserve for a snapshot of unspoilt Suffolk.

PAGE 185

2. THE RIVER BARN

Much of the produce at the fantastic River Barn is sourced from the Fonthill Estate, so if you've time to spare it's worth stopping to take a turn in the grounds and explore the Nadder Valley. Walks of varying length take in the extravagant country mansion, ruins of the infamous Fonthill Abbey (which collapsed not long after being built) and the tranquil lake.

PAGE 275

3. WOTTON FARM SHOP

For spectacular views from the edge of the Cotswolds, stop at Wotton Hill. The route between here and the North Nibley Monument is easy to follow and offers an uplifting panorama over the Severn Valley, as well as working up an appetite for the food at Wotton Farm Shop.

PAGE 341

4. THE FLEECE INN

The Wyresdale Lakes were formed when the pits that supplied the gravel used to build the M6 were abandoned, and today the route between them and Scorton, at the edge of the Forest of Bowland, makes an excellent place to work up a hunger before dining at the welcoming Fleece Inn.

PAGE 454

5. FFIN Y PARC

It's impossible to miss the grandeur of Snowdonia National Park from Ffin y Parc, so get outside and lap some of it up at the neighbouring section, Gwydir Forest Parks. The Llyn Parc route follows an old miner's path from Pont-y-Pair and has wonderful views of the Conwy Valley.

PAGE 412

6. SPEYSIDE CENTRE

There are four official long-distance routes in Scotland, and the Speyside Way tracks the river Spey linking the Grampian Mountains with the Moray coast. You can sample a section of its 65 miles before tucking into refreshments at the bucolic Speyside Centre while watching out for red squirrels.

PAGE 20

Old Hall Farm

OUR TOP 6 FOR
Meeting the animals

When the kids are playing up in the back and no amount of bribery will appease them, break the journey and distract them with an up-close encounter with some animals.

1. CRAIGIE'S FARM DELI

Gather some eggs, meet the piglets (new arrivals are announced via the Facebook page), or watch the pygmy goats gambolling; there are always animals to meet at Craigie's on your way to the brilliant play area.

PAGE 36

2. LOW SIZERGH BARN

Where else can you watch cows being milked as you enjoy a cream tea? A farm trail loops around the pond, woodland and fields too, and includes fairy doors for little ones to spot, so don your wellies and work up an appetite.

PAGE 451

3. WELLINGTON FARM SHOP

The farm shop is ringed with paddocks - home to rare breed sheep, pigs and cows - and there's a fantastic tree house play area where the children can let off steam.

PAGE 373

4. THORNHILL FARM SHOP

Kids will love the purpose-built Pets Paddock at Thornhill Farm Shop where they can meet the resident animals, from alpacas to pigs, ducks to guinea pigs, and at Christmas they're brought into the barn for a nativity extravaganza!

PAGE 389

5. DANIEL FARM

Geese flap, goats bleat, pigs snuffle and alpacas glare in the fields outside Daniel Farm, making this an animal lover's paradise.

PAGE 68

6. OLD HALL FARM

Arrive early and you can watch – even help! – the beautiful Jersey cows being milked in this nurturing microdairy. And when the girls are back in the field, you can spot the peacocks at their various perches around the farm, and sometimes in the café!

PAGE 191

SCOTLAND
& THE BORDERS
A9, M9, M90, A1, A68, M74, A75, A69

A Highland fling through the heart of Scotland

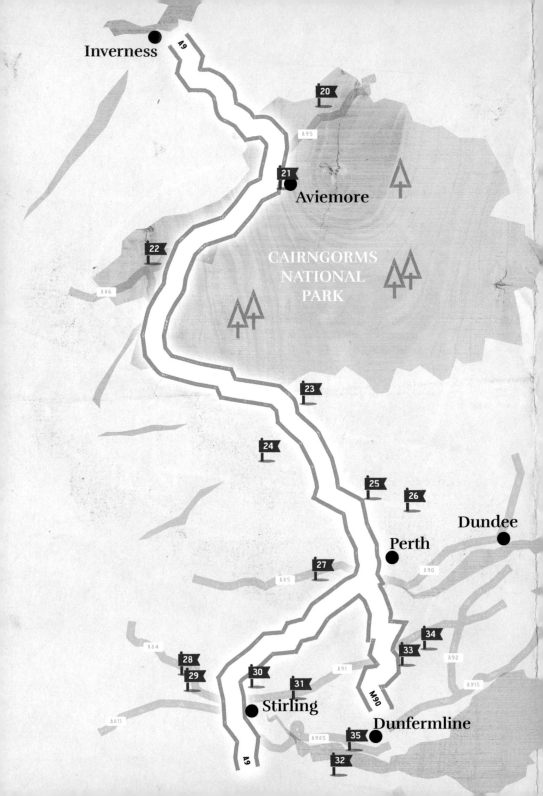

SCOTLAND & THE BORDERS

M90 / A9

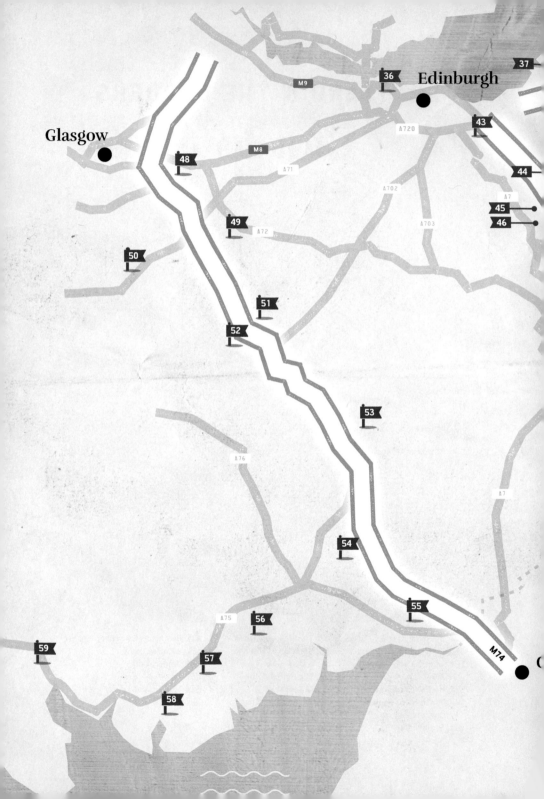

SCOTLAND & THE BORDERS

M74 / A68 / A1

Berwick-upon-Tweed

36 Craigie's Farm Deli	48 Hazel's Butterfly Bakery
37 Fenton Barns Café & Shop	49 Silver Birch
39 Steampunk Coffee	50 Alexander Taylor Bakery & Deli
40 Drift	51 Cairn Lodge Services
41 The Crown and Kitchen	52 The Scrib Tree
42 The Loft Café & Bakery	53 Brodies of Moffat
43 Restoration Yard	54 Pink Flamingo Vintage Tea Room
44 Soutra Coffee House	55 The Maltings Coffee Shop
45 The Spotty Dog	56 Loch Arthur Camphill Community Farm Shop
46 Cloudhouse Café-Gallery	
47 The Mainstreet Trading Company	

57 Streetlights Coffee House
58 Station House
59 Tree Bar & Café
60 Bite
62 House of Meg
63 Jill's Catering Tea Room
64 The Station Coffee House
65 The Angel of Corbridge
66 The Hearth
67 The Coffee Tree
68 Daniel Farm

GARDEN CENTRE
Speyside Centre
JUNCTION: A95; 9 MINUTES

A local landmark, the Speyside Centre is tucked among the boughs of a pine forest at the edge of the Cairngorms. It was nearly destroyed by a fire four years ago but, undaunted, the family have shuffled the buildings around to accommodate the garden centre, antiques shop and café while work is completed on a glittering new building (due to open in autumn 2019).

The plant selection is excellent, the antiques well worth a rummage and the playground ideal for little ones to burn off some energy. There's something for everyone here – even before you've eaten.

Grandad's old workshop has been colonised by the tearoom, famous for its clootie dumplings (a spiced fruit pudding, for the uninitiated), which can also be bought to take away. The lunches are equally good: be sure to have a slice of carrot cake. Grab a table on the terrace (known here as the 'Sitooterie') to watch the red squirrels, butterflies and birds drift around as you eat. Magical.

Opening hours
Mon-Sat 9am-5pm
Sun 10am-4pm

Speyside Centre, Skye of Curr, Dulnain Bridge PH26 3PA
WWW.HEATHERCENTRE.COM   01479 851359

FARM SHOP

Rothiemurchus Centre

JUNCTION: AVIEMORE; 4 MINUTES

The rambling Rothiemurchus Estate covers one of the largest remaining areas of ancient Caledonian pine forest, which once enveloped the whole of Scotland. Stretching from the River Spey to the Cairngorm Mountains, it's a precious pocket of wildlife and sweeping scenery.

It's been under the stewardship of the Grant family since the 16th century, and they encourage visitors to come and enjoy the landscape. Take a pony trek, fish the loch, try an all-terrain Segway, hire bikes or enjoy an easy stroll to Loch an Eilein, voted the UK's best picnic spot – keep your eyes peeled for red squirrels, osprey and turkey-like capercaillies as you go.

And if it's a picnic you're after, look no further than the fantastic farm shop and Druie Café. It's stuffed with produce from the estate and surrounding area – Highland beef, heather honey, smoked salmon sandwiches, homemade fudge and artisan cheeses – while the bright café does an excellent line in light lunches, fluffy cakes and locally roasted coffee.

Opening hours
Mon-Sun 9.30am-5pm

Rothiemurchus Centre, Rothiemurchus Centre, Rothiemurchus PH22 1QH
WWW.ROTHIEMURCHUS.NET   01479 812345

CAFÉ-SHOP-GALLERY

Laggan Coffee Bothy & Gallery

JUNCTION: DALWHINNIE; 10 MINUTES

You're not imagining things if you hear the squawk of a parrot as you walk into Laggan Coffee Bothy and Gallery: Kara the African grey is a popular resident and loves to entertain visitors to the café, gallery and gift shop. You'll get also a warm welcome from owners Stuart and Gordon who stock a beautiful range of Scottish gifts. Bread and croissants are baked fresh daily, while the excellent coffee will set you up for any onward drive. Better still, settle by the wood burner and enjoy lunch as you admire the fantastic local photographs taken by Stuart, while Kara entertains you with her vocabulary.

The handsome, gabled shop (featured in the hit TV series 'Monarch of the Glen') stands on a bend in the road where Laggan Bridge crosses the River Spey. Visitors are often on their way to Fort William or Aviemore but there's plenty to divert you here at the edge of the Cairngorms, particularly the Corrieyairack Pass, which leads across the Monadhliath Mountains.

Opening hours
Mon, Tues, Thurs, Fri 8am-5pm
Sat 9am-5pm (Sun 9.30am)
Seasonal opening hours apply – please check

Laggan Coffee Bothy & Gallery, Laggan Bridge, Laggan PH20 1AH
WWW.LAGGANSTORES.CO.UK   01528 544737

Hettie's Tearooms

JUNCTION: PITLOCHRY; 2 MINUTES

Clare named her tearooms after her daughter but was inspired by her granny, Eunice, to honour the family talent for baking and a blether (chat, for the non-natives). Behind the enticing turquoise and pink front, the dog-friendly café rings with the bustle of busy waitresses and happy chatter, especially from twinkly eyed, good-humoured Clare. Hettie's Loose Leaf Teas – all 31 flavours – are blended in-house and have become so popular they're now shipped all over the world. Newer on the scene is the coffee, roasted on the premises in Donnie the roaster, this time named after grandad.

You can lunch on sandwiches (served with pink coleslaw), salads and jacket potatoes, but it's the cake that people really come for. Try the signature triple-layer cake or strawberry tart and be warned that if you let kids loose on the eye-widening ice cream selection, you'll need to take them for a riverside walk (where you can also find free parking) before piling them back in the car.

Opening hours
Mon-Sun 9am-7pm

Hettie's Tearooms, 93-95 Atholl Road, Pitlochry PH16 5AB
WWW.HETTIESTEAS.CO.UK   01796 473991

CHOCOLATE HOUSE-EXHIBITION-SHOP

Iain Burnett Highland Chocolatier

JUNCTION: A827; 7 MINUTES

Pull in here if you're hankering after a hot chocolate on your way through Scotland. Iain Burnett has won international awards for his chocolates, notably his smooth-as-silk Velvet Truffles, and this is his factory. You can peer into the workshop to watch the team blend Perthshire cream with cocoa imported from São Tomé to make the sensational (if pricey) chocolates in the shop.

Service in the tartan chocolate lounge is slick, friendly and slightly formal (but don't let that put you off). Chocolate is the star here so expect to gorge yourself on the good stuff. The thick hot chocolate – an espresso-cup full of molten Velvet Truffles – is a regular crowd pleaser, and the chocolate tastings are unmissable: an audio tour from Iain himself will guide you through a flight of gourmet chocolates or the secret art of the chocolatier.

Even non-chocolate lovers will enjoy getting off the highway to drink in the rural scenery, the sweep of the River Tay and the forest carpeting the hills behind.

Opening hours
Mon-Sun 10am-5pm
(11am-4pm Jan-Mar)

Iain Burnett Highland Chocolatier, Grandtully PH9 0PL
WWW.HIGHLANDCHOCOLATIER.COM   01887 840775

Scottish Deli

JUNCTION: A923; 1 MINUTE

A grocer's shop has stood on this spot since 1809 when the Duke of Atholl demanded a village store be built for the new crossroads. Today, behind the elegant façade and preserved signage, the shelves and counters of the Scottish Deli are crowded with an enormous array of artisan products, from oatcakes to smoked meats, haggis, chutneys and an enviable cheese selection. They are carefully selected by owners Sarah and Simon and supplied by producers nearby, wherever the quality is high enough: the smoked salmon and preserves scoop the prize for lowest food miles, made just 30 metres down the road.

Grab a spot at one of the handful of convivial tables scattered through the shop to savour gourmet sandwiches, salads and soups at lunch or the delicious tapas menu in the evening, which you can wash down with a glass of wine. Service is relaxed and friendly, lingering is encouraged, and dogs and children are welcome.

Opening hours
Mon-Sun 9.30am-6pm; 6.30pm-10.30pm
(Sat 9am; Sun 10am)

Scottish Deli, 1 Atholl Street, Dunkeld PH8 0AR
WWW.SCOTTISH-DELI.CO.UK   01350 728028

PUB

The Meikleour Arms

JUNCTION: STANLEY; 16 MINUTES

Our aim is to search out the best places to stop within 15 minutes of motorways and main roads, but occasionally a place is so special we allow our self-imposed limit a little flex – the Meikleour Arms is one such place.

Once a coaching inn in the absurdly pretty village of Meikleour, a convenient stop on the journey between Inverness and Edinburgh, the country pub has been revamped into a gorgeous boutique hotel. The style reflects the owners' Franco-Scottish heritage, with heavy drapes and floral wallpapers against slate floors and stone walls.

Much of the food in the restaurant comes from the estate – vegetables and herbs grown pesticide-free in the walled garden, scallops collected by hand on the west coast and venison from the nearby forest. Non-drivers can also sample some quirky finds from the lesser-known vineyards of Bordeaux.

The village grew to notoriety in 1966 for its impressive Meikleour Hedge, officially the tallest and longest on earth, so take a quick look if you're stopping here.

Opening hours
Mon-Sun 10am-11pm

The Meikleour Arms, Meikleour PH2 6EB
WWW.MEIKLEOURARMS.CO.UK   01250 883206

Gloagburn Farm Shop & Coffee Shop

JUNCTION: TIBBERMORE; 4 MINUTES

Skirt the duck pond at the entrance to Alison and Ian's working farm to find this solid, timber-clad farm shop. Set in the gently rolling hills of Perthshire, its view is maximised for those inside by the stunning floor-to-ceiling windows. The shop is a treasure trove, warmly lit by woven wicker lights. Browse the range of regional produce, including the farm's own beef and rare breed pork, eggs, jams, gingerbread, oats and turnips, as well as artisan products such as pottery, art prints, scented candles and homewares. Everything stocked here must pass the family's 'tried and tasted' test before reaching the shelves.

The café and adjoining conservatory are strung with festoon lights and brimming with geraniums. In summer, the glass doors are flung open to let the breeze in, while in winter the wood burner is stoked up to keep the cold at bay. Food is freshly made in the kitchen, from soups and burgers to cheese soufflés and gooseberry tarts. Don't miss the Orkney fudge cheesecake.

Opening hours
Mon-Sun 8.30am-5.30pm

Gloagburn Farm Shop & Coffee Shop, Tibbermore, Perth PH1 1QL
WWW.GLOAGBURNFARMSHOP.CO.UK   01738 840 864

CAFÉ

The Coffee Bothy at Deanston

JUNCTION: A820; 6 MINUTES

Set on the banks of the River Teith, the Deanston Distillery occupies an imposing former cotton mill whose cool, humid weaving shed also proved perfect for ageing organic malt whiskey. The waters that once drove the mill's wheel still power the building today thanks to upstream turbines. It's worth lingering for a tour of the traditional whiskey making methods (it's the national drink after all), especially the chocolate pairing.

Whiskey drinker or not, you should stop in at the Coffee Bothy. Sturdy wooden furniture and green bistro lighting create a warm atmosphere, the food is reliably tasty (try the lentil and haggis soup) and the coffee is great. It's an outpost of the excellent Blairmains Farm Shop down the road and a popular haunt for locals as much as distillery visitors. Old photographs lining the wooden shelves on the wall show the history of the mill. There's plenty of free parking in the distillery car park, and you can buy a bottle of whiskey in the shop for when your journey's over.

Opening hours
Mon-Sun 10am-4.30pm

The Coffee Bothy at Deanston, Deanston Distillery Visitor Centre, Doune FK16 6AG
WWW.DEANSTONMALT.COM/VISIT-US/#COFFEE   01786 843 010

Smiddy Farm Shop, Butchery, Deli & Café

JUNCTION: 10; 5 MINUTES

The spacious Smiddy Farm Shop stands on the site of the old village blacksmith's, now transformed into a tantalising local food hub stocking produce from all over Scotland. Browse the shelves for Scottish gifts or artisan ceramics and fill your basket with treats from the deli counter and butchery. The meat is all reared down the road and the game is from the surrounding countryside. Don't leave without picking up a Smiddy's steak pie and some of their home-cured bacon.

In the airy beamed café chefs whip those same ingredients up into delicious dishes (including an outstanding bacon roll). It's busy but staff are smiley and efficient. Grab a pew at the breakfast bar or pull up one of the zingy orange chairs to tuck into panini stuffed with Stornoway black pudding, mature Cheddar and tomato relish, or some homemade banoffee pie or a finger-licking peanut butter slice with a flat white. Don't miss the loos before you head on your way – visitors always remark on the spectacular view.

Opening hours
Mon–Sun 9am-5pm

Smiddy Farm Shop, Butchery, Deli & Café, Blair Drummond, by Stirling FK9 4UY
WWW.BLAIRDRUMMONDSMIDDY.CO.UK   01786 235 024

TEA ROOM

Another Tilly Tearoom

JUNCTION: 11; 4 MINUTES

The magnificent 13th-century cathedral is reason alone for stopping in Dunblane, a picturesque town on the Allan Water river filled with charming architecture. But it's also home to Scotland's oldest private library, which has some 4,500 books dating as far back as 1500, as well as Andy Murray's famous golden postbox.

Wander the pretty streets before refuelling at the comforting Another Tilly Tearoom – recently voted 'Customer's Most Wanted Café' in Scotland – where sensational homebaking is the order of the day. Red gingham cloths dress the tables, to which plates of scrambled eggs on toast, homemade panini, and bowls of lentil soup and soda bread are ferried. Cakes are a real highlight – try a slice of hummingbird cake, a fresh meringue or gluten-free millionaire's shortbread – and the fabulous cooked breakfasts are served all day. Tea is served in vintage china cups from pots warmed by cosies made from recycled jumpers. The Belgian hot chocolate will transform a cold rainy day.

Opening hours
Mon–Sat 9am-4pm
Sun 10am-4pm

Another Tilly Tearoom, 87 High Street, Dunblane FK15 0ER
WWW.TILLYTEAROOM.CO.UK   01786 832968

Blairmains Farm Shop & Coffee Bothy

JUNCTION: 10; 11 MINUTES

Backed by the gorse-strewn slopes of the Ochil Hills and the soaring gothic tower of the Wallace Monument, the unassuming exterior of Blairmains Farm Shop & Coffee Bothy belies the delights within.

Six generations of the Logan family farmed here, before opening a café and farm shop in 2001 (one of Scotland's first). It quickly established itself with a wide range of Scottish produce from local Farm Assured meat and game to fruit, veg and locally brewed beers. The delicious homemade goodies from the Bothy Kitchen are also extremely popular: sausage rolls, quiches, cheeses and pies.

The Coffee Bothy has a selection of daily specials, light lunches and filling soups, all created from the farm shop's fresh produce. Don't forget to satisfy that sweet tooth with a piece of scrumptious Bothy cake or pudding of the day.

Opening hours
Mon–Sat 9am-5pm
Sun 10am-4.30pm

Blairmains Farm Shop & Coffee Bothy, Manor Loan, Blairlogie FK9 5QA
WWW.BLAIRMAINS.COM 01259 762266

CAFÉ

Granary Café

JUNCTION: 3; 4 MINUTES

It may look small, but beyond the smart, awning'd frontage stretches a wonderland of lovely food. The café is a long-held dream for owner Gillian, and a tribute to her granny's healthfood shop – also called Granary – where she used to help after school. Today, Gillian funnels the same passion for tasty, well-balanced dishes into her menus.

Breakfast might be baked eggs with garlic mushrooms or homemade pancakes with crispy bacon (from celebrated Fife butcher Puddledub) and maple syrup; lunch on a loaded Buddha bowl or ciabatta with harissa hummus and grilled courgette. Mouthwatering pastries sit on the counter to tempt you if you're just flying by for coffee.

Free parking is available a short walk away. Take a detour on the way back to your car and stroll around the bank of the small loch and take in the views of the magnificent ruins of Linlithgow Palace, the birthplace of Mary, Queen of Scots. If you're passing in summer, you might be lucky enough to catch the thundering hooves of the annual jousting tournament.

Opening hours
Tues-Fri & Sun 9am-4pm
Sat 9am-5pm

Granary Café, 102 High Street, Linlithgow EH49 7AQ
WWW.GRANARY.SCOT   01506 253408

No.98

JUNCTION: 6; 3 MINUTES

The Lowlands are often overlooked but take some time to drop in to Kinross on your way through Scotland. Centred on a large loch, the sleepy town is ringed with low-lying hills and is a world leader in cashmere production.

On an islet in the loch is the enchanting Lochleven Castle where Mary, Queen of Scots was once held prisoner. Take the ferry out to the castle before meandering over to No. 98, where owners Jim and Jane will indulge you in their love of mouth-watering burgers and Fairtrade coffee. It's far from a two-trick pony, though: there are also excellent brunches (with meat from the butcher down the road) and a good line in vegetarian and vegan dishes.

Kids will love the pink panther milkshake and crunchie rocky road, while sandwiches such as the pulled brisket with slaw and mustard sauce will keep anyone filled up till the Highlands. Service is attentive and the vibe relaxed. A great place to rest road-weary bodies.

Opening hours
Mon-Sat 9am-4.30pm
Sun 10am-3pm

No.98, 98 High Street, Kinross KY13 8AJ
WWW.NO98FOOD.COM   01577 862542

FARM SHOP-CAFÉ

Loch Leven's Larder

JUNCTION: 8; 4 MINUTES

The scenery alone makes a diversion here worthwhile – set between rolling hills the Larder has a panoramic view of Loch Leven. In the food hall, shelves are stacked with a carefully chosen selection of goodies from local producers: cheeses, craft spirits and ales, preserves and confectionary. An artisan bakery creates delicious breads and pastries using high-quality local ingredients.

The Larder stands at the heart of the family's farm and crates of vegetables are delivered direct from the fields, where chefs transform them into imaginative seasonal dishes. The informal, family-friendly atmosphere in the café, where visitors can walk straight in from the Loch Leven Heritage Trail, makes it the perfect place to slow down and appreciate fresh local food. If you're in a hurry the Greenhouse Café is designed for express visits.

There's plenty of parking and the 1.5-mile path around the fields is suitable for buggies. There's also a play area, making it a great place to enjoy some fresh air.

Opening hours
Mon–Sun 9am-5.30pm

Loch Leven's Larder, Channel Farm, Kinross KY13 9HD
WWW.LOCHLEVENSLARDER.COM   01592 841000

Sundial Café

JUNCTION: 1C; 7 MINUTES

Traditional crow-stepped gable, quirky nooks and of course a sundial in the corner, this café is a beautiful glimpse into Scottish life 400 years ago. The building has been lovingly restored and today slate floors, painted panelling, roaring stoves and a cast-iron spiral staircase combine in this super-welcoming neighbourhood café.

Co-owner Sandra bakes brownies and makes soup, which are on the menu next to Molly and Jess's scones, her Mum's loaf cakes, and bacon rolls, toasted ciabattas and ice cream by Di Rollo of Musselburgh. Grab a table upstairs or a comfy window seat to savour a pastel de nata fresh from the oven, and a warming pot of tea.

Limekilns itself is worth a visit, a less-visited side of the Firth of Forth. Referenced in Robert Louis Stevenson's 'Kidnapped', it dates back to the 14th century and has a peaceful fishing village vibe.

Opening hours
Weds-Sun 9.30am-4pm

Sundial Café, 11 Academy Square, Limekilns, Dunfermline KY11 3HN
WWW.FACEBOOK.COM/SUNDIALCAFELIMEKILNS/   01383 873370

FARM SHOP

Craigie's Farm Deli

JUNCTION: 1A; 10 MINUTES

If you're looking for a quick stop near Edinburgh, this is the perfect spot. Savour the fantastic views of the Firth of Forth and Pentland Hills while enjoying a freshly made artisan coffee and good food made with produce direct from the surrounding fields. The café uses only the best local ingredients with a seasonally changing menu – soups, salads, sandwiches, plenty of daily specials and delicious home baked cakes always available.

The farm shop showcases the best that Scotland has to offer and is full of great produce from the farm and its neighbours, with an award-winning butchery, the Buffalo Farm. It's the perfect place to pick up supplies for your journey; you can also buy gifts, farm toys, books and cards.

There's a dedicated Canine Café for dog walkers and you can stretch your legs before getting back into the car with a stroll around Craigie Hill. Pick fruit from July to October or meet the animals on the farm; you may even find a freshly-laid egg if you're lucky.

Opening hours
Mon-Sun 9am-5pm

Craigie's Farm Deli, West Craigie Farm, South Queensferry EH30 9AR
WWW.CRAIGIES.CO.UK   0131 3191048

Fenton Barns Café & Shop

A1

JUNCTION: HADDINGTON; 9 MINUTES

© Angus Bremner

Originally built to serve the RAF airfield that stood here in the war, the former squadron buildings at Fenton are now a fantastic pint-sized shopping village. At the centre is the farm shop, where owner Mhairi thoughtfully manages her trove of Scottish produce and tasteful gifts – cookbooks, kitchenware, cheese, eggs, oatcakes, chocolates and seasonal fruit and veg.

The café at the far end has been remodelled to include an open fire. Food matches the cosy vibe and is home made or locally sourced where possible: quiches, over-filled sandwiches, house-recipe stovies (a Scottish speciality made with meat and potatoes and served with chutney) as well as delicious cakes piled on the dresser. The smoked fish is particularly noteworthy, hooked from the North Sea and smoked down the road. Pick up a cup of freshly made soup to go – the sweet potato, spinach and chickpea is delicious – or try the homemade custard creams or the cheese and chive scones for a tasty snack on the run. We had to prise ourselves away.

Opening hours
Mon-Sun 10am-5pm

Fenton Barns Café & Shop, Unit 16 Fenton Barns Retail Park, North Berwick EH39 5BW
WWW.FENTONBARNSFARMSHOP.COM   01620 850294

Come and stay with us...

Visit the beautiful Easton Estate this year and stay in one of our luxury holiday cottages or new loft apartments.

Whether you choose to stay for one night or a fortnight, our dog-friendly accommodation includes exclusive access to Easton Walled Gardens for the duration of your stay.

easton
HOLIDAY COTTAGES

www.eastonholidaycottages.co.uk
01476 550227

Steampunk Coffee

JUNCTION: ATHELSTANEFORD; 14 MINUTES

North Berwick has been undergoing something of a renaissance as people look beyond the expensive rents of Edinburgh for places to live and work: Steampunk was one of the pioneers.

There's an airy, industrial feel to the steel-framed building, a former joinery warehouse, thanks to on-trend polished concrete, exposed girders, scuffed floorboards and vintage leather chairs. But despite the high ceilings, there's a cosiness here with heaps of books and wood burners.

A vintage Probat roaster roosts in the corner, and supplies beans for the café here as well as others across Scotland; don't forget to buy some to take home. Food is as good as the coffee: imaginative cakes, a different homemade soup every day, sriracha cheese toasties, bagels and other tasty options.

There are charging points if you need to crack open your laptop or top-up your phone, and tables outside if you need a gulp of fresh air.

Opening hours
Mon-Sat 9am-5pm
Sun 10am-5pm
(Fri 8pm-ish while pizza van is there)

Steampunk Coffee, 49a Kirk Ports, North Berwick EH39 4HL
WWW.STEAMPUNKCOFFEE.CO.UK   01620 893030

CAFÉ

Drift

JUNCTION: WEST BARNS; 13 MINUTES

You won't find better views of the North Berwickshire coast. Panoramic windows cut into the converted shipping containers give spectacular clifftop views of the North Sea and Bass Rock so you can watch clouds or waves roll in as you refuel.

Farmers Jo and Stuart opened the doors to their wood-clad container café here in summer 2018 with the simple notion of offering decent coffee, finger-licking cakes, tasty breakfasts and wholesome lunches, and have been expanding ever since. "The scones," says Jo, "have a following of their own."

For those that prefer to dine al fresco, there are picnic tables outside, deliciously bathed in the scent of the herbs planted alongside. If you've got time, wander down the steep hill to walk along the beach for some salty air before you continue your journey.

Opening hours
April-Oct – Mon-Sat 9.30am-5.30pm (Sun 10am)
Oct-April – Mon-Sun 10am-4.30pm

Drift, Canty Bay, North Berwick EH39 5PL
WWW.FACEBOOK.COM/DRIFTEATDRINKRELAX   01620 892817

The Crown and Kitchen

JUNCTION: A199; 7 MINUTES

With baskets of frothy flowers at the windows and a stately Georgian entrance, the Crown and Kitchen has real kerb appeal, matched by the tasteful interior. There's a warmth to the grey wood-panelled walls, dried garlands and mismatched chairs in the dining room.

Owner Billy has been determined to make this a friendly local ever since taking the reins, so you're as likely to be supping a pint next to one of the neighbours as dining alongside a party of walkers. The food is pub grub taken up a creative notch with dishes such as brisket and black pudding stovies, cullen skink with crispy egg and pea shoots, and steak frites.

Retro board games are ideal for waiting out any traffic jams or downpours, though if the fire is crackling you might not want to leave. If you really don't want to, you're in luck as there are five stylish bedrooms upstairs.

You can come off the road at either Haddington or West Barns and track the A1 to the next junction to avoid retracing your steps. If you've got time, consider a short detour to Tyninghame beach which is well-regarded and dog friendly.

Opening hours
Mon-Weds noon-11pm
Thus-Sat 11am-1am
Sun noon-midnight

The Crown and Kitchen, 25-27 Bridge Street, East Linton EH40 3AG
WWW.CROWNANDKITCHEN.COM   01620 860098

CAFÉ

The Loft Café & Bakery

JUNCTION: HADDINGTON ; 5 MINUTES

A lot has changed since Charlotte and Anita took over Haddington Council's former canteen. With an eye for thrifty design they kept the functional stainless steel serving counters and disguised them with piles of food and pallet wood cladding; furniture is second-hand and upcycled. And, with a wave of their wand, they transformed it into a fresh, light-drenched space. A sheltered courtyard in front of the L-shaped, stone building is a fantastic place to pause and unwind on sunny days.

The emphasis here is on good, home-cooked food and there's a strict local sourcing policy for ingredients. Breakfast on shakshuka or pancakes with bacon and maple syrup, lunch on mackerel pâté on homemade oatcakes, pearled spelt salad or the legendary sausage rolls; and indulge in the home-made ice-cream and brilliant cakes – the lime and courgette and bakewell slice are particularly recommended. Coffee is freshly ground and you should try the turmeric latte if you haven't had one before – a cup of golden sunshine.

Opening hours
Mon-Fri 8.30am-4.30pm
Sat 9am-4pm

The Loft Café & Bakery, Peffers Place, Haddington EH41 3DR
WWW.LOFTCAFEBAKERY.CO.UK   01620 824456

Restoration Yard

A68

JUNCTION: WHITECRAIG; 6 MINUTES

© Chris Humphreys Photography Ltd

Just outside Edinburgh the 1,000-acre Dalkeith Country Park is a bucolic stop with something for everyone. Kids will love the enormous Fort Douglas Adventure Park and when you've tired them out on the climbing walls, treehouses and slides, head to the stunning Restoration Yard.

Once the stable block for the Duke of Buccleuch's estate and crowned with a stately clock tower, the yard has been given a radical makeover. Browse the beautiful clothing, homewares, books and gifts in the shop, pick up some artisan deli goods in the fine foods store, even stop for a yoga class. You can refuel in the informal Coffee Bar alongside or grab a table in the slightly more formal restaurant The Kitchen with plate glass windows overlooking the river and herb garden.

Dalkeith Country Park is looped with dog-friendly walking and cycling paths, so stretch your legs before getting back in the car. The longest, two-hour trail takes you through woodlands and along the River Esk – look out for roe deer, otters and buzzards.

Opening hours
The Kitchen: Mon-Fri 9.30am-4.30pm (5pm Sat-Sun)
Store & Coffee Bar: Mon-Sun 9.30am-6pm
Fort Douglas: Mon-Sun 10am-6pm (4pm winter)

Restoration Yard, Dalkeith Country Park, Edinburgh EH22 1ST
WWW.RESTORATIONYARD.COM   0131 322 2572

CAFÉ

Soutra Coffee House

JUNCTION: FALA VILLAGE; 0 MINUTES

Spectacular views and a counter laden with homemade food make Soutra Coffee House a special place to stop. Take a table on the terrace or at one of the enormous windows to drink in the expansive tableau of hills rolling into the distance. In one direction you can see across the Firth of Forth, another looks towards the Bass Rock in the North Sea.

It's the sister café to the gorgeous Carfraemill Hotel just down the road and shares its reputation for great food and warm hospitality. Bacon rolls come with a slice of haggis, sandwiches are hearty, soups are homemade and the cakes are reassuringly indulgent. The chai latte is particularly good.

Parking is plentiful and there's a well-supplied toy corner for keeping children entertained while you enjoy your lunch or coffee. If you fancy a longer stop, stretch your legs in the Lammermuir Hills or visit the nearby medieval hospital at Soutra Aisle before heading on your way.

Opening hours
Mon-Sun 9am-5pm (Apr-Oct)
Mon-Fri 9am-4pm (Nov-Mar)
Sat-Sun 9am-4.30pm (Nov-Mar)

Soutra Coffee House, Blackshields, Fala Soutra Hill, Pathead EH37 5TF
WWW.HOUSEOFSOUTRA.COM   01875 833795

The Spotty Dog

JUNCTION: LAUDER; 0 MINUTES

It would be easy to miss the Spotty Dog, squished into Lauder's high street between the shoulders of two stone houses, but it's well worth breaking your journey here between Scotland and England.

Although primarily a deli, the Spotty Dog's grey-fronted shop also manages to fit in some cafe tables for the lucky few, spilling out onto the pavement when the weather allows. High-quality ingredients from the shop are used to make soups, filled sandwiches and tasty deli boards, while cakes are well-regarded and come in a range of flavour combinations, such as almond and plum or rhubarb and ginger.

Raid the shelves for excellent produce – cheeses, bacon jam, artisan loaves and fine wines – or grab a croissant or scotch egg to keep you going on the move.

Opening hours
Mon-Fri 8am-5pm
Sat 9am-5pm
Sun 10am-4pm

The Spotty Dog, 3a East High Street, Lauder TD2 6SS
WWW.THESPOTTYDOG.CO.UK   01578 722095

CAFÉ

Cloudhouse Café-Gallery

JUNCTION: LAUDER; 9 MINUTES

Just off the A7 and a short but beautiful moorland road away from the A68, the Cloudhouse Café, with its striped awning and glowing windows, stands in the centre of the pretty town of Stow. The building has had various lives as a grocer's and bakery (the delivery horse was once stabled in what is now the kitchen), but now it's Caroline's domain where she and her friendly team serve hearty country dishes amid a collection of local artwork. Full breakfasts might come with duck eggs, bread is freshly cooked and vegan dishes are frequently seen on the menu.

The atmosphere is familiar and there's a play area to keep kids entertained. Cushions soften pew bench seats, upcycled tables are painted in earthy tones and on sunny days tables are set out on the pavement next to pots of lavender. Browse the gallery at the back for a souvenir art piece, pick up a trinket from the counter or a holiday read in the book exchange. It's popular with cyclists (thanks to those wavey moorland roads); a bellwether of good cafés if ever there was one.

Opening hours
Mon-Thurs 10am-3pm
Fri 10am-4pm
Sat–Sun 10am-3pm

Cloudhouse Café-Gallery, 23 Townfoot, Stow TD1 2QN
WWW.CLOUDHOUSECAFE.CO.UK   01578 730718

The Mainstreet Trading Company

JUNCTION: ST BOSWELLS; 1 MINUTE

A magical combination of books, gifts and food, and winner of Britain's Best Small Shop, The Mainstreet Trading Company should be factored into every journey through this part of the Borders. Make time to browse the fabulous bookshop, then refuel on the food that draws inspiration from the recipe books on its shelves; there's always a featured Cookbook of the Moment. Try the tomato, cumin and fig soup, a pastrami and leek jam sandwich or something equally tasty from their seasonal specials. Cakes are all baked in-house and the gluten-free Tunisian cake is particularly good. The café is dog- and child-friendly: we loved the understairs book burrow for kids where they can listen to audio books among piles of cushions.

In the courtyard out the back, a former barn has been developed to add a home shop and deli. The shop, in the old wine cellar, is stacked to the rafters with woven baskets, enamelware, French soaps and beautifully illustrated stationery; while the deli stocks all manner of goodies from independent food producers, with cheese the star of the show.

Opening hours
Tues-Sat 9am-5.30pm (café 5pm)
Sun 11am-4.30pm (café 4pm)

The Mainstreet Trading Company, Main Street, St Boswells TD6 0AT
WWW.MAINSTREETBOOKS.CO.UK   01835 824087

CAFÉ

Hazel's Butterfly Bakery

JUNCTION: 5; 7 MINUTES

A labour of love for Hazel, the Butterfly Bakery is a brilliant neighbourhood café on Uddingston's high street. Occupying one half of a rose-coloured stone building with a handsome bay window the café is bright and inviting with scrubbed wooden tables and walls decorated with pictures of Hazel's finest creations.

She's been conjuring up celebratory cakes for family and friends for years and now they form the centrepiece of her café – multilayered, multi-flavoured and impressive. Try a slice of maple and pecan or white chocolate and cranberry, or go for a lemon curd cupcake. Confectionary is served alongside tasty breakfasts (including great sausages from the butcher across the street) and home-cooked lunches of soups, toasted sandwiches and baked potatoes.

Plentiful parking is available at the back, where you'll also catch a glimpse of the Tunnock's factory – the production house of Scotland's much-loved snowballs and tea cakes.

Opening hours
Mon-Sat 9am-4pm
Sun 11am-3pm
Last hot food orders 30 mins before closing

Hazel's Butterfly Bakery, Unit 1, 54 Main Street, Uddingston G71 7LS
WWW.HAZELSBUTTERFLYBAKERY.CO.UK/HOME   01698 801662

The unassuming car park gives little away but standing in the Clyde Valley between Lanark and Motherwell is the Silver Birch garden centre, homewares emporium and café rolled into one magnificent package.

Tasteful arrangements of ornaments, houseplants, mirrors, furniture and candles in the showroom will whet any interior design appetites, while the sturdy plants in the garden centre are sourced from Scotland where possible.

The coffee shop is perched on a slope with views over the plants and valley beyond, and serves freshly made meals, Mary's impressive cakes and decent coffee from breakfast to tea time. Breakfast might be a stack of pancakes or scrambled eggs and baked tomatoes; lunch a steak pie or charcuterie board.

The Christmas decoration displays are magazine-worthy and famous across Scotland, so if you're passing in the winter it's a great place to distract the family.

Opening hours
Mon-Tues, Thurs-Sun 9am-5.30pm
Weds 9am-5pm

Silver Birch, Lanark Road, Crossford ML8 5QQ
WWW.SILVERBIRCHGARDENCENTRE.CO.UK   01555 860623

CAFÉ-DELI

Alexander Taylor Bakery & Deli

JUNCTION: 8; 12 MINUTES

It's worth every extra drop of fuel to make the detour to Strathaven (pronounced 'Stray-ven'), a colourful market town set around a traditional square, just south of Glasgow. The castle ruins and independent shops are ripe for exploration while the beautifully manicured park is perfect for a breath of fresh air. Stroll around town before rewarding yourself with a visit to the fantastic Alexander Taylor Bakery, facing the river. It was established here in 1820, and six generations of the Taylor family have been producing a vast range of delicious breads and baked goods on the site ever since.

Buy an organic sour dough loaf, pretzel or Opera slice to take away, or have a seat in the rustic tea room across the road to enjoy a bowl of Kype-a-leekie soup (made from St Brides free-range chicken and home-grown leeks), crisp cheese toastie or hot bacon roll made with Ramsay's Ayrshire bacon. The coffee is great and best paired with a pineapple tart or treacle crumpet. A hearty pit stop.

Opening hours
Mon–Fri 8.30am-5pm
Sat 8am-5pm

Alexander Taylor Bakery & Deli, 10-11 Waterside Street, Strathaven ML10 6AW
WWW.ALEXANDERTAYLORBAKERY.CO.UK   01357 521260

Cairn Lodge Services

JUNCTION: 11; 2 MINUTES

The newest addition to the Tebay and Gloucester Services fold, Cairn Lodge has settled seamlessly into the family. It too started life as a home-run business when founders John and Aileen MacInnes spotted an opportunity on the then-new M74 motorway in the early 1990s. They named it after the gothic gateway on site, which is all that remains of an abandoned attempt to rebuild Douglas Castle in the 1700s.

The Westmorland Family took over in 2015 and continued the good work with Donna Hodd, daughter of the founders, at the helm as operations manager. After a major renovation, it's now dressed to impress in the Westmorland signature look. A brand new Farmshop stocks local gifts and artisan foods, while the coffee bar has handy charging points and a gargantuan ceiling planter overhead. The loos and showers are lovely, and the new Kitchen is a mellow place to fill up on a hot meal or quick cuppa. They're also proud to have a Changing Places toilet, one of the first on the Scottish motorway network.

Opening hours
Mon-Thurs 7am-10pm
Fri-Sun 7am-9pm

Cairn Lodge Services, Douglas ML11 0RJ
WWW.CAIRNLODGESERVICES.COM   01555 851880

FARM SHOP-CAFÉ

The Scrib Tree

JUNCTION: 11/12; 3 MINUTES

Cosy and welcoming, in a honeycoloured, slate-roofed building in the heart of the Lanarkshire Estate village of Douglas, The Scrib Tree is an enthusiastic champion of local farm produce and handcrafted gifts. If you're travelling between Glasgow and the Borders, swing in here for excellent coffee (roasted by hand in Glasgow by the Giambastiani family), great breakfasts, home-baked cakes and delicious lunches. The soups are a particular speciality.

Soak up the sun on the little terrace or eat in the lofty café. Here you can also browse the emporium of fresh produce and crafts – hand-thrown pottery, hand-turned wood and homespun woollens are all made by local artisans. Meat, game and vegetables come from the estate or neighbouring farms. Chefs in the kitchen use the same ingredients so if you're impressed by the flavour, fill your shopping bag before you leave. Parking is plentiful and it's worth popping in to Douglas itself – with origins stretching back to medieval times – to visit St Bride's church whose clock is rumoured to have been a gift from Mary, Queen of Scots.

Opening hours
Mon-Sun 10am-5pm

The Scrib Tree, 1-3 Colliers Court, Douglas, Lanark ML11 0RX
WWW.THESCRIBTREE.CO.UK   01555 851262

Brodies of Moffat

JUNCTION: 15; 3 MINUTES

Once a spa destination and centre of the wool trade, Moffat is a handsome market town arranged around a broad high street. Quirkily decorated Brodies is tucked behind the museum to the south of the main square. A much-loved family-run restaurant it's a tea room by day and a relaxed candlelit restaurant by night.

Russell is the man in the kitchen and his much lauded food is almost one of the town's tourist attractions. Lunches are light and flavourful; gutsy, slightly posher dishes are on the evening menu. Even if you're not looking for a full meal, the cakes – baked in-house – and afternoon teas are worth seeking out, while non-drivers might want to sample the enviable selection of gins proudly on show in a beautiful drinks cabinet.

If you've got time, head just out of town to the wonderfully named Devil's Beef Tub, a valley once used by members of the Moffat Clan to hoard cattle stolen in raids.

Opening hours
Mon-Tues 10am-5pm,
Wed-Sat 10am-11pm
Sun 10.30am-9pm.

Brodies of Moffat, 1-2 Altrive Place, Holm Street, Moffat DG10 9EB
WWW.BRODIESOFMOFFAT.CO.UK   01683 222870

Pink Flamingo Vintage Tea Room

JUNCTION: 17; 9 MINUTES

Sensational flavours draw the crowds to Pink Flamingo Vintage Tea Room. The baking is inventive and outstanding, loading the counter with irresistible goodies such as chocolate orange polenta cake and lemon mascarpone cheese cake with homemade pistachio biscuit base. You can also get a hearty lunch here – try one of their famous naan pizzas or the delicious pasty of the day; almost everything is homemade including the jams and chutneys which you'll find served with breakfasts and lunches. There's a cosiness to the tearoom with owner Samin's vintage wingback chairs, brightly painted furniture and ornate stove enclosed by whitewashed stone walls. A box of toys and books will keep little ones occupied; keep a lookout for a teddy bear sitting at one of the tables.

Lochmaben itself is a great place to visit, frequently hosting farmers markets where you can stock up on Scottish goodies. Its castle claims to be the birthplace of Robert the Bruce, and the Annandale Way, which passes through the town, offers superb walking. This is the perfect stop off on the way to the Highlands.

Opening hours
Mon-Fri 9am-4.30pm (Sat 5pm)
Sun open seasonally;
please check website for winter hours

Pink Flamingo Vintage Tea Room, 6a Bruce Street, Lochmaben DG11 1PD
WWW.PINKFLAMINGOVINTAGETEAROOM.COM   01387 810883

Annandale Distillery Visitor Centre

JUNCTION: 20; 9 MINUTES

A sleeping beauty, restored to life after a nearly hundred-year hiatus, Annandale Distillery flung open its doors and casks again in 2014. Handsome red sandstone buildings, set around a cobbled courtyard, are topped by an elegant chimney and spired roof, beneath which lie the magical rumblings of a working distillery, where you can pick up a take-away dram for later. The friendly team offer tours and will tell you about the history of the area: this is Robert the Bruce and Robert Burns land; you can try the whiskys named after them.

The dog-friendly Maltings café is open to all and serves finger-licking cheese scones fresh out of the oven alongside soup and huge filled sandwiches (try the cheese and haggis). The towering cakes are impressive: courgette and avocado, and cranberry and white chocolate tiffin. Waney-edged wood, exposed beams, rosy stone walls and iron pillars create a soothing spot. Cluster around a striking triangular table or relax on the deep, purple sofa and enjoy a rich, strong coffee or loose leaf tea. Once you're refreshed you can release your inner Celt and take a look at the actual costumes used in the Robert the Bruce film Outlaw King, and have your photo taken with some of the gory props.

There's bags of parking a short walk away in the car park, with closer options for disabled visitors.

Opening hours
Mon-Sat 9am-5pm
Sun 10am-5pm

Annandale Distillery Visitor Centre, Annandale Distillery, Northfield, Annan DG12 5LL
WWW.ANNANDALEDISTILLERY.COM   01461 207817

FARM SHOP

Loch Arthur Camphill Community Farm Shop

JUNCTION: CARGENBRIDGE; 8 MINUTES

It's easy to wax lyrical about the fantastic and utterly unique Loch Arthur Farm Shop. It stands next to a peaceful pond in the working Camphill Community, which offers independent living and working opportunities to people with learning disabilities. Their numerous workshop activities produce an array of lovingly made items which are then sold in the shop. Whether organic vegetables, cheeses, freshly-baked breads, woven goods or wood-worked crafts, the fruit of the Community's labours are first-rate, and the farm shop is a showcase.

The shelves provide almost everything you could want for your onward journey – cakes, pies, biscuits, meat and eggs as well as pottery and gifts – while the oak-framed café is a tranquil spot to pause over a slice of cake or a light meal. Take a seat by one of the many windows to soak up the rural views and bask in the warmth of this wonderful social enterprise. Coffee is organic and best served with homemade biscuits.

Opening hours
Mon-Fri 9.30am-5pm
Sat 9.30am-4.30pm

Loch Arthur Camphill Community Farm Shop, Beeswing DG2 8JQ
WWW.LOCHARTHUR.ORG.UK   01387 259669

COFFEE SHOP
Streetlights Coffee House

JUNCTION: CASTLE DOUGLAS; 2 MINUTES

Handsome Castle Douglas is an 18th-century market town in the heart of one of Scotland's most productive farming regions. Its high street has a selection of wander-worthy shops and cafés, but our favourite place to refuel is Streetlights.

Katrina makes as much food in the kitchen as possible, cheerily serving delicious plates from behind a wood clad counter hung with vintage lights. The bacon baps are frequently praised and the baking prowess evident in the multi-layered cakes and meringues. Grab a table at lunch for a bowl of homemade soup or a barista coffee and slice for an afternoon pick-me-up, perhaps sticky date or banoffee. Dogs are welcome and will be showered with fuss and treats.

Galloway Forest Park was the first in the UK to be designated a Dark Sky Park, so stargazers should consider a longer stop in the area for a real glimpse of the universe.

Opening hours
Mon-Sat 10am-4pm

Streetlights Coffee House, 187 King Street, Castle Douglas DG7 1DZ
WWW.FACEBOOK.COM/STREET-LIGHTS-COFFEE-HOUSE-370797449635859/   01556 504222

COOKERY SCHOOL-CAFÉ

Station House

JUNCTION: TARFF BRIDGE; 6 MINUTES

Kirkcudbright (pronounced kir-coo-bree) is a fantastically vibrant and artistic town in Scotland's south west. It alone warrants a break from the A75 to explore its boutiques, pastel-coloured houses and fishing harbour, and to refuel, it has to be the Station House Cookery School.

Nick and his team set up the cookery school (well worth looking up if you're staying in the area) and café after a thorough search of the country for the right spot, and his enthusiasm for good food is positively infectious. Their range of cookery classes is impressive from International Cuisine such as Indian, Thai or Eastern European to skill-based courses such as bread-making, fresh pasta or pastry and there are classes for children.

Nick's a fierce advocate of local produce, carefully sourcing from individual suppliers as close to the café as possible, and frequently makes from scratch, whether baking bread to churning the butter. You can taste the benefits in the café, where the rustic counter is piled with quiches, pies, scones and cakes to supplement the menu options – soups, frittata and mouthwatering breakfasts.

Sunday is pizza night, so call in for a superior take-away if you're passing.

Opening hours
Weds-Sat 9am-5pm
Sun 10am-8pm

Station House, St Mary Street, Kirkcudbright DG6 4DN
WWW.STATIONHOUSECOOKERYSCHOOL.CO.UK   07484 915709/ 07493 242792

Tree Bar & Café

JUNCTION: A714; 1 MINUTE

A huge bar made from a single piece of Douglas fir and propped on granite blocks makes a dramatic statement at the entrance of the Crafty Distillery in Galloway. It's home to Hills and Harbour gin, an award winner flavoured with seaweed from the coast and pine needles from the forest; that commitment to offering regional flavours extends to the café and bar in their visitor centre.

In the unique picnic system here, visitors are invited to choose from the deli-style goodies in the well-stocked fridge – smoked fish, cheese, pâté – and take them to a table at the stunning picture window to eat with crusty bread and butter. Decent coffee is supplied by the Good Coffee Cartel in Glasgow, and will pep you up for any ferry crossings to Northern Ireland.

While you're stopped, consider the tour (for an entertaining insight into the team's gin-creating journey), and then pop into Wigtown itself, officially named Scotland's National Book Town, with some 20 shops to browse.

Opening hours
Mon-Sat 10am-6pm
(winter times vary – see website)

Tree Bar & Café, Wigtown Road, Newton Stewart DG8 6AS
WWW.CRAFTYDISTILLERY.COM   01671 404040

CAFÉ
Bite

JUNCTION: A6071; 2 MINUTES

The food miles could not be lower for the trout that owner and chef Linda serves up at Bite. It's fished from the lake right outside the door and turned into tasty pâtés, lasagne, fishcakes and chowder. The same goes for the rest of the ingredients, which are sourced from local producers wherever possible, and all the tastier for it.

The café and upstairs bistro occupy a former mill building within New Mills Trout Fishing Park and have striking bare stone walls, exposed beams and wooden floors. Menus vary in each: simple sandwiches, nachos, salads and cakes in the cafe, and a more filling, frequently changing menu upstairs, such as Stornoway black pudding with apple, beef stroganoff, or fillet of beef with local haggis.

Take a seat outside to hear the Quarry Beck stream trickling past while kids explore the fairy trail. Wonderful.

Opening hours
Tues-Sun 10am-4pm

Bite, New Mills Trout Fishing Park, Brampton CA8 2QS
WWW.NEWMILLSTROUTFISHINGPARK.CO.UK/BITE-CAFE   016977 42235

Over
700
alternative
places to
stay off the
beaten track

CANOPY & STARS

canopyandstars.co.uk

CAFÉ

House of Meg

JUNCTION: B6318; 4 MINUTES

The name for this charming tea room was inspired by the house's connections with a local landlady from the 17th century who gained notoriety for fatally drugging her monied guests. Thankfully Andi has gained his notoriety for truly excellent baking instead, so much so that he is now invited to judge other people's baking.

There's a real homeliness to the café, with two rooms leading from the entrance corridor, so there's plenty of space to find a table and enjoy a proper refuel. Ample breakfasts are served alongside crispy jackets, bowls of stew and, of course, a range of cakes, biscuits, brownies and scones.

Outside, in the pretty garden, there's a shelter for al fresco dining, or those needing sustenance with their dog after a walk, and the village play area is just round the corner if energetic children need to be worn out.

Opening hours
Mon-Fri 7.30am-4.30pm
Sat 10am-4.30pm
Sun 10am-4pm

(V) (GF)

House of Meg, 4 Hall Terrace, Gilsland CA8 7BW
WWW.HOUSEOFMEG.CO.UK   016977 47777

Jill's Catering Tea Room

JUNCTION: A686; 10 MINUTES

We couldn't put it better than one customer, who said, "the views of the valley are reason enough to visit, but these are matched by home baking and cooking". The cedar-clad barn-style building clings to the hillside in Catton, at the northern edge of the North Pennines with a blissful vista over the hills and fields. From it Jill produces her fabulous home cooking, a natural extension of her successful catering business: pies, broths, hot meals, scones and sandwiches; the cheesecakes come particularly recommended.

Tea is served in china pots with dainty cups for a traditional tea room experience, and staff are delightfully friendly. The space is bright and clean, tables are dressed with gingham cloths and patio doors are opened wide on fine days.

Opening hours are limited and it's not open every day, but if you're passing at the right time you're in for a treat. This is a proper escape from the road.

Opening hours
Fri-Sat 10am-4pm
Sun 11am-4pm

Jill's Catering Tea Room, Folly House, Folly Lane, Catton NE47 9LT
WWW.FACEBOOK.COM/JILLSCATERING/   07957 571885

CAFÉ
The Station Coffee House
JUNCTION: STYFORD ROUNDABOUT; 5 MINUTES

Friends and next-door neighbours Pam and Chris set up The Station Coffee House to bring good coffee and a community hub to their corner of Northumberland. As the name suggests, they've adopted the ground floor of an old railway station house – still on an active train line – and installed a hugely welcoming village café. You're as likely to meet dog walker's chatting at a picnic bench here as commuters grabbing a coffee to go.

There's a wonderful homely feel to the compact space, helped by the pair's beaming smiles and home baking (Chris's cheese scones are particularly tasty). They've taken pains to source their products as locally as possible so you can expect to find sausage rolls made with pork reared nearby, pies from North Acomb farm up the road and Newcastle's very own Mark Toney ice cream. Coffee comes from Pumphrey's, a favourite Northumberland supplier, and soft drinks are all Fentimans, which originated close by in Hexham.

Packaging is compostable, so you can take away with a clear conscience.

Opening hours
Tues, Thurs, Fri 9am-4pm
Weds 9am-8pm
Sat 10am-4pm

The Station Coffee House, Dene Close, Ridingmill NE44 6JD
WWW.FACEBOOK.COM/THE-STATION-COFFEE-HOUSE-RIDING-MILL-1954889081481523/   01434 239 274

The Angel of Corbridge

JUNCTION: CORBRIDGE; 4 MINUTES

At the very fringe of what was once the Roman Empire, Corbridge is steeped in history. It was once a busy market town acting as a supply base for the Roman legions based here. The Corbridge Hoard on display in the museum is one of the most significant finds of the era and well worth a peek if you have time.

Fast forward several centuries and it's still a paradise for shoppers with its streets of independent boutiques and cafés. When you've finished exploring, head to the Angel to refuel. The 16th-century coaching inn is a great gathering place for all day dining with bar, dog-friendly dining lounge, restaurant as well as a fish and chip shop! The food is hearty, seasonal, homemade and locally-sourced; the lunch menu is particularly good value and the Sunday roast with beef drippping roasties is not to be missed.

There's plenty of outdoor seating at the front; a great place to watch the world go by. There's a small car park at the rear and the town's petrol station is, conveniently, next door.

Opening hours
Mon-Sat 7.30am-11pm
Sun 8.30am-10pm

The Angel of Corbridge, Main Street, Corbridge NE45 5LA
WWW.THEANGELOFCORBRIDGE.COM   01434 632119

CAFÉ
The Hearth

JUNCTION: HORSLEY/B6528; 2 MINUTES

Ten minutes from the A1, two minutes from the A69 and a mine of North Eastern creativity, the Hearth is a great place to stop for a taste of the region. The 17th-century manse house was restored in 2004 to provide Horsley with a community hub and nine studios where full-time artists create ceramics, jewellery, paintings and textiles, which are for sale downstairs; you may also be able to tour the studios.

The café is in the front two rooms, just beyond the porch, and its windows are frequently fogged up in winter with the hubbub of happy visitors and dog walkers warming themselves within. Snack on delicious home baking, such as peanut butter flapjacks or cheese scones, washed down with proper coffee, or opt for something more substantial. One visitor claimed the eggs Benedict were the best they've ever had (breakfast is served all day), and lunches are filling: duck hoisin panini, hunters chicken or roasted sweet potato.

There are a couple of tables on the front terrace, with gorgeous views over the Tyne valley, for al fresco dining on fine days. Parking is just up the hill behind.

Opening hours
Mon-Fri 9.30am-4pm
Sat-Sun 10am-4pm

The Hearth, Main Road, Horsley NE15 0NT
WWW.THEHEARTH.CO.UK   01661 853563

The Coffee Tree

JUNCTION: WYLAM; 3 MINUTES

Chocolate
Fudge Cake

Walkers of the Hadrian's Wall path often miss this little gem of a café as they track the Tyne just below Main Road, and we feel sorry for them as this is blissful respite from the trail, whether you're on foot or wheel.

Suzanne took over the honey-stoned café a few years ago and has been treating the village to her fabulous cooking ever since. Once she's stocked the counter with an array of teetering cakes, scones and meringues, she turns her attention to sending hearty plates of brunch, soups, sandwiches and cream teas out to eager tables. The interior is simple, with some hints of the building's history in the rugged beams and bare stone walls, but it's the warm, chatty service that sets this café apart.

It's popular with the locals too, so you're as likely to sit alongside with mums after their yoga class as retirees catching up over a coffee.

Opening hours
Mon-Fri 9am-4pm
Sat 8.30am-4pm
Sun 10am-3pm

The Coffee Tree, Main Road, Wylam NE41 8AQ
WWW.FACEBOOK.COM/THECOFFEETREEWYLAM   01661 852422

FARM SHOP
Daniel Farm

JUNCTION: WYLAM; 6 MINUTES

Geese flap, goats bleat, pigs snuffle and alpacas glare in the fields outside Daniel Farm, making this an animal lover's paradise. It's a working farm, tucked down a country lane in the Tyne Valley, and owners Danny and Jane added a farm shop and tea room in 2015, keen to share the beauty of the hills and ancient woodland with the public.

It's fast become a popular spot, and the scrubbed farmhouse tables are often abuzz with people enjoying the fuss-free farmhouse menu: cooked breakfasts, quiches, paninis, salads, and hearty slices of cake. The atmosphere is homely, with wallpapered walls and farm-themed art hung on the walls, and a pair of glazed swing doors lead through to farm shop where you can buy the farm's meat from the butchery counter or browse local produce on the shelves.

Entertain kids with a tour of the animals before you leave.

Opening hours
Mon-Fri 9.30am-4.30pm
Sat-Sun 9am-4.30pm

Daniel Farm, Sled Lane, Wylam NE41 8JH
WWW.DANIELFARM.CO.UK   01661 853849

Love pubs?
You need a
pub guide

A wonderful mix of warm, buzzy and
welcoming places run by passionate people.
We look for special. We've visited every one
of them and written about them honestly.
We love them, we know you will too.

Visit sawdays.co.uk/pubs

The 👉 A1

Travel the length of the country the Roman way

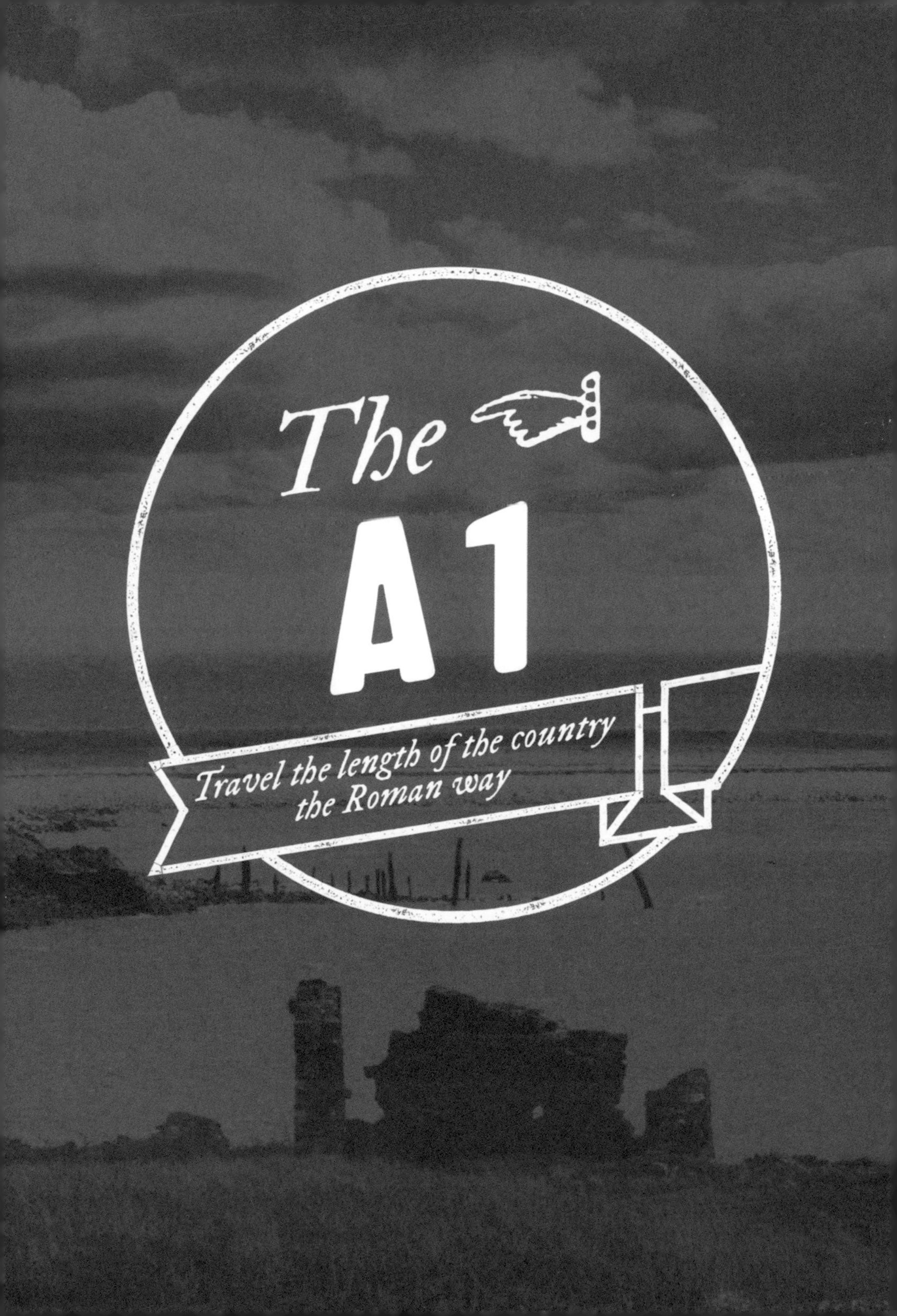

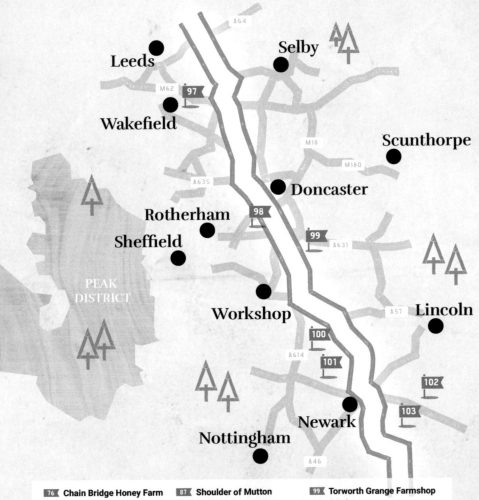

A1 NORTH

Leeds

Selby

Wakefield

Scunthorpe

Rotherham

Doncaster

Sheffield

PEAK DISTRICT

Workshop

Lincoln

Newark

Nottingham

76	Chain Bridge Honey Farm	87	Shoulder of Mutton	99	Torworth Grange Farmshop & Lakes
77	Doddington Milk Bar	88	Kiplin Hall & Gardens	100	The Hay Barn Café
78	Carnaby's Café	89	Lister's Farm Shop	101	Newfield Dairy Ice Cream Parlour
79	The Old Stables Tea Room	90	Bowe & Co	102	Leadenham Teahouse
80	Grannies	91	Minskip Farm Shop	103	JandJ Alpacas
81	Moorhouse Farm	92	Hideaway Kitchen		
82	Broom House Farm	93	Fodder		
83	Tea with Alice	94	The Castle Inn		
84	Cross Lanes Organic Farm	95	Don't Tell the Duke		
85	Mainsgill Farm	96	Tom Foolery		
86	The Coach House at Middleton Lodge	97	Farmer Copleys		
		98	Garden Room Café		

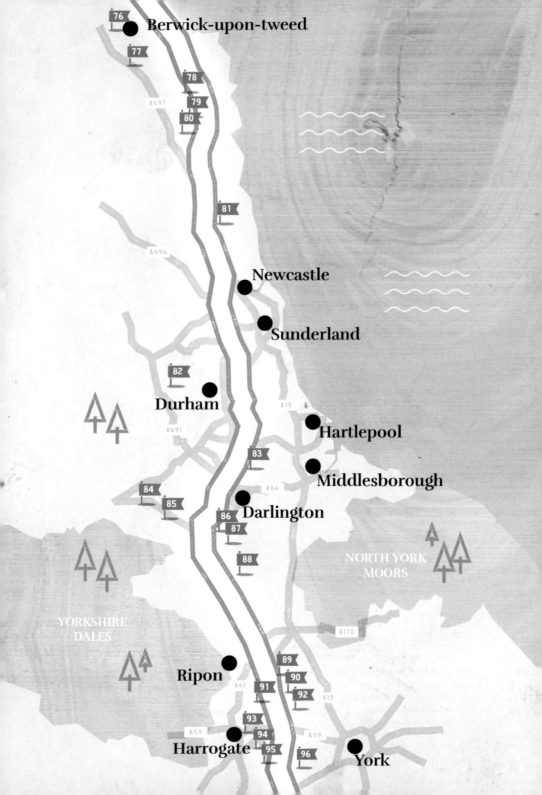

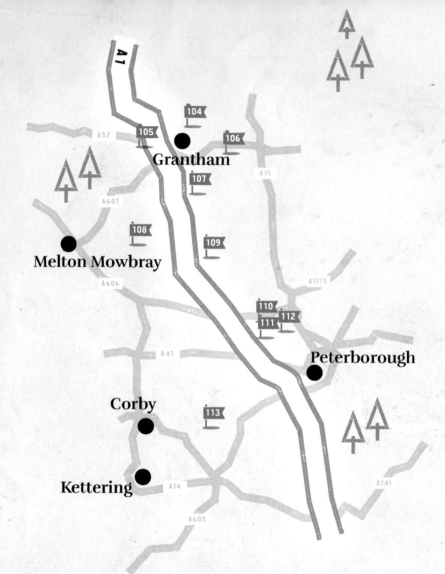

A1

104   Grantham
105

106

107

A52

A15

A607

Melton Mowbray

108

109

A606

A1175

110
111   112

Peterborough

A47

Corby

113

Kettering

A14

A141

A605

104 **Syston Park Farm Shop & Café**	109 **The Olive Branch**	114 **Tea at Tapps**
105 **Dougie's**	110 **Café au Chocolat**	115 **River Cottage Kitchen**
106 **The Green Man Ropsley**	111 **The William Cecil**	**at Hatfield House**
107 **Easton Walled Gardens**	112 **The Bull & Swan at Burghley**	
108 **The Lodge Country Café**	113 **The Crown Inn**	

A1 SOUTH

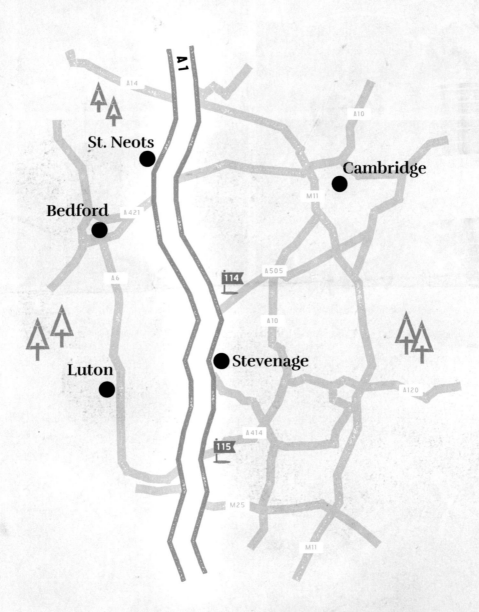

AI Chain Bridge Honey Farm

JUNCTION: A698; 6 MINUTES

© Walter Baxter, Creative Commons

On your travels in Northumberland,you will see W. S. Robson's honey for sale in farm shops. Most outlets stock the solid heather variety; harder to source are tubs of their intensely fragrant and runny flower comb honey. For this sensory delight, you may need to go direct to the source, high above the wooded slopes of the River Tweed. A short walk from the early 19th-century suspension bridge that gives the farm its name, Mr Robson's shop sells beeswax beauty products, polish, candles – and, of course, honey.

Outside you will see a double-decker bus, now a tea room run by the farmer's daughter, Frances. The interior of this Café Bus will take you back to the 1950s with its gingham curtains and original aluminium-framed bus seats. Farm produce is used wherever it tastes good; try honey flapjacks, honey lattes and heather honey ice cream made by Doddington Dairy. A lady in the local village bakes many of the cakes, including a honey and beer sponge.

Opening hours
Tues–Sun 10am–5pm
(from early April–end October)

Chain Bridge Honey Farm, Horncliffe, Berwick-upon-Tweed TD15 2XT
WWW.CHAINBRIDGEHONEY.COM   01289 382362

Doddington Milk Bar

JUNCTION: BELLSHILL; 15 MINUTES

Ice cream and milkshake lovers, hold your horses here. Painted a shade of powder blue and guarded by a life-size model cow, the cutesy Doddington Milk Bar sells meals and snacks fresh from the Maxwell family's dairy farm. It's a little way off the A1 at the edge of Northumberland National Park, but a fun diversion on the way to or from Scotland.

The interior is decked out like an American diner – baby blue and navy booths, breakfast bar and zingy orange lamps – and service is faultlessly friendly to match. Breakfasts are free range and delicious. Doddington's own cheese goes into the scrumptious lunchtime rarebits – pick up a piece at the small cheese counter if you're seduced.

But it's the ice cream that people (especially little people) really come for. The counter has around ten varieties, such as lemon meringue and caramel and sea salt, that can be served in cones or tubs, or whizzed up into a milkshake and devoured in seconds.

Opening hours
Tues-Sat 7am-5pm
Sun-Mon 9am-5pm

Doddington Milk Bar, 11 South Road, Wooler NE71 6QE
WWW.DODDINGTONMILKBAR.CO.UK   01668 282357

CAFÉ

Carnaby's Café

JUNCTION: BROWNIESIDE; 1 MINUTE

Metres from the A1, Carnaby's is the perfect stop for weary travellers on the move through Northumberland. The chic, airy venue is the vision of two sisters, dreamt up over a cup of coffee. The menu is written on rolls of paper fixed to the wall, and might include blueberry and banana pancakes, courgette and sweetcorn fritters, chicken club sandwiches, smoked salmon flatbreads and sausage rolls using pork from their own rare breed pigs. Grab a table in the dining area to make the most of the wood burner in winter while doors open onto the courtyard in warmer months

The modern, airy building is arranged in a L-shape against a hillside, so while the road thrums to one side, the sheltered courtyard to the rear is surprisingly peaceful. It's enclosed so parents can enjoy an al fresco cuppa while kids enjoy the play area, miniature picnic benches and ride-on tractors.

A shop section at the entrance stocks a relatively small but very tasteful selection of gifts and homewares – stationery, toys, toiletries and clothing.

Dogs are welcome in the courtyard, but not inside.

Opening hours
Mon-Sun 9.30am-4pm

Carnaby's Café, Brownieside, Chathill NE67 5HW
WWW.CARNABYSCAFE.CO.UK

The Old Stables Tea Room

JUNCTION: DENWICK; 1 MINUTE

For travellers looking for a quick pit stop close to Alnwick who don't want to navigate through the town, this friendly, secluded café is the place. The stone stables that give the tea room its name adjoin the small kitchen garden and courtyard. The dog-friendly courtyard is a wonderful suntrap in the afternoon with views of farmland and the distant A1 (which can be seen but delightfully hardly heard). For the most part the only sounds are the wind in the trees and buzzards calling overhead.

On the food front, there's no escaping the huge cakes on the counter: pistachio, raspberry, lemon and mascarpone Victoria sponge, coffee and walnut. Sandwiches and soups are served with really good homemade bread. As for the coffee, it's got to be Pumphrey's, a regional favourite.

They also sell homemade treats and local products including Northumberland honey, so don't forget to stock up before you leave.

Opening hours
Weds-Sat 10am-4pm

The Old Stables Tea Room, Broomhouse, Denwick, Alnwick NE66 2LB
WWW.OLDSTABLESALNWICK.CO.UK   07594 044904

Alnwick is a delectable, medieval gem, with a proud castle, dubbed 'the Windsor of the North', serpentine streets and an appealing mix of old buildings. The castle and fabulous gardens are well worth exploring (don't miss the enormous tree house).

Below the stronghold in the traditional stone high street, you'll spy Grannies, a charismatic tea room with large windows and handsome, blue and gold shop front. The deli upstairs is a hoard of toothsome Northumberland delicacies – cheeses, jams, pickles and honey. The tea room is downstairs in the old cellar where the remains of a coal chute indicate its former life. It's a cosy room (though the claustrophobic might disagree) with chunky furniture, antique curiosities decorating the shelves and grannie's bloomers pegged out on the ceiling. Food is generous and tasty: perhaps smoked salmon croissants, jacket potatoes, paninis with homemade coleslaw, hunks of homemade cakes and huge scones.

Opening hours
Mon-Sat 9am-5pm
Seasonal Sun 10.30am-4pm

Grannies, 18 Narrowgate, Alnwick NE66 1JG
WWW.GRANNIESTEA.CO.UK   01665 602394

Moorhouse Farm

JUNCTION: STANNINGTON; 2 MINUTES

A super farm shop and café on the edge of a 500-acre family farm, where home-grown is the buzzword. "If we don't produce it ourselves, we know somebody local who does," says farmer Ian. The farm shop is well-stocked with Northumberland produce: from fresh bread to home-reared meat, jams, farmhouse cakes and cheeses. Pick up some spicy jalapeno sausages and minted lamb burgers for a delicious BBQ. A convenient click-and-collect service means you can order ahead and whip a bag of groceries away with you.

The coffee shop serves honest, home-cooked food – cooked breakfasts, pie of the day, fresh sandwiches, burgers, sponge puddings with ice cream and lunch boxes for kids. Grab a cup of Rington's tea and a slice of cake, then take in the country views from the terrace. Children will enjoy the free play area, sandpit, ride-on tractors and visits to the animals – catch Ian at the right time and you might even be able to help him hunt for eggs.

Opening hours
Mon-Sat 9.30am-5.30pm
Sun 10am-4pm

Moorhouse Farm, 21 Station Road, Stannington, Morpeth NE61 6DX
WWW.MOORHOUSEFARMSHOP.CO.UK   01670 789016

FARM SHOP-CAFÉ

Broom House Farm

JUNCTION: 63; 15 MINUTES

© Anna Iermolaieva

Broom House Farm sits at the top of a hill looking out over the dip and roll of the countryside towards Durham cathedral. The coffee shop is cosy in winter with a wood burner and gleaming domes of cakes, whilst in summer there is seating outside, overlooking a huge grassy play field and meadows stocked with sheep and cattle. During the warmer months there's nature-based family action in the Forest Adventure (buy a ticket at the coffee shop) – let off some steam here before heading back to the café to enjoy home cooked snacks and freshly ground coffee.

Ingredients sourced from the farm and surrounding area are whizzed into irresistible bites, such as bacon sandwiches, beef burgers and toasties. Traybakes and cakes are summoned daily from the oven. Fill your bags in the farm shop on the way out: our picks include Durham honey and Broom House chutney.

Opening hours
Mon-Sun 9am-5pm

Broom House Farm; Witton Gilbert, Durham DH7 6TR
WWW.BROOMHOUSEDURHAM.CO.UK   0191 3718382

Tea with Alice

JUNCTION: 58; 2 MINUTES

A1

"We only use the best ingredients, we give free smiles with every visit, we will always fuss over your children or dog and appreciate your handbag," say Mark and Mary, owners of Tea With Alice. We can't disagree. They set up their friendly neighbourhood café after the arrival of their daughter, Alice, and have devoted boundless energy to making it a haven for travellers. There are toys, games and colouring for kids; bowls of water and biscuits for furry visitors.

The neon sign gleams in the window, colourful vintage furniture fills the café and personal trinkets litter the shelves. In the summer holidays workshops and activities – from pizza decorating to bread making – keep the little ones happy while you enjoy your meal.

Tea is loose leaf and the coffee is excellent. In the kitchen brother-in-law Paul cooks everything from scratch using the best ingredients in Country Durham. Home-made bread and Weardale artisan brie create a cheese sandwich to remember.

Opening hours
Tues-Sat 8am-4.30pm

Tea with Alice, West Park, 4 Tilage Green, Darlington DL2 2GL
WWW.TEAWITHALICE.CO.UK   01325 360397

Cross Lanes Organic Farm

A1

JUNCTION: SCOTCH CORNER; 13 MINUTES

Sustainable living is the watchword at the fabulous Cross Lanes Organic Farm, set on the theatrical A66, which links the glorious North Pennines to the Lake District. Owners Peter and Sue have woven eco-principles into the very fabric of the business. Sheep occasionally graze on the meadow-turfed roof, the compost loo is thatched with heather, solar panels heat the water, toilet doors are made from recycled plastic bottles and straw bales line the building.

The restaurant serves a wide range of delicious meals using organic, fresh, wild, local and home-grown ingredients. Home-cured bacon and homemade sausages feature on the breakfast menu; koftas, salads and wood-fired pizzas at lunch; cakes and scones for tea. The shop has a butcher's counter, deli, bakery and a craft section, all focused on local producers and ethical ranges.

Three infamous resident geese will entertain children if they tire of the sturdy, wooden adventure playground.

Opening hours
Mon-Sat 8.30am-5pm
Sun 10am-5pm

Cross Lanes Organic Farm, Cross Lanes, Barnard Castle DL12 9RT
WWW.CROSSLANESORGANICS.CO.UK   01833 630619

Mainsgill Farm

JUNCTION: SCOTCH CORNER; 6 MINUTES

From the camels – Doris, Delilah and Camelot – grazing in the field to the zip wire and adventure playground there's a lot to love about Mainsgill Farm. Just off the thunderous A66 overlooking the northern edge of the Yorkshire Dales, it's a gargantuan farm shop with butchery, food hall, tea room, gift shop and homewares.

Step through the front door and you come face-to-face with a 28-metre deli counter filled with cheeses, cold meats, pies, antipasti and fresh meats. The vegetable aisle has a picture window giving onto those rolling dales, as if to remind you where it all comes from. Most of the goods on offer have their roots (and hooves) in the Mainsgill family's 500-acre farm; the rest is carefully selected from British and continental suppliers.

The café prides itself on freshly baked cakes, meringues, country breakfasts and award-winning soups. The menu is simple and comforting, the service friendly. A fabulous place to break a journey.

Opening hours
Mon-Sun 9am-5pm

Mainsgill Farm, East Layton, Richmond DL11 7PN
WWW.MAINSGILLFARM.CO.UK   01325 718860

The Coach House at Middleton Lodge

A1

JUNCTION: 56; 4 MINUTES

Scotch Corner is a milestone in many journeys, so if you've got there and need a break, take it at The Coach House. It's part of Middleton Lodge, a grand Georgian estate at the fringe of the Yorkshire Dales, and current owners Becky and James have turned it into a luxuriously modern get-away, with food to match.

The Coach House is the more informal of the two restaurants, and occupies the former stables. Make your way from the car park, laid out among a copse of pine trees, to find the restaurant in the elegant lavender-scented courtyard. Despite lofty ceilings, there's a cosiness to the dining room's slate floors and buttoned banquettes. Much of the produce comes from the estate's kitchen garden, and the menu is otherwise dedicated to showcasing Yorkshire's bountiful harvest, cooked to order. You could have eggs Benedict for breakfast, fish pie for lunch or seared beef and popped capers for dinner. You are, of course, just as welcome to drop in for coffee and cake.

And if you're weary or fancy treating yourself in the cocktail bar alongside, book in to one of the sumptuous rooms for the night.

Opening hours
Mon-Fri 7.30am-9pm
Sat 8am-9pm
Sun 8am-9pm

The Coach House at Middleton Lodge, Kneeton Lane, Middleton Tyas, Richmond DL10 6NJ
WWW.MIDDLETONLODGE.CO.UK   01325 377977

Shoulder of Mutton

JUNCTION: SCOTCH CORNER ; 1 MINUTE

An ideal pit stop at just a minute's drive from the A1, and a cut above your average pub food. Tasty starters (duck spring rolls, black pudding and pulled pork bonbons, moules marinière with fennel, even snails bourguignon) are followed by imaginative mains, from Korean BBQ rump steak to steak pies, asparagus and mascarpone ravioli to the eponymous shoulder of mutton, slow cooked for hours. Among the usual suspects on the dessert menu are sparks of inspiration like the blackcurrant sorbet and poached pear and lemon tart.

There's a cosiness in the dusky lighting, tartan carpets, inviting nooks and open fires in winter. Tables are spread over several levels, a product of 400 years of history, and serving staff ferry plates to them with friendly smiles.

If you're travelling with four-legged friends, there's a surfeit of footpaths and bridleways fanning out from the village where you can glimpse signs of its copper-mining past.

Opening hours
Mon 5.30pm-11pm
Tues-Sat noon-3pm, 5.30pm-11pm
Sun noon-10.30pm

Shoulder of Mutton, Middleton Tyas, Richmond DL10 6QX
WWW.SHOULDEROFMUTTONMIDDLETONTYAS.COM   01325 377271

Kiplin Hall & Gardens

A1

JUNCTION: CATTERICK; 10 MINUTES

Lawn games to borrow in the porch, flourishing gardens and a barrow selling veg and cut flowers from the garden at the gate, Kiplin Hall is a really special place to stop.

It dates back to 1620, built for George Calvert who went on to found Maryland, USA, and it's well worth a tour if you're a history buff (you'll need to pay for entrance to the house and gardens). Even if it's just a flying visit, the tea room is open to all and a spectacularly atmospheric space. Step through the main doors to find the darkly panelled room decorated with grand portraits and heavy drapes. Ice cream is made using home-grown fruit, and the walled garden supplies ingredients for the sandwiches, chutneys, jams and soups. There's also an excellent selection of gifts along the dresser at the entrance so be prepared to leave with souvenirs.

If you want to stretch your legs there are plenty of footpaths through woodland and open parkland (sometime with grazing sheep) as well as a circular one-mile lakeside walk. Come in the early Spring for spectacular snowdrops.

Opening hours
Sat-Weds 10am-5pm
(Please check website for seasonal opening hours)

Kiplin Hall & Gardens, Nr Scorton DL10 6AT
WWW.KIPLINHALL.CO.UK   01748 818178

Lister's Farm Shop

JUNCTION: DISHFORTH; 3 MINUTES

From farm to fork, Listers is a wonderful place to enjoy a taste of Yorkshire. It's run by the Lister family, with Grace at the helm, third generation farmers who keep Aberdeen Angus cattle, pigs and sheep as well as an arable enterprise. In the farm shop you'll be tempted by counters of home-reared meat, handmade sausages and home-cured bacon as well as a selection of deli goodies, including home-cooked meats, local cheeses and pies, jams and chutneys.

The café has wooden tables topped with posies of flowers where you can enjoy homemade sausage rolls, salads, tray bakes, cakes, toasted tea cakes, grazing boards and filling sandwiches. There's a small but perfectly formed veggie selection and the breakfasts are award-winning – a plateful of Listers' bacon, sausages, black pudding, tomatoes, mushrooms and eggs will satisfy even the most ravenous.

Children are very welcome and will love the dedicated play area. They can have the run of the pedal-on tractor course, sandpit, swings and Wendy house, and maize maze when in season.

Opening hours
Tues-Fri 8.30am–5.30pm
Sat 9am-4pm (Sun 10am)
(Café closes about an hour earlier.)

Lister's Farm Shop, Leeming Lane, Langthorpe, Boroughbridge YO51 9DE
WWW.LISTERSFARMSHOP.CO.UK   01423 326452

Bowe & Co

JUNCTION: 48; 4 MINUTES

Pretty Boroughbridge is bounded by gently rolling hills and pockets of history. Stretch your legs by the River Ure or walk to the edge of town to find three ancient standing stones, known as the Devil's Arrows and said to have been flung there by Satan himself. Refuel at Bowe & Co, a relaxed and friendly café-deli on the high street. Lunch is wholesome, generous and freshly made. Regulars rave about the salads, which are served alongside soups (maybe beetroot and horseradish), quiches and frittatas.

The go-to Yorkshire platter is an enormous plate of salads, cooked ham, cheese, crisps and a pork pie; cakes are playful – try the coconut and Malibu, raspberry and amaretto or orange and almond. Coffee is deliciously smooth; the tea is Yorkshire, of course. The deli counter is ripe for the picking – fabulous cheeses, sandwiches (maybe pastrami or local roast beef) and anti pasti.

Opening hours
Mon-Sat 9am–4pm

Bowe & Co, 27 High Street, Boroughbridge YO51 9AW
WWW.BOWEANDCO.COM   01423 323037

Minskip Farm Shop

JUNCTION: 48; 1 MINUTE

A1

Food miles are so low at the Minskip Farm Shop near Boroughbridge that you can see vegetables growing in the field in front. Chickens scratch around for grubs in the field at the back, supplying golden-yolked eggs to the shop, and you can visit the lambs in spring.

Third-generation pig farmer Ben and his novelist wife Emma took over the farm business in 2017 and have been busy evolving the popular farm shop into a local food hub. They stock a wide range of fresh and store-cupboard products from the local area, 96% of which are sourced less than 30 miles from the door. These goodies include Aga tray bakes and jams from Bessie's Yorkshire Preserves, bread from the village down the road, pork pies from Whixley, pâté and smoked mackerel from Mackenzies Yorkshire Smokehouse. Plunder the selection for a sensational picnic or the makings of a delicious dinner.

Keep an eye out for the café, which is due to open soon and promises good things.

Opening hours
Mon-Sat 8.30am-5.30pm (7pm Fri)
Sun 9.30am-4pm

Minskip Farm Shop, Minskip Road, Boroughbridge YO51 9HY
WWW.MINSKIPFARMSHOP.COM   01423 329 063

Hideaway Kitchen

JUNCTION: 48; 8 MINUTES

Hideaway by name, hideaway by nature, you'll find this smashing, on-trend restaurant tucked away in the North Yorkshire countryside, yet still within easy reach of the A1.

The atmosphere is relaxed and informal, perhaps in homage to the building's former life as the village pub, but also because co-founders Amelia and Georgina want you to feel like you're eating at a friend's house. And a stylish house at that. The interior has been updated with a liberal splash of white paint and hundreds of soothing plants. Even the piano, standing at the entrance for visitors to play, hasn't survived the whitewash.

Food is simple and seasonal – "We use lamb and pork raised in the village and neighbours frequently leave baskets of apples and other such goodies on the door step," says Amelia. The menu changes every three weeks to showcase Georgina's magic in the kitchen. Expect anything from breakfast waffles to lobster bisque and mezze sharing platters, all served on beautiful hand-thrown ceramics.

Opening hours
Thurs-Fri: 10am-2.30pm & 5-9pm (food)
Sat: 10am-9pm (food)
Sun 10am-5.30pm (food)

Ⓥ Ⓟ

Hideaway Kitchen, Lower Dunsforth, York YO26 9SA
WWW.HIDEAWAYKITCHEN.CO.UK   01423 320700

Fodder

JUNCTION: 47; 9 MINUTES

A1

Fodder is a paragon of the local food movement, a thriving food hub supporting a staggering 430 producers. It was set up when the Yorkshire farming community had been hard hit by the foot and mouth crisis and designed to provide a more sustainable, long-term plan. It's just on the outskirts of Harrogate and for a taste of Yorkshire, there's no better place: pick a cut of meat from the butchery counter, browse the tweed in the gift shop or grab a pie from the deli counter.

The modern and sustainable building – stone walls, large windows and a wooden pergola – also houses a café turning all those ingredients into hearty, affordable meals. Breakfast might be creamy porridge or a Great Yorkshire breakfast, lunch a chargrilled chicken Caesar salad or chickpea and courgette burger. For those in a hurry, takeaways are available from a gleaming Airstream outside – Fodder on the Hoof – with peaceful views of the wonderfully named Crimple Valley.

And you can shop with a clear conscience as all profits are ploughed back (pardon the pun) into the farming charity, and any spare food is donated to a nearby homeless charity.

Opening hours
Mon-Sat 8.30am-6pm
Sun 9.30am-5pm
(café and take-away times vary)

Fodder, Railway Road, Great Yorkshire Showground, Harrogate HG2 8NZ
WWW.FODDER.CO.UK   01423 546111

The Castle Inn

JUNCTION: 46; 8 MINUTES

A beautifully updated stone pub in the Yorkshire countryside with 12 very stylish bedrooms. The original bar and pretty dining room have been transformed and extended with the addition of a relaxed courtyard and two private dining rooms. A sliding glass roof, wood-clad walls, wicker chairs and jolly blankets give the whole space a modern breezy style.

Food is freshly prepared and beautifully presented. Begin your day with a brilliant breakfast and enjoy an excellent choice of starters, mains and desserts, from noon. Little diners can choose from their own menu and there's a good selection of light bites if you are short of time.

Drop into the free-to-visit Spofforth Castle while you're in the area; once the family seat of William Percy, a close associate of William the Conqueror, this is reputedly where rebel barons drew up the Magna Carta.

Opening hours
Mon-Sat 7am-11pm
Sun 7am-10pm

The Castle Inn, 35 High Street, Spofforth HG3 1BQ
WWW.THECASTLEINNHARROGATE.COM   01937 590200

Don't Tell the Duke

JUNCTION: 45; 4 MINUTES

Wetherby is precisely the mid-point between London and Edinburgh; two hundred miles in either direction will land you in a capital city. That alone would make it a perfect staging post, but on top of that you have Don't Tell the Duke, a brunch joint, steak restaurant, wine bar and café rolled into one, with real personality to boot.

The atmosphere is friendly and relaxed, and the décor quirky, so you'll feel as comfortable popping in for one of the generous, rich coffees as a full meal. Order a treacle-cured bacon bap or sweet potato and cumin rösti for brunch, Buddha bowl or chicken burger for lunch or perhaps a grilled Cajun seabass or juicy steak for dinner. If you're hungry, go for the decadent sharing boards, a big pile of steak, crab, pork and salads served on an almost equally big slab of wood; If you fancy just having nibbles or prefer tapas style dining, there's an extensive small plate menu to choose from. There are also deliciously creative cocktails, local ales, and an impressive selection of gins and wine; if you're driving, never fear – you can chose from one of the tasty fresh juice mixes.

It is in the town, but the nearby Wilderness car park on the river bank (by the very pretty bridge) is a short stroll away and free of charge.

Opening hours
Mon-Thurs 11am-11pm
Fri-Sat 11am-midnight
Sun 10am-11pm

Don't Tell the Duke, 6-8 Bank Street, Wetherby LS22 6NQ
WWW.DONTTELLTHEDUKE.CO.UK   01937 587897

CAFÉ-BAR

Tom Foolery

JUNCTION: 45; 3 MINUTES

A light-hearted café-bar on Boston Spa's high street, Tom Foolery is decorated whimsically with umbrella light fittings, John Lennon artwork and metal Tube signs. It's community-focused (weekly quiz on Tuesdays) and informal, so you're as welcome to slump into a sofa with a coffee and raspberry blondie from their delicious cake and pastry selection, as sit at a table and order the works.

Varied breakfasts will suit all appetites – toasted teacakes, Nduja and avocado on sourdough, chicken and waffles with 24-hour chicken gravy (yes really - try it) and big fry-ups with local sausages, treacle-cured bacon, black pudding and flat mushrooms. Salads and sandwiches are on the menu at lunchtime – speck ham, spiced peach and peppers; cumin roasted falafel with spiced squash purée – along with bread baked in house; if you're hungry, the burgers will more than fill a hole. In the evening enjoy their Neapolitan-inspired pizzas or small dishes such as Cajun salmon croquettes, calamari, halloumi fries. There's a good choice of gluten-free, vegetarian and vegan dishes so no-one will miss out. And pity the designated driver with the extensive cocktail menu, every-changing selection of craft ales and carefully curated wine list on offer.

Opening hours
Mon-Sun 10am–midnight

Ⓜ Ⓥ Ⓟ
⎙ ⒼⒻ

Tom Foolery, 179 High Street, Boston Spa LS23 6BD
WWW.TOMFOOLERYBOSTONSPA.CO.UK   01937 541500

Farmer Copleys

JUNCTION: M62 32/33; 9 MINUTES

The family has been farming here for over 140 years but Farmer Copleys as it is seen today began 15 years ago and is a fantastic showcase of sustainable agriculture and British food.

You'll struggle to resist the homemade jams, fudge, chutneys and gelato in the farm shop as well as farm fresh fruit and vegetables. Plunder the lovely deli and 10m-long butchery counter for ingredients for your dinner, and peek into the Jam Kitchen to see the cooks at work.

Quirky Bowler hat lampshades hang from the rafters of the award-winning Moo Café next door, where friendly staff serve home-cooked food from breakfast till tea time. Bread and cakes come from the farm's own bakery; other ingredients from the fields outside.

It's a great place for kids to learn about farming – we didn't know that alpacas keep foxes away! You'll have to peel little ones away from the close-up animal experiences.

Opening hours
Mon-Sat 8.30-5.30pm
Sun & bank hols 8.30-4pm

Farmer Copleys, Ravensknowle Farm, Pontefract Road, Pontefract WF7 5AF
WWW.FARMERCOPLEYS.CO.UK   01977 600200

CAFÉ

Garden Room Café

JUNCTION: 36; 9 MINUTES

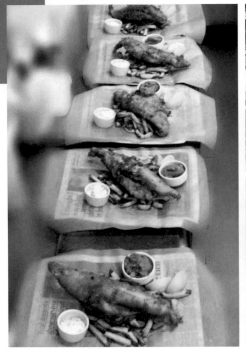

Unpretentious homemade food is the promise from Gina and Stuart at the Garden Room Café, and that's exactly what you get. Whether you order a healthy breakfast, weighty tuna melt, delicious afternoon tea or gargantuan slice of carrot cake you won't go hungry. Ingredients are sourced from nearby farms wherever possible, and on Fridays you can sample fish 'n' chips made with the daily catch at Filey. Everything is cooked to perfection and the staff are welcoming and efficient.

The café is swamped by blooming plants and shrubs (make the most of the lush courtyard on fine days) and housed in a low stone building. Light pours in from country-cottage windows; walls are decorated with delicate floral patterns and the wood panelling is painted a soft olive green. You'll find it in a handsome village just south of Doncaster and near Sheffield, so it's a great place to break a long journey north or south.

Opening hours
Tues-Sun 10am-4.30pm

Garden Room Café, High Street, Braithwell S66 7AL
WWW.GARDENROOMCAFE.CO.UK   01709 790790

Torworth Grange Farmshop & Lakes

JUNCTION: 34; 7 MINUTES

However arduous your journey the sound of wind rustling through the reeds in the lake at Torworth Grange will calm you down. Farm shop, café, campsite and fishing spot, this family business occupies an idyllic corner of Nottinghamshire and stocks almost everything you could want for your onward journey. Artisan bread, regional cheeses, homemade meat pies, freshly baked cakes and craft beers.

The decked terrace, looking over the lake, is festooned with flowers and is the perfect spot for a relaxed lunch while watching the children play. Inside is bright and comfortable with a lovely homely feel. Tea is served in china cups and saucers collected over the years and food is inspired by family classics.

There's something for everyone on the menu – hearty breakfasts, handmade scotch egg salad served with crunchy pickles and coleslaw, or homemade fishcake with poached egg and chips. Just make sure you leave room for one of their delicious cakes.

Opening hours
Mon-Sun 9am-5pm
(winter 9am-4pm)

Torworth Grange Farmshop & Lakes, Great North Road, Torworth DN22 8NY
WWW.TORWORTHGRANGE.CO.UK   01777 816439

CAFÉ

The Hay Barn Café

JUNCTION: CARLTON-ON-TRENT; 10 MINUTES

For a warm, country welcome look no further than the Hay Barn Café. The ladies who work here are interminably friendly and don't bat an eyelid at muddy footwear, muddy paws and messy children. They're expert bakers to boot, and scones are served warm from the oven (try the cherry and almond if you're there on the right day), always with locally made jam and Chantilly cream.

Freshly made quiches, filled rolls and tasty sandwiches are on the lunch menu. Prices are reasonable, the coffee is smooth and the gravelled, suntrap courtyard is ringed by tall, red-brick walls and filled with bright plants and sage-coloured furniture – a lovely spot for listening to the chirrup of birds over a pot of tea or a Haybarn breakfast.

The shelves at the back harbour local produce to take away such as plum bread, pickles, biscuits, pressed apple juice, honey and real ales, ciders and gins.

Opening hours
Mon-Sat 9am-4pm

The Hay Barn Café, Old Hall Farm, Kneesall NG22 0AD
WWW.HAYBARNCAFE.CO.UK   01623 862677

Newfield Dairy Ice Cream Parlour

JUNCTION: NORTH MUSKAM; 10 MINUTES

With views reaching over the Nottinghamshire countryside and 16 delicious ice cream flavours, which often imaginatively use seasonal fruits (damsons and cream, apple and cinder toffee ripple, liquorice and elderberry), Newfield Dairy has become something of an institution. Try their award-winning raspberry macaroon or ginger and honeycomb ice cream.

The flavours are born in the fields around you, and that farm-fresh ethos applies to excellent café fodder too: a farmer's fuel breakfast, hot steak baguettes and homemade quiches. Coffee is locally roasted and, as you'd expect, the floats and milkshakes are legendary. Gluten-free, skinny and dairy-free dishes are available, as well as yummy sorbets and gluten-free cones.

The breezy café overlooks the fields and a safe play area. It's warmed by the wood burner in winter and has plenty of games to keep everyone amused. Outside there's lots of seating for taking in those views, and a grassy lawn for lolling about in summer.

Opening hours
Mon-Sun 10am-4.30pm

Newfield Dairy Ice Cream Parlour, Caunton Road, Hockerton, Southwell NG25 0PN
WWW.NEWFIELDICECREAM.COM   01636 636600

Leadenham Teahouse

A1

JUNCTION: CODDINGTON; 13 MINUTES

Leadenham stands on the southern edge of the Lincoln Cliff which rises up from the famously flat county, and makes for panoramic views from its winding footpaths.

The views alone are worth a detour, but it's worth every extra drop of fuel for a stop at Leadenham Teahouse, recently voted Lincolnshire 'Tearoom of the Year'. Just along from the polo club, this classic English tea room is uniquely located in the village Post Office. Pastel-painted, it is strung with bunting and has posies of fresh flowers on each table. It's run by sisters Katie and Kirsty, who initially set up a deli in the village Post Office – run by their mum – to save it from closure. Since starting life with shelves of honey and cheese, the enterprise has grown into a tea room and gift shop with a beautiful selection of local gifts and cards. It enjoys a wide range of customers, and you're as likely to find locals in for a quiet cuppa as tourists settling down for a light lunch. There are tables outside where you can enjoy the brimming country cottage borders on a fine day.

It's a short spin off the A1 and is a great stop if you're heading down the A17 to Norfolk. Please note that as it's located n the Post Office it is unable to open independently so is closed on Saturday afternoons and Sundays.

Opening hours
Mon-Fri 10am–4pm
Sat 9am–12.30pm
Please check website for seasonal opening times

Leadenham Teahouse, Leadenham Post Office, 10 Main Road, Leadenham LN5 0PY
WWW.LEADENHAMTEAHOUSE.CO.UK   01400 318497

ATTRACTION

JandJ Alpacas

JUNCTION: DODDINGTON LANE; 8 MINUTES

When you've had enough of the tailbacks, few things will cheer you up more than a field full of woolly-faced alpacas. The family have been rearing alpacas here since 2005, specialising in the Huacaya variety for their colourful wool, on display in creative patterns in the shop. The herd has grown from four to more than 90, and so has the farm business, with the most recent addition – a café and visitor centre in funky converted shipping containers.

Large windows onto the fields mean you can watch the animals gambolling around (or even gazing in) while you tuck into toasted paninis, bacon rolls, and generous slices of cake. The coffee is very good, endorsed by even the strictest coffee snobs, and for a small fee you can wander the Alpaca Trail. A restorative stop.

Opening hours
Weds-Sun 10am-5pm
(10am-4pm in winter & on Bank Hol Mondays)

JandJ Alpacas, Meadow Farm, Clensey Lane, Dry Doddington NG23 5HT
WWW.VISITALPACAS.CO.UK   01636 626990

Syston Park Farm Shop & Café

JUNCTION: B1174; 9 MINUTES

Syston Park Farm Shop & Café sits on a low hill above Lincolnshire's gentle fields, just outside Grantham, and makes the most of its sunny position with a wrap-around veranda, solar panelled roof and al fresco seating in the gravel courtyard.

Its productive fruit fields are open to the public to pick their own (in June & July with Christmas trees in December), but they also supply the cafe kitchen with ready ingredients, whether asparagus in spring, soft fruit in summer or pumpkins in autumn. That pipeline leads to freshly baked cakes topped with plump raspberries, asparagus soup and redcurrant jam, while much of the menu also showcases produce from the rest of Lincolnshire. Keep an eye on the specials board for some of the best dishes, such as a light curry, tomato and vegetable risotto or smoked haddock with hollandaise sauce.

The café is popular so it's sometimes worth calling ahead to reserve a table, especially if you'd like one of the prized seats overlooking the parkland.

Opening hours
Tues-Sun 10am-4pm

Syston Park Farm Shop & Café, Syston Park, Grantham NG32 2BZ
WWW.SYSTONPARKFARMSHOP.CO.UK   01400 250000

Dougie's

JUNCTION: A52; 2 MINUTES

Dougie's, The Cake Hole or however you know it, is a cracking place to break from the A1. "It caters for many regulars as well as passing trade," said one customer, "including walkers, cyclists and 'stray' motorists."

Be one of those motorists. Kirk set up the deli, café and bistro after a career as a chef with the RAF and makes almost everything in-house. You'll have to time it right for the lunch window, but if you do you'll be treated to seasonal dishes: pâté and redcurrant jelly on rye bread, stilton and walnut sandwiches or a slice of the much-loved carrot cake. Book ahead if you'd like to treat yourself to an afternoon tea. This is a community affair: jams and chutneys are frequently made with the glut from neighbours' allotments, meat comes from the butcher down the road and bread is supplied by Hambleton in Rutland.

In the evening, it goes up a notch with a widely praised 8-course set menu showcasing Kirk's skills. Arrive hungry.

Opening hours
Weds-Thurs noon-2.30pm
Fri-Sat noon-2.30pm, 7.30pm-midnight

V **GF**

Dougie's, 1 Main Street, Barrowby NG32 1BZ
WWW.BARROWBYCAKEHOLE.CO.UK   01476 564250

PUB
The Green Man Ropsley

JUNCTION: LITTLE PONTON; 10 MINUTES

Like many village ale houses, it was nearly curtains for The Green Man in 2015. At least, it was until Leanne and Phil stepped in to give it a breath of new life. They've since ploughed energy into the food offering and turned it into a community asset: tea room and drinking hole by day, excellent eatery from breakfast till dinner.

Posies of flowers decorate the tables and there's a crackling log burner to warm yourself by on crisp days. As for the food, it's true to its pub roots, with all the classics well represented (crispy fish and chips, sausage and mash in a Yorkshire pudding), but run alongside exotic specials such as game, crocodile steak and seafood, so there's something to suit every taste. Afternoon teas are served on miniature picnic benches, which you can have at a full-sized version in the grassy garden if the weather allows.

Whether you're a foodie or ale swiller, this is a cracking village pub.

Opening hours
Tues-Sat 11am-11pm
Sun 11am-10.30pm

The Green Man Ropsley, 24 High Street, Ropsley, Grantham NG33 4BE
WWW.THE-GREEN-MAN-ROPSLEY.COM   01476 585897

Easton Walled Gardens

JUNCTION: COLSTERWORTH/B6403; 3 MINUTES

Once famously described as 'a dream of Nirvana, almost too good to be true' by Franklin Roosevelt, the gardens of Easton were nearly lost forever when the original house, Easton Hall, was demolished in 1951.

Thankfully Ursula and Fred Cholmeley took over the family property in 2001 and have been restoring the 12-acre gardens. There's a turf maze, yew tunnel, meadows, rose garden, orchards and a pickery (Easton's unique term for its cut flower garden). A Sweet Pea Week is held every July and showcases both heritage and modern varieties.

A garden-themed gift shop smells evocatively of English country gardens and is a rich hunting ground for souvenirs. The tea room serves simple but flavourful meals: filled baguettes, cream teas, excellent cakes, a gardener's ploughman's and vegetable soups. Wash it down with hot cups of tea or homemade elderflower cordial in the summer. You'll need to pay the entrance fee even to access the café so make it a leisurely stop.

Opening hours
Wed-Fri, Sun, Bank Hol Mon 11am-4pm (from March-October)

Admission fee: £7.70 adults; £3.50 children 4-16 yrs.

Easton Walled Gardens, Easton, Grantham NG33 5AP
WWW.VISITEASTON.CO.UK   01476 530063

CAFÉ

The Lodge Country Café

JUNCTION: STRETTON; 7 MINUTES

Ten acres of open meadowland, big skies, tables of homegrown plants for sale out front and a sturdy wooden playframe make The Country Café at the Lodge a tranquil place to pause from the road.

It's run by the Lodge Trust, a charity which provides support and training to adults with learning disabilities, some of whom supply the friendly welcome. Inside the larch-clad hut is warm and relaxed, lined with shelves selling pots of homemade jam and chutneys alongside wooden handicrafts made here. Food is honest and uses local and Fairtrade suppliers – fry ups and sausage and egg sandwiches for breakfast, omelettes, paninis and Caesar salads for lunch. Grab a table inside or take tea and cake to one of the picnic benches on the grass, washed with bird song.

Car parking is plentiful and – as you'd expect – there's excellent access for the elderly and less able.

Opening hours
Mon-Sun 8.30am-4pm

The Lodge Country Café, Main Street, Market Overton LE15 7PL
WWW.LODGECOUNTRYPARK.ORG.UK   01572 767234

The Olive Branch

JUNCTION: STRETTON; 2 MINUTES

A model country pub with a relaxed upmarket vibe, the Olive Branch is as comfortable as a slipper. The pub was formed in 1890 when three cottages built to house farm labourers were knocked together. Since 1999 it has been lovingly developed by owners Sean, Ben and Marcus. A line of pegged wellies stand at the front door for guests to borrow; there's a help-yourself basket of blankets to stave off evening chills; chestnuts roast on the fire in winter. Outside, a lush lawn is fringed with burgeoning borders beyond the pergola, heaven on summery days.

Great lunches and dinners are crafted from the best seasonal produce the kitchen team can lay their hands on, perhaps a lightly smoked sea trout, cucumber and apple, or lamb rump and belly with ewe's milk curd. Cocktails are made with herbs from the paddock. If you like what you taste, loot the dinky shop for local swag including recipe books, restaurant wines, local woodwork and jars of beef dripping.

Opening hours
Mon-Sat noon-2pm, 6.30pm-9.30pm
Sun noon-3pm, 7pm-9pm

The Olive Branch, Main Street, Clipsham LE15 7SH
WWW.THEOLIVEBRANCHPUB.CO.UK   01780 410355

CAFÉ

Café au Chocolat

JUNCTION: A6121; 4 MINUTES

The crêpes at Café au Chocolat are to die for – 'as good as in Brittany' one French visitor remarked. Lunch on the savoury varieties, made with buckwheat flour so naturally gluten free, perhaps stuffed with mushroom and spinach or hummus, rocket and sundried tomatoes. Follow up with a strawberry and salted caramel version if you've got a gap for something sweet.

You'll find the sky-blue fronted café tucked up a side street in the pretty Georgian town of Stamford. Vintage furniture, a 17th-century cast iron range and scuffed panelling give a sense of tousled Parisienne chic inspired by owner Krystyna's travels around Europe. That leaning also translates into deliciously straightforward food: rich, single origin coffee, freshly squeezed juices, french-style pâtisseries, not to mention its chocolate namesake, which is present in many forms. The raspberry and white chocolate brownies are noteworthy, as are the orange-scented hot chocolate and luxury French truffles.

Opening hours
Mon-Sat 8.30am-5pm
Sun 10am-4pm

Café au Chocolat, 2 Ironmonger Street, Stamford PE9 1PL
WWW.CAFEAUCHOCOLAT.CO.UK   01780 437080

The William Cecil

JUNCTION: KETTERING ROAD; 2 MINUTES

This attractive townhouse hotel stands yards from the gates of the Burghley estate. Inside, interiors offer a pleasing mix of English quirkiness and splendour, and informality reigns downstairs.

There are armchairs in front of the fire in the bar, smart wicker tables in the conservatory, doors onto a lovely terrace in summer, and hanging lamps and half-panelling in the colourful restaurant. The food is fresh and local with seasonal delights that include game from the estate. You might find pan-fried stonebass with pak choi and Thai green curry broth, king prawn and sundried tomato linguine, salted caramel tart with peanut butter powder and candied peanuts. Staff recommend booking ahead as it's so popular, for good reason.

Walk it all off through historic Stamford or spin over to Burghley for one of the finest Elizabethan houses in the realm.

Opening hours
Mon-Thurs 7am-9pm (Fri 9.30pm)
Sat 8am-9.30pm (Sun 9pm)
(see website for details)

The William Cecil, St Martins, Stamford PE9 2LJ
WWW.HILLBROOKEHOTELS.CO.UK/THE-WILLIAM-CECIL   01780 750 070

The Bull & Swan at Burghley

JUNCTION: KETTERING ROAD; 2 MINUTES

A beautiful renovation of an ancient inn that stands a short walk from the middle of glorious Stamford, part of the Burghley estate. Step inside and find varnished wood floors, golden stone walls and fires smouldering. The inventive comfort food that flies from the kitchen is hard to resist, perhaps heavenly bites of deep-fried feta and paprika, pan-seared calves liver with mustard mash and a red wine jus, then spiced apple crumble with English custard. If you're stopping on the fly, there are scotch eggs at the bar and decent coffee.

The new kitchen garden is a great venue for pizza and film nights – weather permitting – and rugs are provided to keep the cold at bay.

Don't miss Burghley, one of Britain's finest Elizabethan houses, just a five-minute stroll away.

Opening hours
Food service
Mon-Fri 7-9.30am, noon-3pm, 6-9.30pm
Sat-Sun 8-10am, noon-9.30pm

The Bull & Swan at Burghley, St Martins, Stamford PE9 2LJ
WWW.HILLBROOKEHOTELS.CO.UK/THE-BULL-AND-SWAN/   01780 766 412

The Crown Inn

JUNCTION: 17; 5 MINUTES

A1

The Crown is a proper village pub, from the spreading chestnut tree in the small courtyard at the front, to the enormous hearth in the bar and thatched roof.

Food is a point of pride here, so arrive hungry. Starters might be ham hock and smoked chicken croquettes or crispy fried squid with chilli-pickled cucumber, perhaps steak, ale and mushroom pie or a spicy black bean burger – all made with the best local ingredients owner Marcus can find. You'll find lighter bites on the lunch menu, all served in the round dining room or on the terrace outside on warmer days.

If you're breaking a long journey here, consider overnighting in one of the comfortable bedrooms to make the most of both the ale and the surrounds. Fotheringhay church up the road is enormous and is steeped in Plantagenet and Tudor history, the historic town of Stamford is a short drive away, or you can take a wander along the river that supposedly inspired 'Wind in the Willows'.

Opening hours
Mon-Sat noon-11pm
Sun noon-10.30pm

The Crown Inn, 8 Duck Stree, Elton PE8 6RQ
WWW.CROWNINNELTON.CO.UK   01832 280232

Tea at Tapps

A1

There's always a warm welcome at Tapps, a plant nursery housed in a long barn overlooking a patch of allotments and Hertfordshire countryside. Tea at Tapps is off to the right, a roomy, rustic café with floor-to-ceiling windows, decorated with greenery and local artwork.

Teas are loose leaf, coffee is strong and the atmosphere is relaxed. Owner Louise is a maestro in the kitchen, priding herself on home-cooked food,. She conjures up lip-smacking cakes from the oven every day: warm scones slathered with clotted cream and jam, passion fruit and white chocolate loaf, vegan fruit cake with cherries, macaroons and orange and poppyseed cake.

Lunches are hardy and filling: quiches from the oven, jacket potatoes, stuffed sandwiches and Gardener's lunches. Parking is plentiful and muddy walkers are welcome, so you can work up an appetite exploring the many footpaths that thread through the fields in front.

Opening hours
Mon–Sat 10am–5pm
Sun 10am–4pm

Tea at Tapps, Wallington Road, Baldock SG7 6RS
WWW.TEAATTAPPS.COM   01462 896302

River Cottage Kitchen at Hatfield House

JUNCTION: 3; 10 MINUTES

Built in 1611 by the Earl of Salisbury and once the childhood home of Elizabeth I, Hatfield House is a breathtaking Jacobean mansion, well worth a visit for its rich history, exquisite decoration and tales of Tudor intrigue.

The horses have long since been evicted from the Stable Yard, which is now host to a range of boutiques – gunmaker, dog-grooming salon, goldsmith – as well as a year-round programme of events, from the monthly antiques and farmers markets to face painting and buskers. River Cottage has taken over the coach house restaurant, where large windows give onto the paved courtyard. From either side of the glass, depending on the weather, you can enjoy light bites or full meals, cooked from scratch using the best local ingredients chefs can get their hands on.

Entertain the kids at the farm (you'll need to buy a ticket) where they can play in sand pits, visit animals grazing in the paddocks and enjoy tractor rides, which are free, just like the parking.

Opening hours
Tues–Sun 10am–5pm

River Cottage Kitchen at Hatfield House, Hatfield House, Hatfield AL9 5NQ
WWW.HATFIELD-HOUSE.CO.UK   01707 262030

The

NORTH
M60, M62, M180

Coast to coast through the peaks and the dales

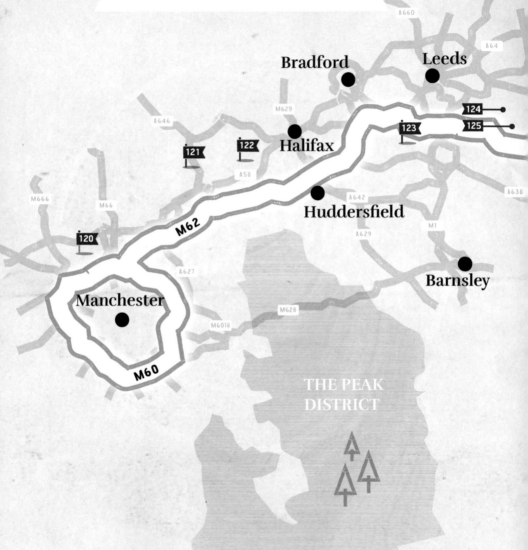

M60 / M62 / M180

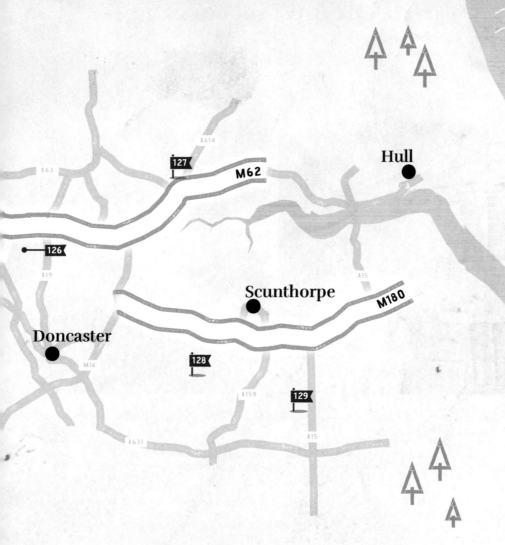

A614

A63

127

M62

A19

126

Hull

Scunthorpe

Doncaster

M18

A15

M180

128

A159

129

A15

A631

120	Farrars café	124	Rivers Meet	128	Tiggy's Tea Room
121	Waterfall Tea Rooms	125	The Twisted Tree	129	Uncle Henry's
122	The Larder Delicatessen	126	The Courtyard Tearoom		
123	BREW Coffeehouse & Brunch Bar	127	That Tea Room		

If you're stuck in the confusion of motorways that is Manchester's ring road system, give yourself a break and pull in here.

Radcliffe Market is one of the new wave of food halls sweeping the country and regenerating tired markets and large industrial spaces into vibrant culinary hubs. It was set up by Jodie Bannister to bring good food and arts back into the town, and there's a youthful buzz to the retro furniture and varied food stands.

At the far end, Farrar's is one of the permanent fixtures, and serves a decent range of considered lunches and snacks, all provided by small artisans companies nearby. The coffee is excellent, and roasted nearby by Ancoats Coffee Co while tea is the house's own blend. Bread and pastries are fresh daily, from croissants to seed-loaded flapjacks and pastel de nata, and friendly staff are happy to steer you through the menu.

We agreed with the number of delighted customers calling this a 'hidden gem' and left reluctantly.

Opening hours
Mon-Tues, Thurs-Sat 9am-5pm

Farrars café & tea rooms, Market Hall, Radcliffe, Manchester M26 1PN
WWW.FACEBOOK.COM/FARRARSCAFEANDTEAROOMS01/   07824 441925

Waterfall Tea Rooms

JUNCTION: 21; 13 MINUTES

Antique chairs, farmhouse tables and soft grey-painted walls make the low-key Waterfall Tea Rooms at the roadside an appealing stop. Sharon and Susan set up the tea room to indulge their love of baking, which emerges in tantalising cakes with flavours such as After Eight, double chocolate, rosewater and raspberry and apple drizzle.

But it's not just cakes. The cheerful staff also ply tables with homely cooked breakfasts, warming lunches and dainty afternoon teas, cooking up ingredients from Pennine and Yorkshire suppliers: sandwiches, jackets, quiches, rarebits and filling pies.

There's a peaceful garden at the back where dogs are welcome and children can safely let off steam, and the canal path that stretches away in either direction is a great way to see the Pennines and moorland that inspired Ted Hughes's and Sylvia Plath's work when they lived in nearby Mytholmroyd.

Opening hours
Tues-Sun 9.30am-3.30pm

Waterfall Tea Rooms, Dean Head, Todmorden Road, Littleborough OL15 9LZ
WWW.FACEBOOK.COM/WATERFALLTEAROOMS/   01706 378877

One customer described The Larder Delicatessen quite succinctly: "It looks pretty small from the outside, but inside it's like Mary Poppins' handbag!". The unassuming shop front stands on Ripponden's elongated main street, smart after a recent refurb. The welcome is almost invariably warm and you'll be drawn quickly into genuine conversation.

Sizzling bacon rolls and cooked breakfasts are on the morning menu and you can lunch on sandwiches made with home-roasted meats and deli goodies, fresh salad boxes, in-house sausage rolls, chicken pies and filled jacket potatoes. Food is freshly made daily in the implausibly compact kitchen (given the volumes), and it's a hotbed of experimentation: visitors will frequently be asked to taste and review morsels.

The café is similarly bijou so while you can grab a perch at the beautiful wooden breakfast bar if there's space, gourmet take-aways are readily supplied.

Opening hours
Mon-Fri 8am-4pm
Sat 8am-3pm
(last hot food orders 2.30pm; 2pm Sat)

The Larder Delicatessen, 170 Oldham Road, Ripponden HX6 4EB
LARDERDELI.WORDPRESS.COM   01422 822218

BREW Coffeehouse & Brunch Bar

JUNCTION: 28; 9 MINUTES

After his extensive travels, Mohamed decided that Batley was missing a brunch spot and meeting point, and immediately resolved to fix that. Leaping on the opportunity of an empty job centre, he enlisted the help of his family and set about stripping out the office fittings and replacing them with tiled walls, modern lighting and a wood-clad counter that wouldn't look out of place in any major city worldwide. (If you think it looks familiar it was used as a set for BBC's 'Last Tango in Halifax'.)

A steady stream of happy groups flow to tables beneath the luminous sky lantern to either linger over smooth coffees or order up hearty plates. Fresh bread and cakes are handmade by a local bakery; gourmet sausages and rashers from another nearby producer. Creative flavour combinations are a nod to the team's travels and heritage, perhaps shakshuka, Indian-style thali breakfast, cinnamon buns or croissant loaf with berry compote.

Somewhat uniquely for brunch joints like this, it's also halal.

Opening hours
Mon-Thurs 10am-4pm
Fri-Sun 10am-6pm

BREW Coffeehouse & Brunch Bar, 26 Wellington Street, Batley Carr WF17 5HZ
WWW.FACEBOOK.COM/BREW-COFFEEHOUSE-AND-BRUNCH-BAR-614819758948722/ 01924 694758

The combination of home cooking and crafts make this a cosy place to pause on your journey. Rivers Meet is an unassuming café in the village of Methley. The building was once a pub but today its rooms play host to numerous microbusinesses selling their arts and crafts – leather handbags, natural skincare, dream catchers and clothing – as well as a range of classes and workshops. Drop in and you might find a kids' activity in full swing, a book club chattering enthusiastically or a local WI meeting discussing jam or climate change.

Given the business ethos, it's only right that food is homemade to match. This is plain from the delicious smells that greet you on arrival. Lunch might be a pulled pork scuffler (Yorkshire bread cake) or a freshly baked quiche, warm from the oven.

A modest amount of parking is available just beyond the bend in the road.

Opening hours
Mon-Fri 9am-4.30pm
Sat-Sun 8.30am-4.30pm

Rivers Meet, 102 Leeds Road, Methley LS26 9EP
WWW.RIVERSMEETCRAFTCAFE.CO.UK   01977 279729

The Twisted Tree

JUNCTION: 31; 2 MINUTES

Not so long ago the Mexboro' Arms Hotel was down on its luck, languishing by the roadside, but that was before the Beal family stepped in to reshape its fortunes. Seeing the building's potential, they have created a stylish gift shop and vintage emporium with the adjoining Twisted Tree café.

There's a charm to the rustic décor, with its wood-clad counter, industrial coat hooks and old maps wallpapering the dining room. Food is all freshly cooked and never processed, so you could stop in for a croque madame, halloumi fries or steak, morning to night. Take your platefuls through to the sunny conservatory at the back if you can grab a table – it's a fantastic spot with the bi-fold doors flung back on a summer's day.

But it's the service that really sets The Twisted Tree apart from its peers. Staff make a noticeable effort to make every customer welcome. The steady procession of regulars is testament to owner Chris's simple philosophy: 'We don't want to do anything clever; I want my customers to come in, have a great coffee and leave with a smile on their face.'

Opening hours
Mon-Sat 10am-late
Sun 10am-4pm

Ⓥ ⒼⒻ

The Twisted Tree, Mexboro' Arms Hotel, Whitwood Common Lane, Whitwood WF10 5PT
WWW.THETWISTEDTREE.MENU   01977 516174

The Courtyard's low-set building was originally built as a Navy, Army and Air Force Institute in the grounds of Womersley Park, when the stately home was turned over to support the war effort. Since then the building has been used as an apple store and craft centre before settling into its current guise.

Now it's a brilliant tearoom, easily accessed from both the A1 and M62. Owner Jacci is proud of her Yorkshire roots, which filters through to the simple, tasty dishes and relaxed, tea room vibe. Her baking is first-rate – passed down by grandmothers on both sides – and if you can leave without sampling a slice of cake (we had the coffee and raspberry), you've got iron willpower.

A bookshelf at one end is used to sell preserves and books, the proceeds of which provide funds for village amenities, while free-range eggs and local honey are also available to buy.

The dinky car park is over the road, at the edge of a patch of woodland. Dogs are welcome inside but may be asked to sit away from the kitchen.

Opening hours
Thurs-Sun 9am-4pm

The Courtyard Tearoom, Park Lane, Womersley DN6 9BH
WWW.THECOURTYARDWOMERSLEY.CO.UK   01977 621190

That Tea Room

JUNCTION: 37; 3 MINUTES

The Dickensian windows of That Tea Room in Howden set the scene for Sam and Jo's traditional tea shop. The building itself is fascinating, with internal windows and pillars hinting at a long history of trade, and today it's tasty fare that draws the crowds. The counter is crammed with tantalising homemade cakes, and the chalkboard features regularly rotating specials, perhaps sweet chilli chicken and vegetable flatbread, goats' cheese bruschetta or salmon and dill fishcakes.

There are rooms at the back and upstairs to choose from, but our favourite is the teapot room where the ceiling is hung with hundreds of china pots.

Howden itself has a history stretching back to King Edgar and William the Conquerer, and warrants a wander to see the ruins of the once-famous Minster, learn about the horse fair that drew people from across the continent, and follow the intriguing airship trail.

Opening hours
Mon-Sun 10am-4pm

That Tea Room, 64 Bridgegate, Howden DN14 7JH
WWW.THATTEAROOM.CO.UK   01430 432714

M180 Tiggy's Tea Room

JUNCTION: 2; 7 MINUTES

The pretty Lincolnshire town of Epworth has a robust independent high street, and Tiggy's Tea Room is at the centre of it. Run by Amanda, who named the cafe after her daughter, it's a modern take on a classic, with floral wallpaper, dainty chinaware and cake stands heaving with home baking. Staff add to the ambience with their patterned retro dresses, wide smiles and easy conversation.

Although Amanda is a confirmed vegetarian, the menu is wide ranging, from child-pleasing milk shakes to bacon and brie panini and chocolate orange cake.

Epworth itself is worth exploring, and Tiggy's is a dedicated ambassador, frequently hatching plans to introduce more people to the town. There are a few car parks in town but plenty of free parking in side streets off the main road.

Opening hours
Tues & Thurs 9.30am-5pm
Weds, Fri, Sat 9am-5pm

Tiggy's Tea Room, 46 High Street, Epworth DN9 1EP
WWW.FACEBOOK.COM/TIGGYSTEAROOMS/   07777 653505

Uncle Henry's

JUNCTION: 4; 9 MINUTES

It's a quick dash down Lincolnshire's A15 to Uncle Henry's, a superior farm shop, butchery and café set on the Ward family's arable and pig farm.

Run the gauntlet of enviable gifts and homewares in the shops to reach the café, which draws many of its ingredients from the farm or other producers nearby. You'll find award-winning sausages (made from their own home-reared pork) on the breakfast menu and homemade quiches, soups and ciabattas on the lunch menu (though it's cake and drinks only for the last half hour of café service). In summer, grab a table in the inner courtyard to cool down by the fountain.

You can pick up just about anything you need in the shop for your onward journey – all produce coming from the same range of local suppliers that feed the kitchen. The deli counter has bountiful car snacks, while the butchery has your BBQ covered.

Kids making a nuisance of themselves in the car can burn off energy in the outdoor play area, which has a sand pit, pedal tractor track and climbing frame. If the family is feeling restless, explore the farm trail where you can see Shire horses (Hattie particularly enjoys attention) and the pond. (Free maps available in shop.)

Opening hours
Mon-Sat 9.30am-5pm
Sun 10am-4pm

Uncle Henry's, Grayingham Grange Farm, Grayingham, Gainsborough DN21 4JD
WWW.UNCLEHENRYS.CO.UK   01652 640308

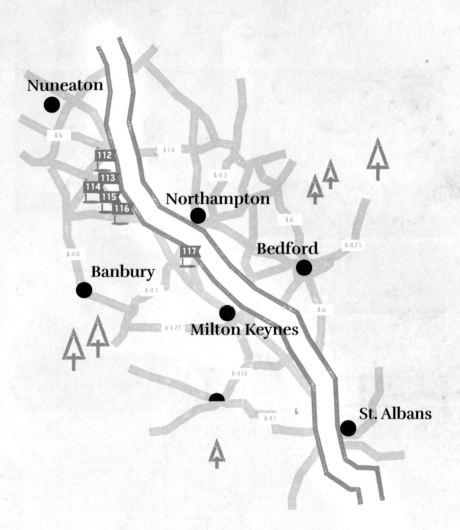

Nuneaton

A6

A14

112

113

114

115

116

Northampton

A43

A6

117

Bedford

A421

A40

Banbury

A43

A421

Milton Keynes

A6

A418

St. Albans

A41

Blacker Hall Farm Shop

JUNCTION: 39; 2 MINUTES

Blacker Hall Farm Shop is an Aladdin's cave of delicious West Yorkshire produce, most of it grown or prepared on the farm and the rest carefully selected from local growers and suppliers who share the same values. The award-winning shop is run by Edward and Cheryl Garthwaite, a hands-on, husband-and-wife team. They pile the shelves high with temptation, from Wakefield rhubarb to Yorkshire ales and Cumbrian charcuterie. Follow your nose to find the in-house bakery making a daily range of cakes, and pies, or pick up some dry-aged beef sirloin, dry-cured bacon and Blacker Hall sausages from the butchery; there's also a deli, greengrocery, fishmongers, gift house and wine loft. Service is friendly and informative – just ask if you'd like some recipe inspiration.

The Barn Café is at the back and serves proper farmhouse food, from full Yorkshire breakfasts to homemade quiche for lunch and delicious afternoon teas, as well as an extensive drinks menu. Sit up in the airy rafters of the beautiful old barn or grab a table either in the courtyard or on the sun-drenched patio where kids can charge about on the lawn beyond.

Opening hours
Mon-Fri 8.30am-6pm
Sat 8.30am-5pm
Sun 9am-5pm

Blacker Hall Farm Shop, Branch Road, Calder Grove, Wakefield WF4 3DN
WWW.BLACKERHALL.COM   01924 267202

PUB

Angel and Harlequin

JUNCTION: 30; 3 MINUTES

The wonderfully named village of Spinkhill is lucky to have the Angel and Harlequin. In fact, the Angel is lucky to have Spinkhill, since villagers stepped in to rescue it from development into flats only a few years ago.

Chris and Jean took the helm instead, metamorphosing the former pub into a cracking and very welcoming bistro. It's open from 9am each day for breakfast and continues whizzing seasonal ingredients into tasty dishes throughout the day: filled bagels, lentil and sweet potato curry, roast tomato soup and wild boar ravioli. Cosy nooks with chevron-detailed tables next to the fire are an ideal spot for a coffee and slice of cake from the in-house pastry chef; it's hard to beat a slice of the coconut and rum.

If you haven't time to stop and make the most of the slouchy Chesterfields and a chat with the natives, the pizza oven produces very good takeaways: call ahead to have it waiting.

Opening hours
Mon-Sat 9am-late
Sun 9am-8pm

Angel and Harlequin, 26 College Road, Spinkhill, Sheffield S21 3YB
WWW.ANGELANDHARLEQUINBISTRO.CO.UK   01246 432315

The Café at Renishaw Hall

Grade I-listed Renishaw Hall, surrounded by award-winning Italianate gardens, has been the Sitwell family seat for nearly 400 years. Not far from the M1 and Chesterfield, the rural grandeur will pacify any road-frayed nerves. Parking is plentiful (you'll need to buy a £1 ticket) and a short walk away from the estate's old stable block. Horses have been hoofed out and the buildings around the cobbled courtyard beautifully renovated to host a range of small businesses, including the Sitwell Museum.

The café is here too, a large, beamed space with dovecote towers at either end and the walls hung with some of the family's collection of art and antiques. Food is seasonal and tasty and the coffee good; you can even have a glass of wine from the Renishaw vineyard. Make a day of it by visiting the idyllic, dog-friendly gardens, which are alive with butterflies and dragonflies and well worth the entry fee. Guided tours of the Hall itself are available every Friday in the season, and weekends in August.

Opening hours
Weds-Sun 10.30am-4.30pm (Mar-Sept)
Fri-Sun 10.30am-4pm (Oct-Nov)
Thurs-Sun 10.30am-4pm (last week Nov-1st week Dec)

The Café at Renishaw Hall, Renishaw Park, Chesterfield S21 3WB
WWW.RENISHAW-HALL.CO.UK   01246 432310

Welbeck Farm Shop

JUNCTION: 30; 11 MINUTES

© Welbeck Farm Shop

© Welbeck Farm Shop

© Welbeck Farm Shop

© Marcel Walker

An enormous, traditional estate deep in Robin Hood country Welbeck Farm now hosts a chic and well-rounded community of artisan food producers and entertainments. The large shop sources two-thirds of its produce from the estate, stocking its own meat, raw milk, Welbeck Abbey ales, Stichelton blue cheese, artisan chocolates from in-house chocolatier Shelly Preston and sensational sausage rolls.

Across the courtyard, the Harley art gallery has activities for kids, an irresistible gift shop and contemporary exhibitions alongside the Portland collection. In a building nearby, there's an independent café with a hip, minimalist interior where hungry hoards are fed with classic fare, delicious daily specials and a unique coffee blend. If you have time to spare, park up, grab some snacks and meander round one of the three downloadable walking routes around the rural estate. Heaven.

Opening hours
Mon-Sat 10am-5pm
Sun 10am-4pm

Welbeck Farm Shop, Worksop S80 3LW
WWW.WELBECK.CO.UK   01909 478725

PUB
The Elm Tree

JUNCTION: 30; 10 MINUTES

Swathed in ivy with two gabled windows peeping from the roof, the Elm Tree is a welcome sight during a long journey. When Chris and Jean took it over some years ago, it was a standard pub serving standard, ready-made food, but they have ploughed heaps of energy into reviving it with fresh ingredients and decent cooking, and they're reaping the rewards.

Regulars and visitors alike find a friendly reception in the low-beamed, cosy inn, and in summer can take a seat on the terrace outside, rustic with its chunky tables and festoon lighting.

The food is pub classics done well, perhaps prawn cocktail with lemon grass, gammon steak with triple-cooked chips or leek, pea and spinach risotto. At lunchtime there's a good value set menu as well as stuffed sandwiches featuring the kitchen's own bread and chutneys. Portions are generous so you won't go hungry.

Opening hours
Mon, Weds-Sat noon-9pm
Sun noon-6pm

The Elm Tree, Elmton, S80 4LS
WWW.ELMTREEELMTON.CO.UK   01909 721261

The Pump Tea Rooms

JUNCTION: 29A; 5 MINUTES

Frequently described as a hidden treasure, The Pump is a captivating tea room alongside the mighty Bolsover Castle. It's housed in a sturdy stone building on the town square and takes its name from the water pump just outside. Inside the vibe is warm and welcoming: tables are clustered with colourful chairs, a stove stands in the original stone hearth and a mural of fields brings a bolt of sunshine to one wall.

For breakfast, lunch and dinner the food is honest and flavoursome (sandwiches, salads, soups; hot meals after dark) and very reasonably priced. Book ahead if you want to try the very popular Sunday roast or build-it-yourself afternoon tea. If you can resist the siren call of the towering cakes and home baking beneath glass cloches on the counter, you're stronger than us.

Do pop into the castle if you have time: far from a defensive stronghold, the 17th-century edifice was built as an indulgent gentleman's retreat and is the birthplace of dancing horses.

Opening hours
Mon-Sun 9am-4pm

The Pump Tea Rooms, 21 Market Place, Bolsover S44 6PN
WWW.THEPUMPBOLSOVER.CO.UK   01246 827567

The Old Schoolhouse Deli-Café

JUNCTION: 25; 4 MINUTES

A fabulous little deli-café tucked, as you might guess, behind the old school. It's homely, with a warm welcome and cake-loaded counter – the sort of place you could drop into a sofa with a magazine as music plays softly in the background.

Breakfasts are varied but the signature scrambled eggs and crispy bacon are a must, and the lunch menu may feature jacket potatoes, panini, pork pies, and the speciality crayfish salad. The cakes are killer, made back in the kitchen: from gin and tonic loaf to Bakewell slice. The owners are particularly proud of their coffee, which is sourced from a local supplier who travels the world in search of excellence.

Dogs are welcome outside: ask at the counter for free dog treats.

.

Opening hours
Mon-Fri 10am-3pm
Sat 9am-3pm

The Old Schoolhouse Deli-Café, School Lane, Stanton by Dale DE7 4QJ
0115 930 5699

CAFÉ-RESTAURANT

Buonissima Aperitivo Bar

JUNCTION: 25; 5 MINUTES

Turn off the M1 into the old trading station of Stapleford, an unassuming town with red-brick terraces and a long high street, to find Buonissima. The bright bistro, café and bar rolled into one is open and light: wooden floors, red Chesterfields and clusters of tables invite you to linger. Tables on the wide pavement outside the elegant, charcoal grey frontage are great for people watching and al fresco lunches.

The chef, Pierangelo, is Sicilian and brings that Italian flair for flavours to the menu: homemade tiramisu in individual glasses, frittata with various fillings, antipasti served on lovely wooden platters and weekly pasta dishes. Try the pizzas with crispy bases topped with goodies fresh from the deli – accompanied by a glass of Menabrea (possibly Italy's finest lager) or an Aperol Spritz. Pasqualini coffee is imported from Italy, a rich blend that makes for a killer espresso; teas are loose leaf. Service is relaxed and friendly and kids are welcome.

Opening hours
Tues 9.30am-3pm
Wed 9.30am-10pm (Thurs-Fri 11pm)
Sat 10am-11pm (Sun 4pm)

Buonissima Aperitivo Bar, 14 Station Road, Sandiacre NG10 5BG
WWW.BUONISSIMABAR.COM   0115 939 3256

CAFÉ

Fintons Café & Bakehouse

JUNCTION: 25; 6 MINUTES

The delicious smell of home baking is all the proof you need that the Fintons team make their food in-house. Cosy banquette seating, scatter cushions and white-painted ladder chairs make this a comfortable place to stop and gather yourself while friendly staff ferry plates to your table. A bucket of books and toys will absorb little visitors while you eat.

Breakfast on scrambled eggs and rocket on toast or fluffy omelettes, lunch on generous ploughmans, warm quiche or healthy salads. When it comes to the cakes you've got a counter full of options, but the cornflake tart comes highly recommended. Gluten-free food is a speciality (a pleasant relief for travellers with dietary restrictions) so there's a very good range, and specials are inked up on a roll of brown paper on the wall.

Opening hours
Mon-Sat 9am-4pm

Fintons Café & Bakehouse, 29 Draycott Road, Breaston, Derby DE72 3DA
WWW.FACEBOOK.COM/PG/FINTONSBAKEHOUSE   01332 986 556

No. 11 deli

JUNCTION: 24; 6 MINUTES

Thousands pass Castle Donington on their way to East Midlands airport or to the well-known Donington Park race circuit, but only a handful of people drop into the village itself. They are well rewarded. The charming high street, farmers' market and Saxon history are well worth a look, even if the castle is long gone.

Refuel for the onward journey at No.11 Deli in the village centre, where Liza and her chipper, friendly team serve nourishing breakfasts (almond croissants, bacon butties, homemade smoothies), tasty sandwiches (hot beef, stilton and red onion chutney, pastrami and sliced gherkin, and cheddar crunch), jacket potatoes and pasta pots alongside an array of salads, pies and cakes. Their famous oinkers, giant sausage rolls, have people queuing down the street.

Scoff your goodies and sip your coffee at the small bar in the window while you decide which deli goods you're going to sweep into your shopping basket.

Opening hours
Mon–Sat 8am–5pm

No. 11 deli, 11 Borough Street, Castle Donington DE74 2LA
WWW.NO11DELI.CO.UK   01332 813555

FARM SHOP

Tori and Ben's Farm

JUNCTION: 23A; 10 MINUTES

Tori and Ben's farm shop is a triumph of the field-to-fork philosophy and is set on the family's farm just outside Melbourne: Ben takes charge of the Longhorn cattle and Tori the Jacob sheep. The meat from these compassionately reared animals is sold in the farm shop and the knowledgeable butcher can practically name the animal it comes from, happily advising on the best cut. Look out for the informative butchery workshop if you're keen to absorb some expertise.

As well as the farm's own excellent meats, you'll find free-range pork and chicken from nearby Packington (chosen for its shared ethics), and you can raid the shelves for local vegetables, bread and a delicious selection of salads, also available to take away.

Seating is outside in the the shelter of the marquee, with heaters and a crate of blankets for cooler days. Benches and vintage chairs are clustered round tables and flung with pelts from the farm (also available for sale in the shop). Kids will love the mud kitchens, sand pit and ride-on tractors with mini hay bales in the play area, which frees adults up to savour one of the peerless bacon butties.

Opening hours
Tues-Fri 9am-5pm
Sat 8am-5pm
Sun 10am-4pm

Tori and Ben's Farm, Kings Newton Lane, Kings Newton, Melbourne DE73 8DD
WWW.TORIANDBENSFARM.CO.UK   01332 865698

Three Horseshoes

Opposite the conical 'village lock up', this listed building's former life as a farrier's lends it its name, and the stables are still standing out the back, only now turned over to an artisan chocolate maker and small antiques shop.

Ian and Jennie have revitalised the interior with a good eye for design and pleasing reuse of materials: old floorboards provide wood panelling, a stone window frame has been turned into a grand fireplace and a former garden step now leads to the loos. Reclaimed materials stand alongside seagrass matts, antique pews, tables and chairs, and the crowning glory is the Victorian display counter which proudly displays the chocolates made in the yard.

The menu is filling and expertly cooked: perhaps potato and garlic soup, pork and cider casserole or blackened salmon, and whiskey trifle or treacle tart to finish up. A cracking village pub.

Opening hours
Tues-Sat 11.30am-2pm, 5.30pm-10.30pm
Sun noon-3.30pm

Three Horseshoes, 44-46 Main Street, Breedon on the Hill, Derby DE73 8AN
WWW.THEHORSESHOES.COM   01332 695129

PUB

The Royal Oak

JUNCTION: 24; 8 MINUTES

Slip into the Royal Oak and you'll be greeted by a cosy village pub of tartan carpets, high-backed booths, mismatched chairs, inglenook fireplace and locals sipping ale at the bar. It's a gastropub with 12 bedrooms (in beautifully renovated outbuildings at the back with a cottagey feel) run by brothers Chris and Alex, but you'd be every bit as comfortable popping in for a coffee and a breather as you would for one of their coveted meals.

Service is excellent and portions generous. Start with a sharing platter for a mouthful of all the flavours: pumpkin, feta and pine nut filo parcels, chorizo in tomato sauce, soup shots, and spiced sweet potato wedges. Mains include pub classics, such as fish and chips and juicy burgers, as well as more inventive, seasonal dishes. You're in luck if you're passing on a Sunday as roasts are served at lunchtime followed by their renowned pies in the evening. Save space, if you can, for the chocolate mousse with chantilly cream and chocolate brioche croutons.

Opening hours
Sun-Thurs noon-11pm
Fri-Sat noon-11.30pm

The Royal Oak, The Green, Long Whatton LE12 5DB
WWW.THEROYALOAKLONGWHATTON.CO.UK   01509 843694

Oakley Grange Organic Farm

JUNCTION: 23; 8 MINUTES

If you love organic food, don't miss this beautiful farm, deli and café. Inger and Richard Mee have been farming the natural way on this 600-acre patch of Leicestershire since 2001. As you walk into a tastefully converted brick barn, a bulging deli counter greets you, touting its tempting fresh bread, chutneys, infused oils, cheeses, chocolates and meat produced on the farm, honey, eggs and veg, as well as gifts, jewellery and cards.

Everything in the café is homemade using predominantly organic ingredients: breakfasts of home-cured bacon, Whole Earth beans and artisan bread segue into gourmet sandwiches, farmer's antipasti, mushrooms stuffed with Gruyère cheese and herbs, and chicken and three-cheese pie. Munch cakes, perhaps hazelnut tart or a chocolate brownie, with your coffee.

Service may be leisurely so you can drop the pace on a sunny terrace and lawn (dogs are allowed outside), and enjoy a cup of tea to the sound of birdsong and the light clink of crockery. Bliss.

Opening hours
Mon, Thurs-Fri 9am–5pm
Sat-Sun 8am-5pm
(Closed first 3 weeks in January)

Oakley Grange Organic Farm, Shepshed Road, Hathern LE12 5LL
WWW.OAKLEYGRANGE.CO.UK   01509 842988

SHOP-CAFÉ

The Garden Barn

JUNCTION: 20; 2 MINUTES

Piled with unusual gifts, crockery, homeware, reclamation finds, greetings cards, furniture, plants and garden goodies, the Garden Barn is a veritable emporium comprising a labyrinth of connecting rooms.

The shop began in the mid-1980s as a traditional farm shop and has diversified creatively into a treasure trove – it has an unrivalled collection of Victorian chimney pots, should you need one. It's difficult for even the most hardened minimalists not to walk away with a trinket or two.

In the centre of the action a café offers simple light lunches, rich coffee and sweet treats. The paninis are particularly popular, served with thoughtful extras, such as hummus and crudités or a handful of pistachios. Eat at the open-plan tables by the counter, head for the quieter tea room upstairs with log-burner, reading materials and countryside views, or enjoy al fresco dining in the tumbling gardens during summer months.

Opening hours
Tues–Sat 9.30am–5.30pm
Sun 11am–4pm

The Garden Barn, Rugby Road, Cotesbach LE17 4HS
WWW.GARDENBARN.CO.UK   01455 550900

The Yard Café @ Cotesbach

JUNCTION: 20; 2 MINUTES

Delicious, field-fresh food is served in a rustic, wiggly-roofed Victorian stable block. Breakfasts are filling and tasty; the menu changes frequently to take advantage of seasonal produce, much of it organic. Expect homemade soups, quiches (with inventive fillings such as smoked mackerel, beetroot and horseradish), jacket potatoes and generously filled baguettes, which can be washed down with a local beer. Cakes are freshly baked by the in-house chef and feature flavours such as blueberry and marzipan or chocolate orange.

The café is colourful and homely. Furniture is painted bright colours and there's a bookshelf full of games and books to pass the time. Walls are decorated with local arts and crafts, which you can buy along with baked goodies – the scones are highly regarded.

In winter the wood-burner is fired up; come summer the doors are flung open to a peaceful courtyard with pots of flowers and a canopy for shade. Well behaved dogs are welcome.

Opening hours
Mon-Sat 9am-4pm

The Yard Café @ Cotesbach, Main Street, Cotesbach LE17 4HX
01455 550202

The Barn at Upper Stowe

JUNCTION: 16; 5 MINUTES

A wonderfully ramshackle collection of old farm buildings on a former dairy farm transformed into a micro complex of independent shops, with art gallery, second-hand book shop, photography studio, gift shop and model railway specialist. The Barn stands at the middle, serving generous breakfast and lunches in a tea room that has preserved a distinct farmhouse feel: brick and stone walls, the big belly of a wood-burner in the corner and Cath Kidston-esque tablecloths.

The menu is simple and freshly made: bacon butties, jacket potatoes, halloumi and pepper toasties, overfilled baguettes. Cakes stud the dresser to tempt you (fruit, banana and ginger, rocky road, cranberry and orange sponge), if you're not lured first by the cream teas. Daniel is at the helm in the kitchen and takes any special diets in his capable stride.

You can soak up the rays in the shelter of a gravelled courtyard and kids will be quietly entertained visiting the pygmy goats.

Opening hours
Tues-Sun 10am-4.30pm

The Barn at Upper Stowe, The Old Dairy Farm Centre, Upper Stowe NN7 4SH
WWW.THEBARNRESTAURANT.NET   01327 349911

Boboli

JUNCTION: B6047; 9 MINUTES

If you're looking for an authentic taste of Italy on your way through Leicestershire, you're in luck. Boboli - just off both the A6 and Kibworth's high street - serves up proper pizzas and rustic Italian dishes, practically fresh from the motherland. Behind the whitewashed façade and taupe-painted window frames owners Sarah and Lino Poli run a super-friendly ship that cuddles customers in from breakfast onwards.

If you've never had a Marocchino (coffee with frothed milk and nutella), you absolutely must try the Boboli version, served in the morning with homemade almond biscotti. If that's too sweet for your tooth at an early hour, there's also toast and jam and excellent coffee to start the day right.

Which sets the scene for the menu as the day wears on. Far from run-of-the-mill, dishes are traditional and enormously flavourful, maybe mushroom bruschetta, seafood salad, veal escalope, and Nonna's lasagne. The 'prezzo fisso' menu keeps costs down at lunchtime (including a special one for bambinos), and it's worth every penny. A real gourmet pit stop.

Opening hours
Mon-Sun 10am-9.30pm

Boboli, 88 Main Street, Kibworth LE8 0NQ
WWW.BOBOLIRESTAURANT.CO.UK   0116 2793303

Just off the A6 south of Leicester and painted in coastal teal and white, The Lighthouse is unusual in it's decision to specialise in seafood, right in the heart of the English countryside. Yet fresh fish is shipped in overnight from Cornwall and transformed with finesse into delicious dishes worth stopping for.

The restaurant is the brainchild of Sarah and Lino Poli, who separated it from their sister Italian restaurant - Boboli - and settled in what used to be Kibworth's violin maker's house; how many villages can claim to have a violin maker?!

Inside is cosy and familiar, service is second-to-none and the food is widely fêted for its global influence: Thai fish soup, spaghetti with lobster bisque, cheese soufflé with smoked haddock. And of course they do a mean fish and chips with batter made from local Langton Brewery beer. Vegetarians and meat eaters need not feel left out either: there are plenty of plant and meat based choices, and options of nibbles and mains mean there's something for every appetite.

Opening hours
Tues-Sat from 6pm

The Lighthouse, 9 Station Street, Kibworth LE8 0LN
WWW.LIGHTHOUSEKIBWORTH.CO.UK   0116 2796260

EAST ANGLIA

M11, A14, A12, A140, A47, A11

Criss-crossing the flatlands of East Anglia

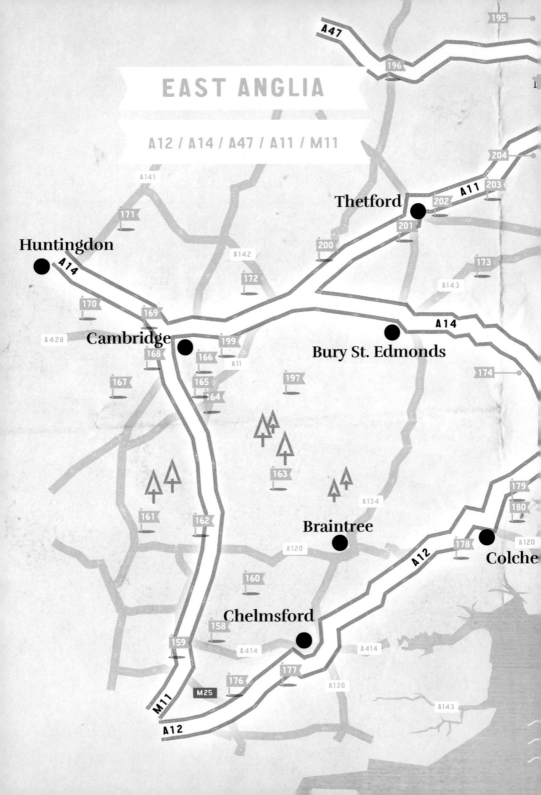

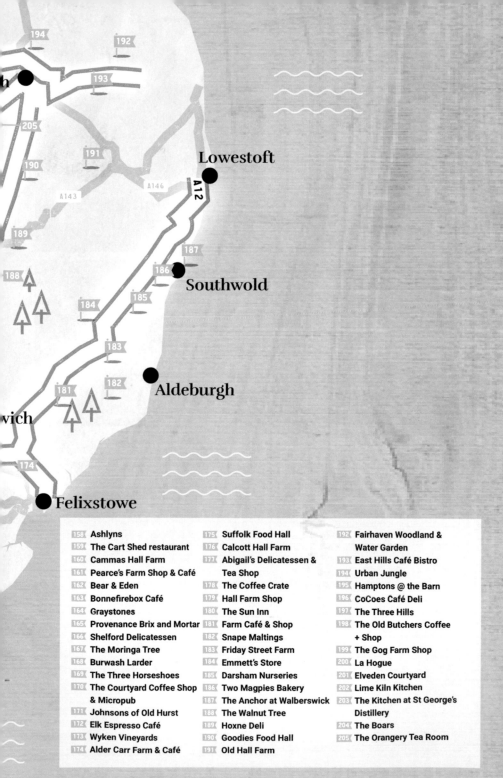

FARM SHOP-CAFÉ

Ashlyns

JUNCTION: 7; 5 MINS

'It ain't easy being green', said Kermit the Frog, but perhaps he had yet to find Ashlyns Farm Shop. It's a beacon of organic food and groceries, the shelves groaning with everything from fennel toothpaste to Ashlyns' own honey; the deli counter sells homemade scotch eggs and sausage rolls, and you can get your fruit and veg fix at the juice and smoothie bar. Much of what you see at Ashlyns is organic; if not, it's ethically sourced.

In the restaurant – open for breakfast, lunch and sometimes dinner – beautifully lettered signboards tempt you with plates to suit all appetites and pockets, from hearty servings of sausage and mash to a more modest smoked salmon salad. Children can tuck into tasty food from their own menu, before burning off some energy in the soft play area or farm park outside. Mum or dad can then raid the wine shop or indulge in a massage in the beauty salon. The chirrup of birds is all you're likely to hear on the garden deck if you want a quieter stop, and the Farm Park trail will point out all the local Essex wildlife.

Opening hours
Mon-Sun 9am-5pm (café 3.30pm)

Ashlyns, North Weald, Epping CM16 6RZ
WWW.ASHLYNSFARMSHOP.CO.UK   01992 525146

The Cart Shed Restaurant

JUNCTION: 7; 4 MINUTES

Vegetarians might want to pass this one by, but if you're a fan of wild meat cooked with European panache, consider stopping here.

Chef and owner William set up the Cart Shed at the edge of the family farm as a means of exploiting his passion for shooting and cooking, a skill he honed working in various kitchens across the continent. The purpose-built, bijou space stands alongside the grand farmhouse, painted in shades of green and seating up to 24 people.

Ingredients are selected from the family farm or suppliers with 10 miles if possible, and cooked in the open kitchen over the fire pit: perhaps saddle of venison, muntjac tartare or a juicy steak served with roasted beetroot, triple-cooked chips or lemon-butter samphire.

You'd be forgiven for thinking you're pulling into the family home when you arrive, but look for the small signs on the wall that steer you towards the low building: the entrance is at the far end.

Opening hours
Thurs-Sat 6.30pm-midnight
Sun 12.30pm-11pm

The Cart Shed Restaurant, Duck Lane, Thornwood, Epping CM16 6NE
WWW.THECARTSHEDRESTAURANT.CO.UK   07701 33 33 23

FARM SHOP-CAFÉ

Cammas Hall Farm

JUNCTION: 8; 13 MINUTES

Cammas Hall Farm, in the beautiful countryside of the Hertfordshire/Essex border, is family owned and pioneered the pick-your-own movement in the 1960s; large letters at the edge of one field proclaiming 'strawberry fields forever' are a nod to that era.

Collect your own car snacks with a stroll through the fields to pick strawberries, raspberries, cherries, blackcurrants, blueberries and sweetcorn, depending on the season. When little people have had enough, a nature trail, children's playground and maize maze (in the summer) will keep them entertained.

In the Tea Barn you'll find homemade cakes, sandwiches, jacket potatoes, cream teas and fresh smoothies made with ingredients from the farm. There are seats inside and out, and a marquee in the garden. Honey direct from the farm's hives can be bought in the shop, along with other farm produce including fresh eggs, chutneys, meringues and preserves.

Opening hours
Tues-Sun 9am-5.30pm
Open April to October (please check website for dates)

Cammas Hall Farm, Needham Green, Hatfield Broad Oak CM22 7JT
WWW.CAMMASHALL.CO.UK   01279 718570

Pearce's Farm Shop & Café

JUNCTION: 8; 16 MINUTES

Once just a shed in a field selling the family's vegetables, Pearce's Farm Shop is now an abundant food emporium and café. Browse the shelves laden with Hertfordshire honey, inspiring fresh fruit and vegetables, smoked meats, artisan cheeses, Granny Pearce's marmalade, homemade strawberry jam and other gourmet goodies. And if you need a present there's a great gift selection plus cards, homegrown flowers, wine and gin.

Stock up on sensational car snacks from the deli then settle at a table in the roomy, oak-beamed café. It's been built with the environment in mind and you can watch the cows grazing in the fields beyond the floor-to-ceiling windows. When the weather's fine, spill out onto the patio terrace and picnic area.

Start the day with a proper farmhouse breakfast, or choose lunch from the menu of freshly-cooked seasonal dishes. Book ahead for three terrific tiers of afternoon tea. Compostable cups and boxes are available if you want food and drink to go, and if you have time to linger in the summer, enjoy picking your own raspberries and strawberries in the fields.

Opening hours
Mon-Thurs 8.30am-5.30pm
Fri 8.30am-6pm (Sat 5pm)
Sun 8.30am-4pm

Pearce's Farm Shop & Café, Hamels Mead, Buntingford SG9 9ND
WWW.PEARCESFARMSHOP.COM   01920 821246

CAFÉ

Bear & Eden

JUNCTION: 8; 7 MINUTES

The brick and clap-board exterior of Bear & Eden does little to prepare you for the striking beamed ceiling once you've ducked through the door. It crowns the newly refurbished and family-friendly café below, set up by a primary school teacher and oil trader couple who were looking for a family-friendly spot to eat with their kids.

The result is a stylish space with a Montessori-style play area at one end, alive with parents, children and locals. There's a quieter space downstairs for a more grown-up-centred visit, which is conveniently close to the counter from where you can keep yourself in a steady supply of excellent coffee – iced, frothed or straight up.

Food is freshly prepared and supplied by local producers, from the creative scotch eggs (arancini and mozzarella; macaroni cheese) to vegan muffins and falafel wraps.

If you're early for Stansted flights, or waiting to pick someone up, this is infinitely superior to a bland chain or a sandwich in the short-stay.

Opening hours
Tues-Sat 9am-4pm

Bear & Eden, Brewery Barn, 31 Lower Street, Stansted CM24 8LN
WWW.BEARANDEDEN.COM   07447 699654

Bonnefirebox Café

JUNCTION: 8/9A; 15 MINUTES

Don't be put off by the misleading 15-minute diversion, as Bonnefirebox is around four miles from the M11 as the crow flies, so a little dog-leg diversion between junctions is all you need to add a smashing stop to your journey.

Jodie and Adam set up their bricks-and-mortar café less than a year ago, a natural extension of their extremely successful street food van from which they've been selling wood-fired pizzas for four years. Adam is a talented chef and makes everything from scratch, right down to the sourdough and pasta. Breakfast on smashed avocado on sourdough or a full English; lunch on loaded sweet potato wedges, salad boxes or rotis piled with falafel or wood-fired meats. And good luck resisting one of their doughnuts if they're on the counter.

Jodie's creative background has been put to good use in the hip interior and the up-cycled kitchen-styled play area in the garden which is being continually adding to along with other hand-built projects.

Opening hours
Tues-Thurs, Sat 9am-4.30pm
Fri 9am-8.30pm

Bonnefirebox Café, Taylors Barns, Wimbish CB10 2XA
WWW.FACEBOOK.COM/BONNEFIREBOX/   01799 521161

CAFÉ

Graystones

JUNCTION: 10; 3 MINUTES

It could have been a tragedy when the Wheatsheaf shut its doors for the last time in Duxford: a name you might recognise from the branch of the Imperial War Museum just over the motorway which stands on the original Spitfire base. Instead Gary and his team took it over, taking advantage of the large beer garden and spacious interior to create a café bistro hub that has swiftly become a village favourite.

Breakfasts are filling, whether you're a meat eater or not, paninis and pasties are popular at lunch and evening might see burger stacks, homemade pizzas or charcuterie platters on the menu. A small deli section at the back means you can take a taste of Cambridgeshire home with you, or simply grab a pint of milk for tea on arrival.

Kids will love the playground in the garden and the naughty milkshakes on offer, while few will turn down the cakes: caramelised orange and white chocolate or lemon and blueberry anyone?

Opening hours
Mon-Weds 9am-4.30pm
Thurs-Sat 9am-5pm
Sun 9am-4pm

Graystones, 4 St Peter's Street, Duxford CB22 4RP
WWW.FACEBOOK.COM/GRAYSTONES-184378925682465/   01223 836200

Provenance Brix and Mortar

JUNCTION: 10; 2 MINUTES

With food cooked over a wood-fired hearth, vegetables grown down the road at a horse-ploughed farm, and a stonkingly good menu reflecting the seasons, it's easy to wax lyrical about Provenance Brix and Mortar.

Provenance put down roots in a formerly bland canteen in the beautiful Cambridgeshire countryside, having started life in an Airstream caravan and horsebox trailer. Bland no longer, owners Kate and Greg have transformed it into a beautifully light and airy space with a large run of bi-fold doors opening onto a courtyard garden, where some of the herbs and vegetables are grown.

The T-shaped space blends deli, restaurant and café spaces, with the open kitchen the centrepiece of the restaurant; a suspended wood burning stove draws the eye. Outside, there's loads of parking, and a huge garden with picnic benches where kids can let off steam and sun can be soaked up.

Stop at the deli on your way out to pick up some of the local ingredients that may have gone into your dishes. If you have time or a plane-mad child, the Imperial War Museum Duxford is just over the roundabout.

Tues-Weds 10am-4pm
Thurs-Sat 10am-4pm, 6pm-10.30pm
Sun noon-4pm

Provenance Brix and Mortar, Hill Farm Road, Whittlesford CB22 4AN
WWW.PROVENANCEKITCHEN.COM   01223 839993

Shelford Delicatessen

JUNCTION: 11; 7 MINUTES

Photo credit: Fanny Bara

It's easy to see why people flow constantly into the Shelford Deli. Within the walls of the stylish, oak-framed building, the menu is crammed with fresh, tasty salads, soups, frittata and proper artisan pizza – all simple and seasonal. Their homemade cakes are irresistible, perhaps carrot, chocolate mocha with hazelnut, or on Fridays the famous Deli doughnuts including honeycomb and salted caramel, washed down with excellent coffee.

Owners Drew and Nikki have been part of the UK's food revolution since 1999, and founded their kitchen on the simple premise of offering Cambridgeshire delicious food made from sustainable, tasty ingredients. It's gone from strength to strength, growing from a tiny shop to the current, purpose-built café and bistro. There's a warming wood burner for colder months and a beautiful sunlit garden for summer with a wooden playhouse for children, but to get there you'll need to pass a gauntlet of temptation: pick up some artisan bread, coffee, salads or gifts on your way.

Opening hours
Mon-Sat 8.30am-4.30pm

Shelford Delicatessen, 8a Woollards Lane, Great Shelford CB22 5LZ
WWW.SHELFORDDELI.CO.UK   01223 846129

The Moringa Tree

JUNCTION: 12; 6 MINUTES

Nothing defines modern life better than coffee and houseplants, and the Moringa Tree brings the two together in a triumphant celebration. The diddy café, no bigger than a garage, is at the roadside in Haslingfield (around the corner from the adorably named Frog End) opposite the village church, but it packs a punch for its size.

Coffee is smooth, tea is loose leaf from Blue Bird, and soft drinks might include homemade raspberry water. Savoury and sweet bites are served from morning till tea time, from avocado toast to Sri Lankan curry and gluten-free orange cake.

A geometric shelf down one wall is filled with plants and trinkets, and the foliage that decorates every surface brings a real sense of calm, pepped up with bursts of colour in the sugar-coloured chairs and flower posies. Pavement seating outside is perfect for shooting the breeze on sunny days.

Opening hours
Mon-Sun 9.15am-4.30pm

The Moringa Tree, 11a Church Street, Haslingfield CB23 1JE
WWW.THEMORINGATREE.CO.UK   01223 870055

Burwash Larder, a farm shop and delicatessen, stands in the converted farm buildings of Burwash Manor's family farm, one of thirteen independent businesses in the pretty, rural courtyard just moments from the M11.

Arrive hungry to enjoy lunch from the well-stocked and frequently changing deli counter, and finish off with delicious cakes baked by talented local bakers. The coffee is excellent and provided by a Cambridge roastery who barista-train the whole team.

Fill a tote with tasty goodies from the deli for your onward journey – the sage and onion Burwash loaf is designed to be paired with their sausages – and in season you'll find the farm's own asparagus and pork from their rare breed pigs. Pick up some store cupboard treats to take home and don't miss the cheese counter – there are 70 varieties to choose from.

Out the back here's an adorable hand-carved Wendy house and play area to amuse the kids, with picnic benches for supervising parents. If you've got time, explore the farm's signposted walks.

Opening hours
Mon-Fri 9am-6pm (Sat 5pm)
Sun 10am-5pm

Burwash Larder, Burwash Manor New Road, Barton CB23 7EY
WWW.BURWASHLARDER.COM   01223 264600

The Three Horseshoes

JUNCTION: 30; 5 MINUTES

Foodies flock to the Three Horseshoes like birds coming home to roost, drawn by its reputation for fine food. The thatched pub is just 20 minutes outside Cambridge, over the road from the grand, copper-topped towers of Madingley Hall and on the fringe of pretty fields.

The pub's large, bright conservatory – brick floor, wicker chairs and view over the landscaped garden – is a beautiful spot for savouring the imaginative, seasonal flavours which emanate from the kitchen. The menu is loosely inspired by the Mediterranean, but not pigeonholed; chefs take cues from around the globe. The menu is considered, varied and seasonal and changes frequently to keep the kitchen and flavours sharp: perhaps pan-fried squid, Tuscan bean soup, a vegetarian mezze board or stuffed guinea fowl. It's on the pricey side, but worth every mouthful.

Opening hours
Mon-Thurs noon-9.30pm
Fri-Sat noon-9pm
Sun & Bank Hols noon-8pm

The Three Horseshoes, High Street, Madingley CB23 8AB
WWW.THREEHORSESHOESMADINGLEY.CO.UK   01954 210221

The Courtyard Coffee Shop & Micropub

JUNCTION: HILTON; 8 MINUTES

A short distance from Cambridge, Papworth Everard stands on the old Roman highway that once linked London with York. Today, a bypass carries the traffic north and south, and the village is a peaceful haven.

The Courtyard Coffee Shop and Micropub is at one edge of a 1960s-style precinct beside the Post Office. It was previously a café for the residents of the Papworth Trust, a charity providing support for disabled people including housing and training. It has now been taken over by Steph and Dave who have turned it into a welcoming community coffee shop by day and an inviting bar by night, serving cocktails and locally brewed tipples.

Dave already had a coffee roasting business which has now joined forces with the coffee shop, so the flat whites are excellent – 'Best in the Cambridge area,' according to one customer.

Opening hours
Tues-Weds 9am-4.30pm, 7pm-10pm (10.30pm Thurs)
Fri-Sat 9am-4.30pm, 6pm-10.30pm
Sun 2.30pm-5pm, 7pm-10pm

The Courtyard Coffee Shop, Unit 2, Pendrill Court, Ermine St North, Papworth Everard CB23 3UY
WWW.FACEBOOK.COM/COURTYARDPAPWORTH   01480 830125

Johnsons of Old Hurst

JUNCTION: HUNTINGDON; 12 MINUTES

Johnson's is a family farm with a difference, on the outskirts of Huntingdon. It's not only home a peaceful tea room, fabulous farm shop and lip-smacking steak house, but also a tropical house, home to the family's collection of crocodiles, turtles, snakes and iguanas. But don't worry you'll also find the more usual farm animals around too.

Don't tell the kids, but you can also buy crocodile steaks from the butchery counter; nearly all the meat on sale is home reared. A quick raid of the farm shop, set around a beautiful, covered courtyard in the old cattle shed, should restock your cupboards in full with pork pies, pasties and bread from the bakery, local fruit and veg, 50 varieties of cheese, home-cooked meats, antipasti, scotch eggs and corned beef.

The tea room serves a range of traditional cooked breakfasts, hot and cold lunches, along with homemade cakes and scones. Finish off your visit with a woodland walk.

Opening hours
Tues-Fri 9am-6pm (4pm Sat)
Sun 10.30am-4pm
Check website for steakhouse opening hours

Johnsons of Old Hurst, Church Farm, Church Street, Oldhurst PE28 3AF
WWW.JOHNSONSOFOLDHURST.CO.UK   01487 824658

CAFÉ

Elk Espresso Café

JUNCTION: 37; 8 MINUTES

Just over the road from the school and in the heart of the village, Elk is a real community hub and owner Emilio actively encourages people to pop in, whether to send a few emails, grab a coffee after the school run or meet friends.

The décor is stylish – white tiles, tan leather seats and a black ceiling – and large windows looking onto the street (a relic from the building's former life as an estate agent) provide the perfect spot for people watching.

The kitchen is teeny tiny so food is largely light, but the menu is very tasty and changes frequently – expect anything from gluten-free cakes to cheese toasties and scones. Coffee is the real focus – with beans from local roastery The Brew Project – and the flat white is excellent. Hot drinks are available to take away, or, if the weather allows, you can soak up village life at one of the pavement tables.

Opening hours
Tues-Fri 8am-5pm
Sat 9am-4pm
Sun 10am-2pm

Elk Espresso Café, 105 The Causeway, Burwell CB25 0DU
WWW.ELKCOFFEE.CO.UK   01638 741031

Wyken Vineyards

JUNCTION: 43 OR 44; 15 MINUTES

A Suffolk stalwart, Wyken Vineyards has been showcasing local and seasonal food for over 20 years. Shetland sheep graze the patchwork of fields and the vineyard produces award-winning wines. Formal gardens crammed with topiary, herbs, roses, fruit trees and meandering peacocks, guinea fowl and chickens surround an Elizabethan manor house.

In a huge 17th-century Suffolk barn you'll find the Country Store selling Wyken's wine, hand-crafted pottery, Irish and Scottish woollens, beautiful books and unusual cards. The renowned Leaping Hare restaurant serves truly local dishes, such as Wyken venison (wild, not farmed) with carrots, celeriac gratin and granola, with an emphasis on flavours and the seasons.

Try the café for lighter and less formal fare. Breakfast eggs come from Wyken's chickens and crab salad or lobster brioche roll use Norfolk seafood. A farmers' market, held here every Saturday morning, sells local bread, cheese, apples and meat.

Opening hours
Sun-Fri 10am-6pm
Sat 9am-6pm

Wyken Vineyards, Wyken Road, Bury St Edmunds IP31 2DW
WWWW.WYKENVINEYARDS.CO.UK   01359 250 287

Alder Carr Farm & Café

JUNCTION: 51; 5 MINUTES

Joan and Nick bought Alder Carr Farm back in 1981 and set about planting various fruit and vegetables to maximise the different soils on the site. During the 'great raspberry glut' of 1987 the pair tried their hand at ice cream making, which turned out to be the nascence of a now-popular Suffolk brand.

Fast forward 30 years and the farm remains a hot bed of entrepreneurialism. Farm shop, craft studio, haberdashery and gift shop have all taken roost in the former farm buildings. The farm shop is well stocked with deli goodies – coleslaw, samosas, cheese, olives – as well as fresh produce and meat from the farm's own animals.

Step through to the Barn Café to taste what those ingredients can become, whether creamy eggs Benedict, pork pies or farm-worthy slices of carrot cake.

If you've got wellies in the boot, make time to explore the farm nature trail, where you can meet the animals and enjoy the idyllic woodland and meadow landscape.

Opening hours
Mon-Sat 9am-5pm
Sun 10am-4pm

Alder Carr Farm & Café, Creeting St Mary IP6 8LX
WWW.ALDERCARRFARM.CO.UK   01449 723359

Suffolk Food Hall

JUNCTION: 56; 4 MINUTES

A Goliath of local produce, the Suffolk Food Hall gathers together top-quality food and crafts from across the county in one enormous warehouse, formerly a cattle barn lest the farming connection be forgotten. Bakers continually stock the baskets with loaves and buns fresh from the oven, butchers prepare all the meat on site and will cheerfully advise on the best cut, while the deli is crammed with antipasti, pies, tarts and salads.

You can grab a bite to take away or enjoy a more relaxing meal in the Cookhouse. The farm's own beef forms the signature dishes, but it stands alongside home-smoked meat and fish, seasonal veg and trout. Lunch could be anything from fish laksa to a steak burger with pickles. It's often busy at this time, so calling ahead is advisable.

If you don't need to rush off, let the kids can wear themselves out on the pillow cushion and climbing frame then wander down the drive to watch the sailing boats tack across the river beneath the soaring pillars of the Orwell Bridge.

Opening hours
Mon-Sat 9am-6pm
Sun 10.30am-4.30pm
(Cookhouse hours vary; see website)

Suffolk Food Hall, Wherstead IP9 2AB
WWW.SUFFOLKFOODHALL.CO.UK   01473 786 610

Calcott Hall Farm

JUNCTION: M25/A1023; 8 MINUTES

Surrounded by fields and backed by the rearing embankment of the Weald Park hill fort, Calcott Hall Farm is a haven from the crush of the M25 and Dartford Tunnel. The timber-beamed shop, partially powered by solar panels, is a treasure trove of delicacies from cloudy pressed juices and Tiptree gin to Colston Bassett stilton and wild rabbit. Load up your holiday hamper with Essex-grown produce, locally reared meat and sustainably caught fish. Many a variety of fruit and veg are grown in the fields just outside.

The shop stands at the edge of the 120-acre farm where the McTurk family have tended the land for decades. Family is still very much the watchword. Daughter-in-law Niki is behind the latest addition, the Barnyard Café, which serves up farm-worthy breakfasts and tasty lunches – crispy baked potatoes, doorstop sandwiches – alongside devilishly good hot chocolate.

Parents can release energetic children into the tractor-themed play area alongside the café. (The farm is not accessible directly from the A12; use A128.)

Opening hours
Tues-Sat 8.30am-5.30pm
(Café 4.30pm)

Calcott Hall Farm, Ongar Road, Brentwood CM15 9HS
WWW.CALCOTTHALL.COM   01277 264164

Abigail's Delicatessen & Tea Shop

JUNCTION: 13; 3 MINUTES

Abigail certainly has an eye for good design, from beautiful homewares to magazine-worthy plates of food. In a unique but entrepreneurial set-up, she's got two shop fronts on Ingastone's high street, one stocking a broad range of enviable lamps and décor for your home, and the other a deli keeping ravenous shoppers well-fed.

The narrow, beamed café leads back to polka-dotted tables, though be prepared to takeaway as it's hugely popular. Service is friendly, amid the hubbub of regulars, and dishes are wholesome, generous and always homemade: specials might include a heritage tomato and rocket salad or roasted vegetable and ricotta frittata.

If you're in the mood to explore, Mountnessing Windmill has been fully restored and is a unique landmark, and Kelvedon Hatch, the cold-war era secret nuclear bunker, is up the road.

Opening hours
Mon-Sat 8am-5pm

Abigail's Delicatessen & Tea Shop, 11A High Street, Ingastone CM4 9ED
WWW.ABIGAILS.CO.UK   01277 355568

CAFÉ

The Coffee Crate

JUNCTION: 24; 4 MINUTES

The Coffee Crate isn't exactly the sort of place you expect to find behind a car wash at the edge of a light industrial estate, but it's right on the pulse, turning a spare plot of unused land at the edge of Tiptree into a small business haven using converted shipping containers.

The mini-complex is festooned with fairy lights, clad with wood and decorated with potted trees, and you'll find coffee in the corner unit (opposite the refill shop). Light floods in through the large sliding doors, with a handful of seats at the front and counter at the back. Coffee is barista standard with a range of plant-based milks alongside standard cow's, tea is by Tea Pigs and hot chocolate devilishly good (try the Black Forest).

Sandwiches are freshly made in-house and ready to take away if you're on the fly, and the cakes are varied and delicious. Although seating inside is limited, there's a gorgeous decked area beneath the boughs of a tree just outside for sunny days, though it's worth swinging in here for decent take-away food whatever the weather.

Opening hours
Mon-Fri 7.30am-5pm
Sat 9am-5pm

The Coffee Crate, Tower Business Park, Kelvedon Road, Tiptree CO5 0LX

Hall Farm Shop

JUNCTION: 30; 2 MINUTES

The moment you crunch into the car park at Hall Farm it's clear that there's a real connection to the land. Farm machinery is parked in an open barn and the red brick farm shop, has trays of plants and vegetables propped outside.

Bistro tables set out on the gravel to soak up the sun guide you towards the café-restaurant, an old cattle byre flanking one side of the farmyard. The light-flooded space is warm and elegant with wonderful views over Dedham Vale. With seasonal menus and rotating specials there is something to suit everyone, whether it is for breakfast, morning coffee, a light bite, a more leisurely three-course lunch or afternoon tea.

Both the café and the shop use local produce in abundance. The farm shop is adored by foodies stocking up on cheese, top-notch deli goods, fresh bread and treats from the bakery. Visitors old and young delight in exploring the farm trail, from which the farm and animals can be seen in action.

Opening hours
Mon-Sun 10am-5pm

Hall Farm Shop, Church Rd, Stratford Saint Mary CO7 6LS
WWW.HALLFARMSHOP.COM   01206 323600

PUB

The Sun Inn

JUNCTION: 30; 5 MINUTES

A 15th-century coaching inn in the quintessentially English village of Dedham, the Sun Inn has an oak-panelled bar and lounge that boast big fires and plenty of comfy sofas and armchairs. It's the perfect place for a relaxed drink or lunch with views of grand St Mary's church and the airy dining room looks out on to the terrace and a large garden.

Both the service and menu are relaxed and unpretentious. Friendly staff serve food featuring local produce with a Mediterranean twist, which benefits the pub's proximity to the coast. Try grilled mackerel, octopus and chickpea salad, or black pork belly with clams, samphire and butterbeans.

The Sun Inn is deep in Constable country; the artist went to school here and Flatford Mill is close by. You can borrow bikes from the pub or take a boat trip down the unspoiled River Stour. With so much to do locally, you may just have to stay a night at the inn.

Opening hours
Mon-Sun 11am-11pm

The Sun Inn, High Street, Dedham CO7 6DF
WWW.THESUNINNDEDHAM.COM   01206 323351

Farm Cafe & Shop

JUNCTION: MARLESFORD ; 0 MINUTES

A favourite with families, the Farm Café has benefited from improvements by new owners to transform it from a roadside caff into a local food destination. Refuel on hearty breakfasts of local bacon and sausages or healthy porridge or granola.

For lunch, find a table in the garden overlooking fields and tuck into Blythburgh free-range pulled pork burgers, Pinney's Smoked Kippers or choose from a selection of sandwiches or paninis. Children's portions are available, and if you haven't got time to stop hot drinks, sandwiches and homemade cakes can be taken away. You can even phone ahead to save you having to wait.

If you enjoyed your food, pick up some ingredients in the shop which stocks local meat, veg, chutneys and jams; there's also a range of the café's popular dishes, such as cottage pie, soups and puddings, both fresh or frozen, ready to warm up when you reach your destination.

Opening hours
Mon-Sat 7am-4pm (shop 8.30am-5pm)
Sun & Bank Hols 8am-4pm (shop 8.30am-5pm).

Farm Cafe & Shop, Main Road, Marlesford, Woodbridge IP13 0AG
WWW.FARMCAFE.CO.UK   01728 747717

On the banks the River Alde, this vast complex of old Victorian maltings looks out over a breath-taking expanse of swaying reed beds. It's well worth a visit to see the world-famous concert hall founded by Benjamin Britten and to enjoy the independent shops, cafés and galleries. If you want to stock up on Suffolk produce, the Food Hall and Fresh Food Pantry will provide everything you need, and if you're passing on the first Saturday of the month make the most of the Farmers' Market too.

For sit-down meals, you're spoiled for choice. Lunch with a panoramic view can be enjoyed at the Concert Hall Café – birdwatchers, don't forget your binoculars. Café 1885 is great for coffee and cake, as well as a seasonal menu inspired by the Farmers' Market. For a more traditional tea room, The Granary Tea Shop offers the best sandwiches, baked potatoes, cakes and scones.

Opening hours
Mon-Sat 10am-5.30pm
Sun 10.30am-4.30pm

Snape Maltings, Snape IP17 1SP
WWW.SNAPEMALTINGS.CO.UK   01728 688303

Friday Street Farm

JUNCTION: A1094; 1 MINUTE

For those heading for the Suffolk coast, Friday Street Farm Shop has to be one of your grocers of choice. Three generations of the Blyth family have been connecting customers to crops from this corner of their arable farm since the 1970s. Behind the salmon-pink façade shelves are loaded with produce grown on the farm or nearby (from almost 100 different producers), alongside butchery and fish counters and a sterling selection of gifts. If any kids are misbehaving, the promise of Friday's Mess – an Eton Mess inspired ice cream with the farm's raspberries and meringue pieces – should buy you some peace.

The café is over the yard in a separate building and adopts the same sourcing policy (the closer the better) to make dishes that a farmer's wife would be proud of: think oozing cottage pies, meatballs and mash, baked salmon and spinach, white chocolate and raspberry cheesecake.

The farm has become a little complex of enterprise, so the curious should follow the signs for 'Weird Stuff' and 'Cool Junk'.

Opening hours
Mon-Thurs 8.30am-5.30pm
Fri-Sat 8.30am-6pm
Sun 9am-5pm

Friday Street Farm, Friday Street, Farnham, Saxmundham IP17 1JX
WWW.FRIDAYSTFARM.CO.UK   01728 602783

Emmett's Store

JUNCTION: YOXFORD; 6 MINUTES

Emmett's has been trading on the same site in the pretty village of Peasenhall since 1820 and is celebrating its 200-year anniversary next year and has a worldwide reputation for its locally sourced ham and bacon. The shop retains some original fittings and is packed with beautifully presented produce. You'll find abundant displays of fresh fruit and vegetables, farmhouse cheese, Sri Lankan chutney and Suffolk apple juice. There's a distinctly Hispanic feel too, with Spanish chocolate, olive oil, almonds and honey.

The small café showcases Emmett's produce and makes a perfect breakfast stop. Don't miss the home-cured ham, free-range bacon and egg or the Spanish equivalent – egg, chorizo picante, tomato and orange. For lunch the generous English, Italian and Spanish charcuterie or the cheese platters are perfect for sharing over a glass of wine. Excellent coffee, tea and cakes are served all day. When the sun shines you can savour the sweet smoke wafting from the smokehouse in the pretty cottage garden.

Opening hours
Mon-Fri 9.30am-5pm
Sat 8am-5pm

Emmett's Store, The Street, Peasenhall IP17 2HJ
WWW.EMMETTSHAM.CO.UK   01728 660250

Darsham Nurseries

JUNCTION: DARSHAM; 0 MINUTES

Step out of the car after a long journey and you'll instantly be revived by the scents of roses and other shrubs sold at Darsham Nurseries. Yet this isn't just another garden centre. The beautiful shop sells a carefully curated collection of ceramics, candles, vases, unusual seeds and designer garden tools, as well as stationery, books and cards.

The stylish café wouldn't look out of place in founder David Keleel's native California, with white wood walls, checkerboard floor and colourful flowers from the garden – which also supplies the kitchen with salad, vegetables, fruit and herbs.

Menus are driven by the seasons; the chefs work with the garden team to produce vegetable-led dishes, such as pea potager fritti misti. Local fish and meat feature – try streaky bacon with house brown sauce for breakfast or Sutton Hoo Chicken leg with leek and potato hash for lunch. For tea, try their cakes and pastries with some intriguing flavours.

Opening hours
Mon-Sat 8.30am-5pm
Sun 10am-4pm

Darsham Nurseries, Main Road, Darsham IP17 3PW
WWW.DARSHAMNURSERIES.CO.UK   01728 667022

CAFÉ

Two Magpies Bakery

JUNCTION: DARSHAM; 0 MINUTES

The counter at Two Magpies is heaped with irresistible goodies, enough to satisfy even the most ardent car munchies: pistachio-topped cakes, vegetarian sausage rolls and picture-perfect cinnamon swirls among them. (Don't forget to pick up a loaf for your destination – they really are excellent.)

Owner Rebecca worked as an art and textiles teacher at a secondary school before taking the plunge to follow her passion for baking in 2013. She and husband Steve started off with an artisan bakery in Southwold before opening a second in Aldeburgh. This is the third, and the jewel in the crown; a former Co-op now transformed into a Magpie mothership housing a café, bakery school and plenty of ovens to supply bread and pastries for all three sites.

Grab a coffee and a bun to go, or find a table in the airy café to enjoy the hubbub while the kids run off some energy in the playground. On Saturdays the pizza oven is fired up for their famous sourdough pizzas, but you'll have to be quick as they soon sell out.

Opening hours
Mon-Fri 8am-5pm
Sat 8am-8.30pm
Sun 8am-5pm

Two Magpies Bakery, London Road, Darsham IP17 3QR
WWW.TWOMAGPIESBAKERY.CO.UK   01986 784370

The Anchor at Walberswick

JUNCTION: BLYTHBURGH; 7 MINUTES

It's true that Walberswick is busy year round, but you'll always find a spot in this large, bustling yet cosy village pub. Whether you've just finished a chilly winter walk through the reed beds, or are in need of après-crabbing refreshments in the summer, The Anchor's changing menu will have just the thing – along with tea or hot chocolate by the fire or a pint of Adam's in the garden overlooking the dunes. Local foods such as Lowestoft smoked fish, Blythburgh ham and Baron Bigod brie are used alongside homegrown vegetables from the allotment in a menu that balances food miles with quality. Bread is baked on site daily.

If you want to work up an appetite or walk off lunch, there's information in the porch.Many of the walks around Walberswick take in a surprising variety of scenery in less than an hour. Or take the rowing boat 'ferry' across the harbour to Southwold and walk back to Walberswick across the Bailey Bridge.

Opening hours
Mon-Sun 8.30am-11pm

The Anchor at Walberswick, Main Street, Walberswick IP18 6UA
WWW.ANCHORATWALBERSWICK.COM   01502 722112

PUB

The Walnut Tree

JUNCTION: THWAITE; 0 MINUTES

Vegetarians and vegans, hold your horses here. Jan Wise, way ahead of the curve, has been impressing everyone with her creative plant-based dishes for a decade. The whole of Suffolk wailed in dismay when her debut restaurant, The Veggie Red Lion, closed. Thankfully it was only to make way for a bigger and better brother – The Walnut Tree at Thwaite, where you'll receive a warm welcome from manager Gaynor.

The pub has been lovingly refurbished without losing the traditional vibe, but it's the food that really sings. Jan and chefs Aston and Chris know their flavours inside out and aren't afraid to experiment with dishes from around the world. Try the Wellington with mushrooms and Suffolk blue cheese, and the renowned vegan peanut butter and Oreo torte, or see what they're cooking up on the specials board. Have the full plant experience by having lunch in the secluded garden where some of the vegetables are grown. If you're travelling between Norwich and Ipswich, you don't want to miss it.

Opening hours
Tues-Sat 11am-3.30pm, 5.30pm-11pm
Sun noon-4.30pm

The Walnut Tree, Norwich Road, Thwaite, Eye IP23 7ED
WWW.THEWALNUTTREETHWAITE.COM   01449 766003

Hoxne Deli

JUNCTION: B1118; 5 MINUTES

With an eye for business, if not specifically Post Offices and delis, David and Joan snapped up Hoxne's Post Office when it went up for sale in 2018 and rescued it from closure. They've added a deli, tea room, shop and some B&B rooms to it and turned it into something of a village fulcrum.

Pause in the morning for a coffee and a leaf through the paper, or drop in for a ploughman's or bowl of soup in the tea room. There's a sunny breakfast bar in one of the handsome double-fronted windows, ideal for people-watching, and a low-ceilinged snug at the rear with a wood burner to stoke up on crisp winter days, and a long garden beyond.

The kitchen uses largely local ingredients, all good-quality, and you can pick up any of your favourites in the deli on the way out – we recommend the Suffolk salami.

Opening hours
Mon-Sun 9am-5.30pm

Hoxne Deli, Post Office, Low Street, Hoxne IP21 5AR
WWW.HOXNE.SHOP   01379 668334

A140 Goodies Food Hall

JUNCTION: BUSH GREEN; 1 MINUTE

The seed for Goodies Food Hall was sown the moment entrepreneurial Stuart began selling the family's potatoes from a humble tractor and trailer at the roadside. When customers began to ask him for other produce, he discovered a talent for sniffing out the best growers, whether strawberries, asparagus or marigolds.

Fast forward a few years and the barn-style building is a treasure trove of goodies, much of it sourced directly from nearby farms. Unusual cuts of game – partridge, duck and rabbit – are stocked in the butchery counter next to chicken, lamb and pork, which makes it easy to stock up for a barbecue. Home made pasties, sausages, scotch eggs, olives and cheeses are ripe for picnic baskets, and the Norfolk ice cream is five-star.

There's a homeliness to the unpretentious café, which is divided from the shop by a glass wall. Chefs send out plates of wholesome food from breakfast to tea time, using the shop's ingredients wherever possible.

Opening hours
Mon-Fri 9am-5pm (Sun 4pm)
Sat 8am-5pm
(café times vary – see website)

Goodies Food Hall, French's Farm, Wood Lane, Pulham IP21 4XU
WWW.GOODIESFOODHALL.CO.UK   01379 676880

Old Hall Farm

JUNCTION: TASBURGH; 12 MINUTES

Arrive early and you can watch – even help! – the beautiful Jersey cows being milked in this nurturing microdairy. Freya, Gaia, Juno and the other cows then head out to the meadows for the rest of the day, where they suckle their calves at leisure. Unlike most dairy farms, the calves at Old Hall Farm aren't taken from their mothers at birth, producing calmer, happier cows – and richer, tastier milk.

Rebecca and Stuart Mayhew adore their 'Jersey Goddesses' and in the farm shop you can buy their award-winning raw milk, milkshakes, cream and butter. The farm's milk-fed pork is sold here too, along with its free-range chickens and eggs, local jams, honey and artisan bread. In the café you can tuck into a sumptuous farm breakfast after watching the milking, or later in the day enjoy a lunch of sandwiches or omelette made with the farm's produce, or a cream tea or 'cheesecake of the day' to set you up for the journey ahead. With a vineyard now planted, Old Hall will be selling its own wine down the line too.

Look out for the peacocks – they roam free and let out piercing calls from their age-old perches.

Opening hours
Mon-Sun 7am-9pm

Old Hall Farm, Norwich Road, Bungay NR35 2LP
WWW.OLDHALLFARM.CO.UK   07900 814252

Fairhaven Woodland & Water Garden

JUNCTION: B1140; 6 MINUTES

A47

© James Bass Photography

Naturalists, twitchers and garden lovers may insist on making a day of it to explore the stunning 130 acres of Fairhaven Woodland & Water Garden. Stretch your legs on four miles of pathways or take a 20-minute boat trip on Fairhaven's private broad, and look out for the 95 different bird species found here.

For those with less time the tearoom and shop are available without paying entry. Park in the field and head over to the low wooden buildings containing the shop and café. If you're early in the day, try the Great Norfolk breakfast. If you're too late for that treat, don't worry – light lunches, homemade specials and fresh local cakes can't fail to satisfy. Luxury ice cream – Ronaldo's, the local favourite – shouldn't be missed either. On warmer days head to the large outdoor area – dogs are welcome here and will find water bowls ready filled and waiting. This is a beautiful spot that feels remoter than it actually is. Grab some local jams and chutneys as you leave through the shop.

Opening hours
Mon-Sun 9.15am-5pm (Garden 10am) Mar-Sep.
Weds, May-end Aug, open until 9pm
Mon-Sun 9.15am-4pm (Garden 10am) Oct-Feb

Fairhaven Woodland & Water Garden, School Road, South Walsham NR13 6DZ
WWW.FAIRHAVENGARDEN.CO.UK   01603 270449

East Hills Café Bistro

JUNCTION: BRUNDALL; 7 MINUTES

Set above a chandlery in Brundall Bay Marina, this café was once the preserve of yacht club members only. Now the pretty Norfolk Broads location is open to all in the friendly East Hills Café Bistro run by local Sophie Hodgkinson. Drive down Station Road, over the level crossing and just as the road is about to peter out, turn left and park. Head up the stairs outside the building and, if it's fine, take a seat on the covered veranda. If it's less clement, there's ample room inside.

Dog beds arranged among the tables say everything necessary regarding pet policy. Afternoon tea laid out on cake stands looks like the real deal. Italian handmade pizza and crispy fish and chips are on offer daily too.

Looking out over the riparian scene in this quiet spot you can feel yourself unwinding. Enjoy life in the slow lane for a while before pulling back out into the traffic.

Opening hours
Mon-Weds 9.30-4pm
Thurs-Sat 9.30-11pm
Sun 9.30-6pm

Ⓥ Ⓟ 🐾

East Hills Café Bistro, Brundall Bay Marina, Riverside, Brundall NR13 5PN
WWW.EAST-HILLS.CO.UK   01603 951850

GARDEN CENTRE

Urban Jungle

JUNCTION: A1074; 7 MINUTES

This is not your average garden centre: you're about to experience a mini-break in the tropics! Banana trees, giant ferns, bamboo, succulents, cacti, climbers all thrive in this extraordinary Norfolk jungle. They invade the glasshouse café too, where scrubbed tables and a pretty assortment of chairs and large, floppable sofas nestle among tropical branches.

Children will vanish into the thick vegetation while you relax among cushions to peruse the enticing menu. It's all gluten free and either homegrown or ethically sourced, and includes cakes through to frittatas, toasties and salads with a definite Middle Eastern vibe (the harissa chicken and slow-cooked pulled lamb were mouth-wateringly delicious). Tea is loose-leaf (hurrah!) and coffee carefully sourced from single estates and served in a cafètiere.

This place is a one off – well, a two off, if we include its other, equally exotic, branch in Beccles.

Opening hours
Mon-Sun 10am-5pm (Café 4.30pm)

Urban Jungle, Ringland Lane, Old Costessey NR8 5BG
WWW.URBANJUNGLE.UK.COM   01603 857196

Hamptons @ the Barn

JUNCTION: B1147; 11 MINUTES

If you're one of the many beginning to discover the hidden gems of Norfolk, add Hamptons @ the Barn to your list.

Low, stone and L-shaped, the barn is half lifestyle shop and half café: a winning combination. Resident chefs Nicci and Sarah took over in 2018 and added their fresh sense of style to the shop and cooking prowess to the menu. Beneath the vaulted ceiling, strung with fairy lights, lucky customers are served delicious breakfasts, lunches and afternoon teas, perhaps beetroot and goats cheese tart, fishcakes, or coconut or Victoria sponge. The menu changes practically daily depending on what's in season, and much of it is cooked on the prized vintage Aga.

There's a small, hedge-trimmed courtyard just outside the run of patio doors so you can listen to the chirrup of birds over a restorative cuppa.

Opening hours
Mon-Sun 10am-4.30pm

Hamptons @ the Barn, Dereham Road, Bawdeswell NR20 4AA
WWW.HAMPTONSATTHEBARN.CO.UK   01362 688094

CoCoes Café Deli

JUNCTION: SWAFFHAM; 2 MINUTES

Hidden in plain sight, CoCoes is easy to miss despite its town centre location. Look out for a tiny alley off Lynn Street and at the end of it is a beautiful courtyard hotel reminiscent of rural France. This is Strattons, luxury and boutique, and CoCoes is the bright, modern café for hotel guests and passers-by alike. The interior is refreshing, cool and stylish with long, bright yellow banquettes. Al fresco seating is available for warmer days and those with dogs. The latter, incidentally, are welcomed as hotel guests so long as they don't chase the resident cats.

The menu is especially good for vegetarians (vegeree, veggie rolls, meze) and presents a challenge for deciding what to eat – a conundrum that can be solved by buying additional deli items and homemade pâtisserie for eating later (who can resist the rosewater and raspberry meringues, or the fudgy nut slice?). Menus change daily and all dishes are made on-site using as much Norfolk produce as possible.

Opening hours
Mon-Fri 7.30am-5pm
Sat-Sun 8.30am-5pm

CoCoes Café Deli, 4 Ash Close, Swaffham PE37 7NH
WWW.STRATTONSHOTEL.COM/COCOES-CAFE-DELI/   01760 723845

The Three Hills

JUNCTION: GREAT ABINGDON; 8 MINUTES

Originally opened as an alehouse in 1847 this rural inn was recently bought and refurbished with aplomb. It's the only pub in this tiny village of a hundred or so souls and doubles up as the village hall, library and all-round buzzing hub. Food is taken seriously: classic British with a twist and locally sourced as much as possible. Touchingly there is also a discount for the villagers.

There's a warm buzz inside with muddy-booted walkers, lycra-clad cyclists and families, who spill outside to the pretty garden on sunny days – there's a pizza oven and barbecue in the garden for the summer. Choose a book from the library and find a cosy spot by the roaring fire, or eat in the light and airy Orangery overlooking the terrace. And if you feel too relaxed after feasting, you can stay the night in one of the beautiful bedrooms.

Opening hours
Tues-Thurs 11.30am-10.30pm
Fri-Sat 11.30am-11pm
Sun 11.30am-6pm

The Three Hills, Dean Road, Bartlow CB21 4PW
WWW.THETHREEHILLS.CO.UK   01223 890 500

CAFÉ

The Old Butchers Coffee + Shop

JUNCTION: BALSHAM; 5 MINUTES

Balsham's former butcher's shop has been at the centre of village life for more than 300 years. But today the sawdust has been swept away, replaced by a lovely café.

Beneath the low thatched roof, tasty local produce is whipped up into quiches, sandwiches, cakes and smoothies. The countryside setting is reflected in the ingredients, so you might find rabbit pie or homemade scotch eggs on the menu, alongside the more usual suspects such as bacon rolls, seasonal soups and Chelsea buns. The wide pavement outside lends itself to kerbside seating, and makes it a popular spot for cyclists and horse riders.

In the shop alongside there's a small but perfectly formed selection of gifts and produce, so if you leave without a loaf of bread, bag of fudge or new favourite mug, you're stronger than us.

Opening hours
Mon-Fri 8am-4.30pm
Sat 9am-2pm

The Old Butchers Coffee + Shop, 35-37 High Street, Balsham CB21 4DJ
TWWW.THEOLDBUTCHERSBALSHAM.CO.UK   01223 892 673

The Gog Farm Shop

JUNCTION: BABRAHAM; 4 MINUTES

The Gog shares its name with one half of a pagan wicker giant duo, Gog and Magog, who also lend their names to the run of low chalk hills on which the farm shop stands. Its position on the outskirts of Cambridge means it enjoys delightful views over the city, and the sunsets are spectacular. The shop is stuffed with seasonal produce, an enviable cheese counter and an amazing butchery – recently voted 'Butcher's Shop of the Year'. Fill your basket with everything you could want for the store cupboard or pack yourself a finger-licking picnic.

Dog walkers and cyclists flock to the grey-painted, beamed café, often after enjoying the rural idyll and country lanes on the doorstep. Beneath felt clouds hung from the ceiling, chunky wooden tables are plied with deliciously simple fare prepared daily. Try a proper farmhouse breakfast, varied sharing platters or the award-winning cheese scone made from Montgomery's cheddar. If you prefer, you can take a seat outside in the covered Shack to catch the breeze: blankets are laid out for keeping knees warm. A great stop on the way to Cambridge.

Opening hours
Mon-Sat 9am-6pm
Sun 9.30am-5pm

The Gog Farm Shop, Heath Farm, Babraham Rd, Stapleford CB22 3AD
WWW.THEGOG.COM   01223 248352

FARM SHOP-CAFÉ

La Hogue

JUNCTION: B1085; 4 MINUTES

Naval battles don't usually lend their names to farms but then battleship timbers are not usually re-used to build farmhouses. La Hogue takes its moniker from a 17th-century sea brawl between Britain and France: the British won and hauled the timbers of the burned-out ships back home. Today, the bucolic farm shop and café sit alongside a working arable farm and if you are lucky you may see the owners' fold of Highland cattle grazing alongside the café. Owners Chris and Jo Reeks have used their farming knowledge to stock the shop with the very best of British produce. The butchery counter is a source of particular pride and if you're planning a BBQ, the farm's own sausages should definitely feature.

You can taste them first in the café as part of the excellent cooked breakfast. Light lunches, quiches, and jacket potatoes are on the menu during the day, best enjoyed on the terrace if the weather allows. Kids can canter about on the lawn and pedal around on toy tractors while parents admire the view down to the Newmarket gallops.

Opening hours
Mon-Sat 9am-5pm
Sun 9.30am-4pm
No hot food after 3pm & no hot drinks 30 mins before closing

La Hogue, Chippenham, nr Newmarket, Ely CB7 5PZ
WWW.LAHOGUE.CO.UK   01638 751128

Elveden Courtyard

JUNCTION: B1106; 2 MINUTES

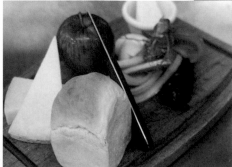

Elveden is the former home of the Maharajah Duleep Singh and the current home of the Guinness family. A few minutes' drive off the A11, onto the B1106 and left again down the wooded drive to a huge car park, with the Courtyard set in the middle of the former stable block.

Foodies won't be disappointed with the range of goods in the Food Hall, both local and exotic – this is an epicurean Aladdin's Cave. The adjacent restaurant's menu serves meals from breakfast to tea and everything in between. Much of what's served is sourced on the Elveden Estate (look out for shot in your game dish!)

The Tea Room 'Teapots & Post' serves light lunches as well as tea and coffee and delicious freshly-baked, homemade scones and cakes; uniquely it is also the home of the village Post Office. After eating, browse the Home & Garden shop which has an array of gifts and homeware or treat yourself to handmade chocolates or macarons.

Opening hours
Mon-Sat 9.30am-5pm
Sun 10am-5pm
(Post Office closes at 2pm on Weds)

Elveden Courtyard, London Road, Elveden IP24 3TQ
WWW.ELVEDENCOURTYARD.COM   01842 898068

GARDEN CENTRE

Lime Kiln Kitchen

JUNCTION: A1075; 2 MINUTES

Within spitting distance of the A11 is the Lime Kiln Kitchen. If weather permits, head out to the deck overlooking the reed beds and Kilverstone Estate – you'll feel like you're in a nature reserve. Inside, the décor is eclectic and there's plenty of seating plus a wood-burner for colder days; dogs are treated to their own area with water, biscuits and even a bed if needed.

A wide menu serves breakfast (including pancakes!), a huge array of sandwiches, salads and daily specials such as hand-battered fish and chips. There's a lavish afternoon tea and the scones are particularly highly regarded, often with a weekly special such as iced coffee and walnut. Children have their own menu and there's a wide range of gluten-free, vegetarian and vegan dishes including cake, so everyone will be happy. Everything is freshly made and the service is excellent.

Don't miss an opportunity to feed the koi in the pond – or send the kids off to feed them while you relax over coffee and discuss how many plants you can fit in the car.

Opening hours
Mon-Thurs, Sat 9am-5pm
Fri 9.30am-7.30pm
Sun 10am-4pm

Lime Kiln Kitchen, Thetford Garden Centre, Kilverstone IP24 2RL
WWW.THETFORDGARDENCENTRE.CO.UK   01842 763267

The Kitchen at St George's Distillery

JUNCTION: B1111; 2 MINUTES

England hadn't had a whisky distillery for more than 100 years when St George's opened its doors in 2007, but peaty Norfolk is surely the right place for a renaissance. Aficionados can take the tour and inspect the stills, but for those who are happy to let the alchemy happen behind closed doors, there's a fantastic café instead.

Tucked at the back of the whisky emporium (featuring more than 200 different types), the Kitchen serves up an enticing range of light bites and mains. Efficient, friendly staff usher you to tables in the modern café before ferrying over hearty plates; the sharing boards are particularly recommended. Whisky has found its way into some of the chutneys, marmalades and sauces, but the menu by no means overworks it: beef dripping fries and butterflied chicken sit next to crab linguine and a Norfolk ploughman's.

Don't let the talk of spirits put families off – children are welcome and tables on the terrace mean they can play nearby on the lawn.

Opening hours
Mon-Sun 9am-4.15pm

The Kitchen at St George's Distillery, Harling Road, Roudham NR16 2QW
WWW.ENGLISHWHISKY.CO.UK   01953 717939

PUB
The Boars

JUNCTION: B1077; 2 MINUTES

There's a wonderful homely feel to The Boars with its vintage furniture, posies of flowers on the table and Jenny's warm welcome at the front. Simon cooks up a storm in the kitchen. He's a self-taught chef, but you wouldn't know it from the imaginative dishes that emerge: Italian coppa (a cold pork cut), Catalan cod, katsu curry, croque champignon are just some of his triumphs.

The pair took over in early 2019 and have been taking the pub from strength-to-strength, adding supper clubs and a hearty breakfast menu, which takes full advantage of their local network of suppliers. The coffee is smooth, so it's worth diving off the A11 for a pick-me-up, even if you're not eating.

When the weather allows, enjoy your meal al fresco at one of the beautifully laid tables on the lawn in the walled garden. Magical.

Opening hours
Mon-Sat 11am-11pm
Sun 11am-10.30pm
(see website for kitchen hours)

The Boars, Spooner Row, Wymondham NR18 9LL
WWW.THEBOARS.CO.UK   01953 605851

The Orangery Tea Room

JUNCTION: WYMONDHAM; 6 MINUTES

Set in 30 acres of woodland, Ketteringham Hall is ideal for dog walkers, ramblers and families. Park among the trees and follow the path around to the back of house to find the timeless Orangery Tea Room, set – as you might imagine – in the elegant orangery. On sunny days you can grab an organic ice cream or homemade cake and satisfy that urge to walk down to the lake, or find a seat on the large terrace; a perfect spot for those just wanting to sit and admire the surroundings.

When it's chillier, settle inside at a linen-laid table and gaze out of the beautiful windows across the lawns. Cakes, pastries, soups, sandwiches and salads are all freshly made and tea is by the pot, small or large – loose leaf, of course – along with the full range of good coffee. For the official Afternoon Tea, phone ahead, but don't worry if you didn't as there are plenty of other tempting tea items.

Opening hours
Tues-Fri 11am-4pm
Sat-Sun 10am-4pm

The Orangery Tea Room, NR18 9RS
WWW.ORANGERYTEAROOM.CO.UK   01603 559224

The ☞ M25, M20 & M23

Circle the city and explore the garden of England

A41
M1
A1(M)
A10
M11
212
Potters Bar
211
Epping
Cheshunt
213
214
210
215
216
M40
Slough
LONDON
M4
Dartford
M3
217
219
A243
Epsom
A232
222
Woking
218
A3
A217
A23
A21
221
220
A24
226

- 210 Norpar Barns
- 211 The Gatehouse Café
- 212 Fred and Ginger Coffee
- 213 The Kitchen Croxley
- 214 The Café in the Park
- 215 The Breadhouse
- 216 The Swan Inn
- 217 Heather Farm Café
- 218 Nest
- 219 The Medicine Garden
- 220 Priory Farm Nursery
- 221 Oldpost
- 222 Riverside Tea Room
- 223 The Potting Shed
- 224 The Kings Head
- 225 The Secret Garden
- 226 The Curious Pig in the Parlour

M25 / M20 / M23

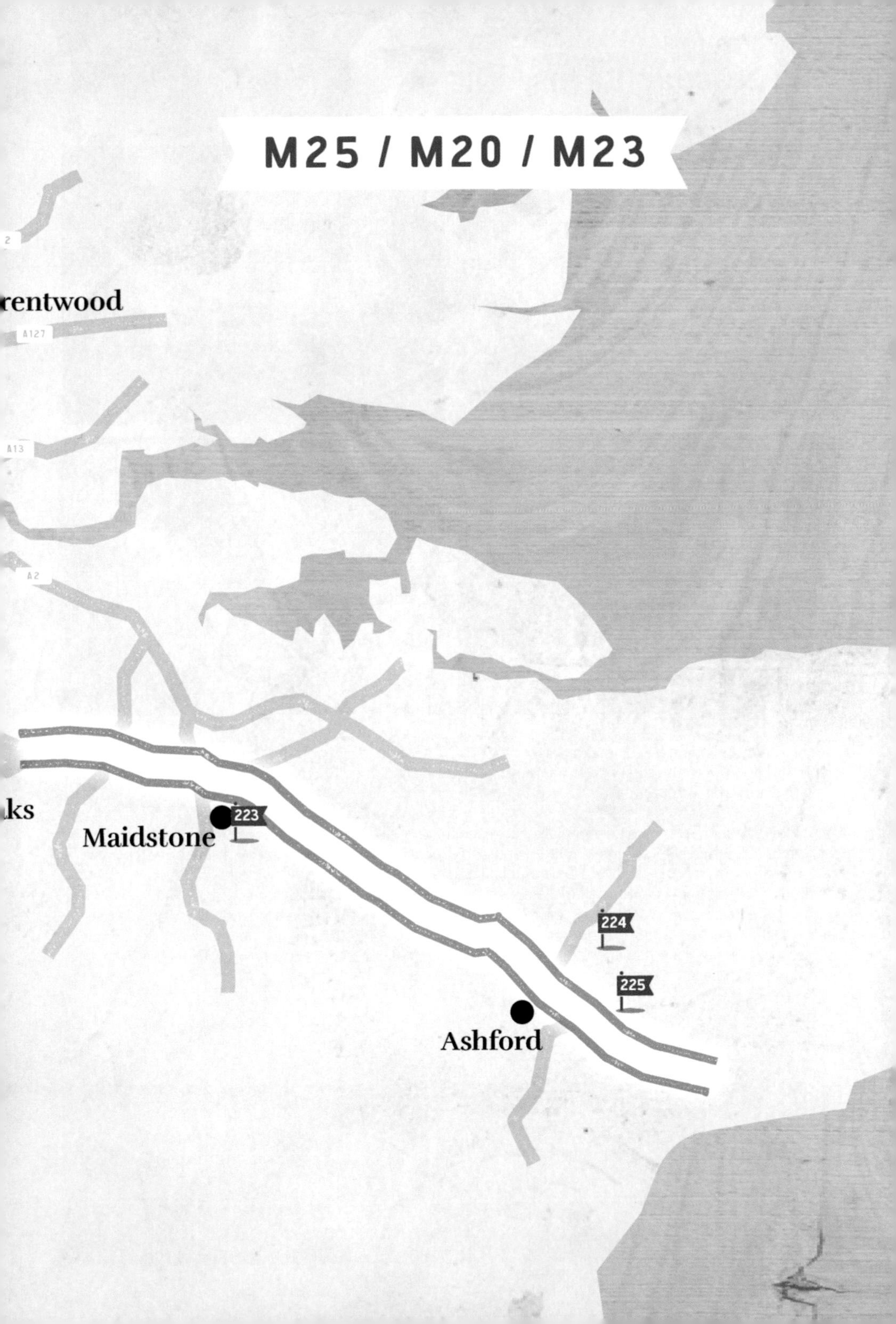

Brentwood

A127

A13

A2

Sevenoaks

Maidstone 223

Ashford

224

225

Hidden down a winding tree-lined track, Norpar Barns is a vision of old country farming. Its medieval clapboard doors were first opened to the public in 1969, selling dried flowers as a diversification to the family's traditional farming.

Today the dried flowers have been replaced by a sensational seasonal emporium of rustic homeware and decorations. Each Easter, summer, autumn and Christmas the whitewashed barn is transformed by a new theme. December is a particular highlight with a woodland, Father Christmas, wreath workshops, pork roast and mulled punch, carol singing and a separate blacked-out Christmas light barn. Individuality and Fairtrade are celebrated. You'll struggle to resist leaving without at least one gorgeous glass bauble or garland, whatever the season. In spring and summer tea and cake is served in a spectacular 14th-century oak barn with wibbly beams decorated with old farm tools, willow boughs and flowers. Don't miss the home-grown apple juice, available to take away.

Opening hours
Tues-Sat 10am-5pm (Sun 11am)
Also open Mon when Christmas & Easter Barns are open
Closed January.

Norpar Barns, Navestock Hall Shonksmill Road, Navestock RM4 1HA
WWW.NORPAR.CO.UK   01277 374969

The Gatehouse Café

JUNCTION: 25; 8 MINUTES

Tucked in a quiet corner of Waltham Abbey, the Gatehouse Café has enviable views over the town's eponymous church and comes into its own in summer when tables and chairs are set out beneath the trees. Frothy hanging baskets are strung up above the pavement tables, and inside there's a warmth to the dark grey panelling, wooden floors and pretty sash windows.

The steady stream of regulars is testament to the warm welcome on offer from Aurelia, Sean and their team. Aurelia brings flavours of her native Italy to the cuisine: gnocchi, panini, sundried tomatoes and pesto served alongside full breakfasts, warm quiches and chocolate vegan cake.

Make time to visit the Norman church, gardens and moat next door. This site has been a place of worship since 600 AD and it's thought to be the final resting place of Saxon King Harold. You can pick up an informative leaflet to guide you round.

Opening hours
Mon-Fri 7.30am-5pm
Sat-Sun 9am-5pm

The Gatehouse Café, 2-4 Highbridge Street, Waltham Abbey EN9 1DG
07971 800727

The handsome charcoal-coloured front of Fred and Ginger Coffee stands on Kings Langley's high street illuminated by filament bulbs and cheery faces and abuzz with enthusiasm for great coffee.

It's a popular local haunt and it's easy to see why: the space is bright and welcoming – decorated with vintage pictures, brass light fittings and soothing palms – and the food delicious.

Whether you're stopping for an expertly made flat white, a flaky almond croissant or a plateful of sumptuous house salad, you won't be disappointed. Vegan options such as pesto, tomato, courgette and onion filo slices stand alongside crisp sausage rolls, teriyaki salmon and a sea of colourful salads in enamel bowls. When the sun is shining sit at the Parisian tables outside to watch the world go by.

Juices freshly squeezed on site and soya milk chai lattes will pep you up for the onward journey. Parking outside is free for an hour.

Opening hours
Mon-Fri 8am-5pm
Sat 8.30am-5pm
Sun 9am-4pm

Fred and Ginger Coffee, 38c High Street, Kings Langley WD4 9HT
WWW.FREDANDGINGERCOFFEE.CO.UK   01923 262420

The Kitchen Croxley

JUNCTION: 18; 7 MINUTES

The Kitchen is not just a tearoom and coffee shop but also a studio for the cake artists at work here. Cupcakes, chocolate dripcakes, classic Victoria sponges and their legendary lemon drizzle adorn the counter, served alongside tasty sandwiches: perhaps blue cheese, mango and rocket or free-range egg and mayo. Coffee is smooth and the afternoon tea, with bottomless teapots, is highly recommended so book ahead if you've time for a longer stop.

It's a family business which shows in the cheerful, accommodating service; they even baked a special batch of scones for one customer who was sorry to miss them. They support and welcome community groups such as the local book club, and 'Knit and Natter' for the local hospice.

There's a licensed bar too so non-drivers can savour a craft beer or try a cheeky cocktail for the road. Parking is available in the bays adjacent, in Croxley Station opposite or at the car park adjacent to the Red House pub just down the road.

Opening hours
Mon call ahead to check
Tues-Sat 9am-5pm
Sun noon-5pm

The Kitchen Croxley, 198 Watford Road Croxley Green WD3 3DB
WWW.THEKITCHENCROXLEY.CO.UK   01923 805896

Nature lovers stuck on the M25 should stop off at the Rickmansworth aquadrome, a 41-hectare reserve in the hollow of an old gravel quarry. Filled by the River Colne, it throngs with wildlife and a stroll around the easy mile-long trail will still any frayed tempers.

To match the eco-minded location, Café in the Park is a family friendly spot and draws many of the ingredients for its wholesome meals from local farms. Bread and pastries are all baked fresh in the kitchen and dishes are tasty and reasonably priced: rice falafel bowls, harissa chicken salad and a counter full of cakes.

The ethical philosophy spills over into the adjoining shop where you can fill your tote with organic vegetables, bamboo homewares, posies of flowers and loose grains. You can even grind your own nut butter here.

Kids are encouraged to get back to nature in the mud kitchen outside, and you can hose them off in the toilets before returning to the car. The queues are only proof that this is a winning formula.

Opening hours
Mon-Sun 9am-5pm

The Café in the Park, The Aquadrome, Frogmoor Lane, Rickmansworth WD3 1NB
WWW.THECAFEINTHEPARK.COM   01923 711131

The Breadhouse

JUNCTION: 17; 12 MINUTES

© Paul Upward Photography

There's a cheery welcome and a real sense of community at the Breadhouse, encouraged by lovely initiatives such as crochet workshops, guided walks, art exhibitions and seminars. Set in the town's central marketplace, it's a hub for Chalfont St Peter. Step through the door and you're greeted by a beautiful cherry-wood counter laden with home baking, from sausage rolls and banana loaf to chocolate mud cake.

It's family-friendly and kids will be kept occupied by the play area in the corner, though with tables spread over two levels, it's easy to find a peaceful spot too.

A roll of brown paper hung on the wall displays the often-changing specials, ranging from Moroccan porridge to sautéed asparagus with poached egg and bacon, mini roast pumpkin stuffed with puy lentils and smoked mackerel salad. There's lots for vegans and vegetarians here as well, and probably the best almond coffee near the M25!

Opening hours
Mon-Sat 8.30am-4pm

The Breadhouse, 8 Market Place, Chalfont St Peter SL9 9EA
WWW.BREADHOUSE.CO.UK   01753 885371

Though it's just within the London Orbital, you can also reach The Swan from the M40 and A40, so if you're heading West from London to Oxfordshire (or vice versa) and looking for a rural pub in leafy village, you've just struck gold.

Brick and timber-framed and draped in wisteria, it's a welcoming sight even before you step through the door, where dark wood furniture and heritage paints intermingle with vases of fresh-cut flowers and decorated mantlepiece.

Provenance and welfare a big deal for the team here, so ingredients are largely free-range and organic, delivered by producers nearby and turned by talented chefs into dishes such as slow-roasted garlic with rustic bread, sundried tomato and almond pesto linguine or harissa-spiced tiger prawns. Specials change regularly, but the bubble and squeak, served with hollandaise and a poached egg, draws consistent praise, so be sure to add it to your order.

The Harefield Place nature reserve a walk away on the other side of the Grand Union canal warrants a visit if you need a post-prandial stroll.

Opening hours
Mon-Fri 11.30am-11.30pm
Sat 9.30am-11.30pm
Sun noon-11pm

Ⓥ Ⓟ

The Swan Inn, Village Road, Denham UB9 5BH
WWW.SWANINNDENHAM.CO.UK   01895 832085

The Horsell Common meadows and wetlands are an enormously popular spot with dog walkers, whether striding over the boardwalks or throwing sticks for their charges in the river.

Set among the reeds is the equally popular Heather Farm Café, which opens with the larks to warm the early morning walkers with piping hot tea and hearty breakfasts. The sunny yellow walls, farmhouse kitchen style and Amy's cheery team welcome visitors in, and staff won't bat an eye at muddy paws and damp coats. Blankets are provided on the terrace next to the chunky benches to stave off the chill on crisp days.

Grab a pew inside or out to fill up on healthy bowls of porridge, warm waffles, giant Yorkshire puddings and varied salads: check the chalkboard behind the counter for specials. Dogs are indulged with special pet ice creams and a jar of treats, and little people will be kept occupied for a while with the colouring crayons and paper.

Opening hours
Mon-Fri 8.30am-5pm
Sat-Sun 8.30am-5.30pm

Heather Farm Café, Chobham Road, Horsell Common, Woking, GU21 4XY
WWW.HEATHERFARM.CAFE   01483 726556

Large Dickensian bay windows stand either side of the front door, one piled with an enticing and eclectic range of ceramics, tableware, books and gifts, the other a window onto the goodies in the café within.

Breakfast on almond croissants baked that morning, lunch on sandwiches, frittata and salads – perhaps quinoa with feta, mango and pomegranate – or pep up your afternoon with a Green and Blacks hot chocolate and a slice of home-baked pistachio and lemon drizzle cake. You can sit at one of the tables inside among the trinkets and fresh flowers or grab a pew on the sunny terrace at the front (though you'll have to beat the cyclists to it; Nest is a popular mid-ride stop). Blankets are provided for world-watching on cooler days.

Dogs are very welcome and there are great walks around this pretty town for wearing them out before browsing Nest's exquisite antiques and enjoying its Italian coffee.

Opening hours
Mon-Fri 9am-5pm
Sat 9am-5.30pm

Nest, High Street, Ripley GU23 6AQ
WWW.NEST-HOME.COM   01483 211111

CAFÉ
The Medicine Garden

JUNCTION: 10; 6 MINUTES

The Medicine Garden has adopted a Victorian walled garden, saving it from ruin and restoring the glasshouses to turn it into a nurturing space where visitors can reconnect with nature, take a little time out, stretch out in a tai chi class or shop the community of small businesses.

You'll find the café in one of the former potting sheds, a comfortable shabby chic affair serving sandwiches, jacket potatoes and very good cakes. The garden and its borders are beautiful and have a run of tables beneath awnings along one wall, so you can enjoy them to the full over a meal. There's a sand pit and play area for children to burn off some steam too.

Speaking of gardens, RHS Wisley is a short spin up the road and a mecca for horticulturalists, though if you're anything like us, you won't want to leave here.

There's parking on site but there's a (small) pay & display fee.

Opening hours
Mon-Sat 9am-5pm
Sun 10am-4pm

The Medicine Garden, Downside Road, Cobham KT11 3LU
WWW.THEMEDICINEGARDEN.COM 07754 677747

Priory Farm Nursery

JUNCTION: 6; 9 MINUTES

Priory Farm Nursery, at the edge of the Sussex Downs, is a positive haven from the motorway. You could easily lose an hour or so to browsing the healthy plants and carefully chosen selection of gifts, but if you're weakening with hunger, head directly to the bright café.

There's a homeliness to the mismatched chairs, tea is served in pots with knitted cosies, and cakes and treats stand temptingly on the wood-clad counter. For more substantial sustenance, turn to the menu and specials board for dishes such as mushroom soup, sausage and mash, and vegan nachos, made with ingredients from local producers; their very popular breakfast menu is served till 11.30am. If you need a moment to unwind from the frenetic M25, the Potting Shed area is designated for grown-ups only, so you can quietly leaf through a paper or savour a coffee.

If you've got restless kids in the back, there's a really brilliant play area with a tractor to sit on and pirate galleon to hijack, and the farm's discovery walk is a great excuse to grab a breath of fresh air.

Opening hours
March-Oct Mon-Sat 9am-5.30pm; Sun 10am-4.30pm
Jan-Feb Mon-Sat 9am-5pm; Sun 10am-4.30pm

Priory Farm Nursery, Sandy Lane, South Nutfield, Redhill RH1 4EJ
WWW.PRIORYFARMNURSERY.CO.UK   01737 823500

Oldpost

JUNCTION: 6; 7 MINUTES

Many things to many people, Oldpost is a brilliant reinvention of Nutfield's former Post Office. A gift shop, fitness studio, beauty salon and more jostle for space with the café in what is an inspirational combination. You can browse for a birthday card, sniff scented candles or get your nails done while you wait for your coffee to brew.

Entrepreneurial owner Joe Chandler originally started his career as a graphic designer. He then launched a home accessories range – Chickidee Homeware, which you can find for sale in the shop – before turning his attentions to creating a neighbourhood hub.

Food is good too – breakfasts, baguettes, salads and quiches – served to tables in front of tall bright windows, or out in the landscape courtyard on fine days.

Opening hours
Mon-Sat 8am-4pm
Sun 10am-4pm

Oldpost, 19 High Street, Nutfield, Redhill RH1 4HH
WWW.OLDPOST.CO.UK   01737 652 131

Riverside Tea Room sits overlooking the ford in pretty Eynsford, its window boxes brimming with flowers. Reminiscent of childhood sweet shops, it has a pastel pink door and leaded windows strung with bunting. Breakfast might be eggs Benedict with local honey-roasted ham, lunch could be a jacket sweet potato or filled baguette and if you're lucky you'll catch the afternoon scones warm from the oven. Dietary requirements are cheerfully accommodated and ingredients are sourced as locally as possible.

Business and family life intermingle here, with owner Lizzie's kids often found doing their homework at tables after school, wading in the stream or kicking a football around outside. The kids' menu shows that she knows how to get small children eating!

Visitors often drop in after visiting the heavenly lavender farm up the road. Pre-book Riverside's Vintage Afternoon Tea for a princely Kentish stop.

Opening hours
Mon-Fri 9am-4.30pm
Sat-Sun 9.30am-4pm

Riverside Tea Room, 21 Riverside, Eynsford DA4 0AE
WWW.RIVERSIDE-TEAROOM.CO.UK   01322 861551

The Potting Shed

JUNCTION: 8; 8 MINUTES

If you're looking for a quick pit stop on your way to or from Dover, The Potting Shed is it. Spacious and down-to-earth it has plenty of room for the whole family, and will shortly have some quirky, underground bedrooms to stay in too, should you fancy a night in Middle Earth.

Walk through the bar and past the decadent leg of Spanish jamón to find the breezy dining room. Felt clouds hang from the lofty vaulted ceiling, above a mismatch of brightly coloured chairs. Watch the chefs at work in the open kitchen as they prepare the flavourful menu. It's a notch up from pub grub, offering tapas, Lebanese platters and wood-fired pizzas alongside Sunday roasts and burgers.

The sunny terrace is shaded by awnings on sunny days, and deck chairs are set out on the large lawn. History buffs should not depart before heading to the magnificent, if confusingly-named, Leeds Castle. The Norman stronghold is exactly as a castle should look – moated and crenelated – and was used by Henry VIII and his first wife Catherine of Aragon.

Opening hours
Mon-Thurs 8am-11pm
Fri-Sat 8am-11.30pm
Sun 8am-10.30am

The Potting Shed, Sutton Road, Langley ME17 3LZ
WWW.ELITEPUBS.COM/THE-POTTING-SHED   01622 862 112

If you're searching for an award-winning gourmet destination in an historic spot, you've struck lucky. Welcome to a grand old pub in very pretty Wye run by "a couple of down to earth boys from the North" (their words).

Mark and Scott have created an up-to-the-minute village pub where you're as welcome to drop by for coffee and croissants as order a good meal – french toast with poached rhubarb or a vegan breakfast to start the day, crayfish croquettes, corn-fed chicken kiev or lamb from the nearby community farm later in the day. Almost everything is made in-house so it's a foodie's delight.

This pub is a cool place to be – suave antler chandeliers, purple feature wall – but not so cool that they don't keep dog biscuits behind the bar (handmade by the chef). So settle into a leather wing back chair, and soak up the vibe. There's a welcome for all, and if you're going to hole up in the countryside, you'd do well to do it here. Bedrooms upstairs are simple and uncluttered with a sunny feel.

Opening hours
Mon-Weds 8am-10pm
Thurs-Sat 8am-11pm
Sun 8am-10pm

The Kings Head, Church Street, Wye, Ashford TN25 5BN
WWW.KINGSHEADWYE.COM   01233 812 418

CAFÉ

The Secret Garden

JUNCTION: 10; 5 MINUTES

It's easy to see why The Secret Garden is so popular with brides. Squirreled away in the old coach houses of the Mersham Le Hatch Estate, the rambling collection of Victorian buildings, topped with a stately clock spire, are adrift in a sea of gorgeous gardens. Though the M20 thrums past not far away, remarkably it can barely be heard.

Luckily you don't have to wait to tie the knot to see it for yourself. Breakfast and light lunches are served seven days a week (when wedding parties haven't invaded), transforming produce from the garden and Kentish fields into wedding-worthy plates. It's worth booking ahead to have an afternoon tea in the dining room flooded with natural light or on the shady veranda.

If you're not in a rush for a ferry, make time to explore the estate beyond the gardens, which has been in the Knatchbull family since the reign of Henry VII. Public footpaths thread through the woodland passing a large deer park, ornamental lake and some impressively ancient trees.

Opening hours
Mon-Sun 10am-6pm

The Secret Garden, Merhsam-le-Hythe Business Village, Hythe Rd, Ashford TN25 6NH
WWW.SECRETGARDENKENT.CO.UK   01233 501586

Sash windows, gabled porch, abundant hanging baskets and wood-clad extension, The Curious Pig in the Parlour is smart in its rural setting. Friendly staff greet you on arrival, and you're as welcome to pop in for coffee or a leisurely lunch, as stay overnight on your way to Gatwick (which is just 7 miles down the road).

The dining room is chic and clean, with panelling in duck egg blue offset by red upholstery and scrubbed wooden tables. Specialities on the menu are tasty wood-fired pizzas and charcoal oven steaks, but it's no two-trick pony and the menu also features the likes of pan-fried duck, cauliflower burgers and three-cheese arancini.

When the sun shines, make the most of the stylish beer garden, where wagon wheels and vintage lights bring out the best of the landscaping as you watch the planes soar overhead.

Opening hours
Mon-Sat noon-11pm
Sun noon-10.30pm

The Curious Pig in the Parlour, Effingham Road, Copthorne, Crawley RH10 3HY
WWW.THECURIOUSPIGINTHEPARLOUR.COM   01342 716202

Go the Extra Mile
THE FARM - STRATFORD #254

COTSWOLD &
COUNTRY

A46, M42, M40 & A40

*Explore the heart
of England*

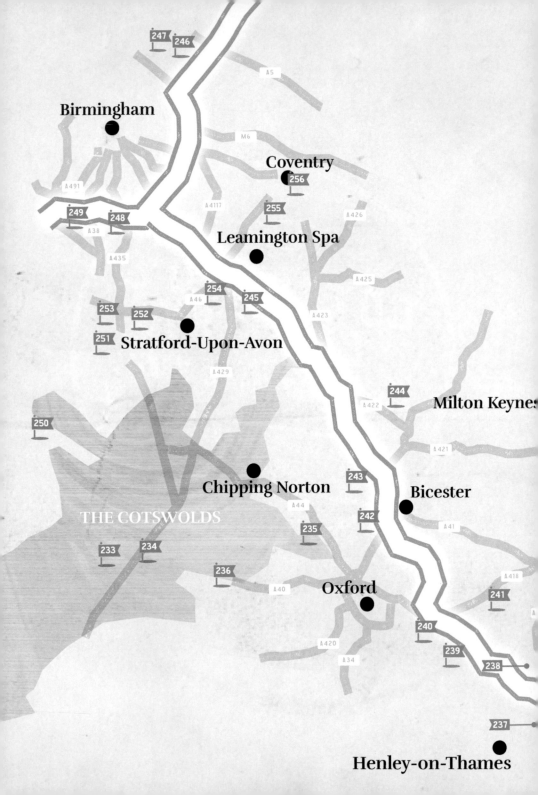

M40 / M42

M25

igh Wycombe

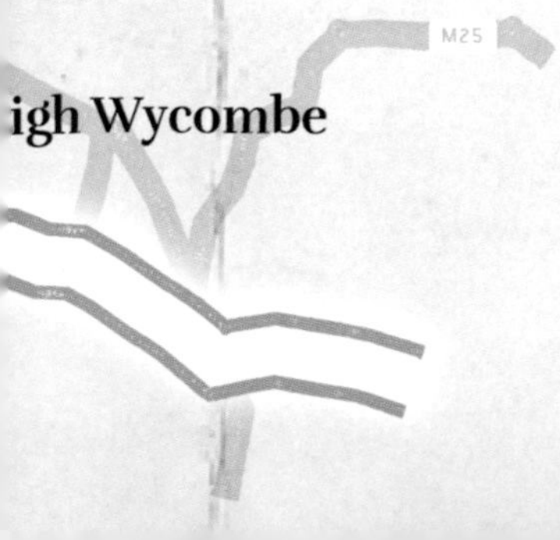

A46 & A40

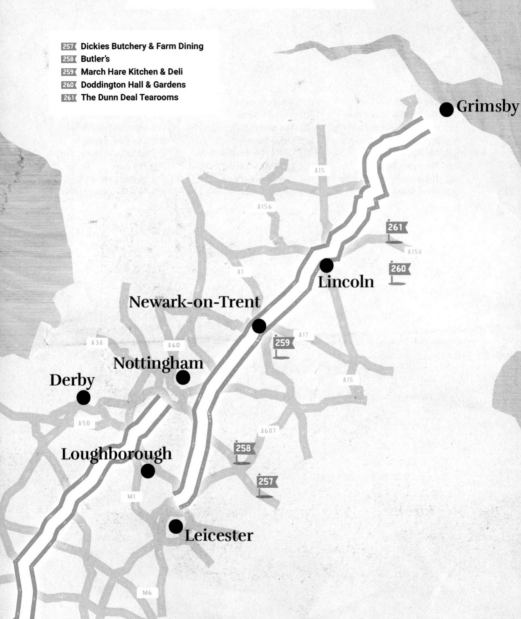

257 Dickies Butchery & Farm Dining
258 Butler's
259 March Hare Kitchen & Deli
260 Doddington Hall & Gardens
261 The Dunn Deal Tearooms

Grimsby

A15

A156

261

A158

260

A1

Lincoln

Newark-on-Trent

A17

259

A15

A38

A60

Nottingham

Derby

A50

A607

258

Loughborough

257

M1

Leicester

M6

The Hayloft

JUNCTION: A429; 5 MINUTES

Sprawl on a beanbag in the yurt, take a table in the mellow cafe or bask in the sun on the grass: The Hayloft is a dramatic change from the road scenery. It's in the middle of the Cotswolds and so ringed with greenery and bathed with bird song.

Eloise is your chirpy host, and ensures the team keep the tasty plates flowing: enamel bowls of homemade soup, woodfired pizzas, quinoa salad, filled paninis and chewy flapjacks just some of the decent fare on offer. Coffee is good and there are plenty of low sugar, vegetarian and gluten-free options.

The grey-painted shelves around the room stock deli produce from some of the carefully selected local companies supplying the kitchen, so if you liked the smoked fish, Cacklebean eggs, apple juice or coffee, you can fill you tote on your way out.

There's a climbing and bouldering centre next door as well as an expansive camp site, so if you're looking to split your journey with a fun overnight stop, this is a strong contender.

Opening hours
Mon, Weds-Fri 9am-7pm
Tues 9am-8pm
Sat-Sun 9am-5pm

The Hayloft, 1 The Hayloft, Far Peak, Northleach GL54 3AP
WWW.HAYLOFT-CAFE.CO.UK   01285 700370

Northleach, a delightful (and mercifully comparatively quiet) Cotswold town, was once at an important crossroads on the Roman Fosse Way but grew to Europe-wide notoriety in the fifteenth century as the centre of the wool trade.

The Curious Wine Cellar perches on one side of the Market Place, which has changed little since those wool-trading days (perhaps with the exception of the car park), and is a very welcome break from the road. Smiley staff are almost always happy to chat and you'll often find locals sharing news at the bar.

Pastries are brought in every morning for breakfast, lunch might be a Parma ham and sundried tomato salad or goats cheese, thyme and apricot jam ciabatta, and substantial bar snacks are served in the evenings; there's also the occasional pop-up restaurant. Coffee is very good can be supped at the breakfast bar in the window while you watch the world go by, but of course with a name like the Curious Cellar, non-drivers really should exploit the wine expertise.

Opening hours
Tues-Sat 9am-11pm
Sun-Mon 9am-9pm

The Curious Wine Cellar, The Ox House, Market Place, Northleach GL54 3EG
WWW.CURIOUSABOUTWINE.COM   01451 860650

Hampers Food and Wine Co.

JUNCTION: EYNSHAM ROUNDABOUT; 9 MINUTES

"Homemade, hearty, happy and healthy" is how the Hamper's team describe their food, and it's hard to disagree. Homemade quiches, scotch eggs, brownies and salads vie for attention in the deli counter, while laden plates are ferried to tables in the cafe, perhaps eggs Benedict, spanakopita, or beef and stilton rolls.

Owner Deb sold a deli in Oxford on a few years ago, but the entrepreneurial streak runs deep and she's back to work her magic in Woodstock. The cafe and delicatessen stands on the vibrant high street, and is appealing for its smart, sea green sash windows and brass lamps, not to mention excellent coffee brewed with wood-roasted beans from local roastery, UE.

It's round the corner from Blenheim Palace so if you're taking your time over your journey, this is a diverting place to stop.

Opening hours
Mon-Fri 8.30am-5.30pm
Sat 8.30am-6pm
Sun 10am-5pm

Hampers Food and Wine Co., 31-33 Oxford Street, Woodstock OX20 1TH
WWW.HAMPERSFOODANDWINE.CO.UK   01993 811535

From the moment you swoop past the elegant landscaped entrance you'll be revived by Burford's 15 acres of plants and gardens. Horticulturists will find the show gardens entrancing, but if you're not so green fingered there's plenty to divert you in 'Le Souk' – once the glasshouses now a large shop filled with covetable furniture, gifts and books. Founder Nigel and his team have dubbed it a 'magical emporium', and we agree.

The cafe is at the heart of it: a contemporary, light-flooded space that's abuzz with happy customers. If you'd like a moment of peace there's a quiet zone outside in one of the greenhouses where you're welcome to take your coffee. Food here is well regarded – supplied by seven chefs and a full-time baker behind-the-scenes, it often uses ingredients grown on site as well as lamb from the local Burford flock. Anything the Company doesn't grow is sourced from suppliers elsewhere in the Cotswolds. Wonderful.

Opening hours
Mon-Sat 9am-6pm
Sun 11am-5pm

Burford Garden Company, Shilton Road, Burford OX18 4PA
WWW.BURFORD.CO.UK   01993 823117

The Royal Oak

JUNCTION: 4; 10 MINUTES

A cracking country pub, the Royal Oak stands at the edge of the Chilterns, not far from the Thames-washed town of Marlow. It's informal yet stylish with rugs flung over tiled floors, scrubbed pew seats and dogs asleep by the wood burner. The garden is beautiful, big enough to lose your kids in and perfect for slothful lunches in summer. Keep a lookout for red kites overhead.

There's a wonderful sense of a local economy here: bees bob about in the garden to make the pub's honey and ingredients are foraged from the hedgerows or swapped with local allotment holders. Food is uniformly excellent and moves with the seasons – try the bubble and squeak with bacon and hollandaise or pan-roast Devon hake fillet with creamed spinach and salt fish fritters. And there are dedicated menus for vegan, dairy- and gluten-free diets.

Before you depart take a stroll through the beech trees of Marlow Common, where you'll find trenches used for practice during the First World War.

Please note, the Royal Oak is currently recovering from a recent fire so please do check ahead to ensure they're open.

Opening hours
Mon-Thurs noon-9.30pm
Fri-Sat noon-10pm
Sun noon-9pm

The Royal Oak, Frieth Road, Bovingdon Green, Marlow SL7 2JF
WWW.ROYALOAKMARLOW.CO.UK   01628 488611

Goods have been sold out of this building for hundreds of years. Once a posh merchant's house, the Apple Orchard is now an upmarket furniture and homeware store with a warren of rooms filled with tasteful pieces selected by owners Huw and Carolyn. They are both often on hand greeting customers like old friends.

After wending your way through the maze of rooms you finally reach the café at the top, where you're rewarded with delicious cakes and smooth coffee, which you can enjoy curled up in the snug. Staff are open and friendly, and will happily steer you through the choices on offer, including homemade quiches, generous salads and cream teas. After the higgledy-piggledy 16th-century interior of the house, the courtyard garden just beyond the café door is a bright and spacious surprise. The car park is just beyond for those with buggies or mobility issues.

If there's time, head to the curious Hellfire Caves behind the house – a labyrinth of tunnels and elaborate chambers dug into the hillside.

Opening hours
Mon-Sat 9.30am-5pm
Sun 10.30am-4.30pm

The Apple Orchard, The High Street, West Wycombe HP14 3AG
WWW.THEAPPLEORCHARD.CO.UK   01494 528328

The Granary Delicatessen

JUNCTION: 6; 5 MINUTES

Watlington is the sort of town that tourists travel to see: a vision of handsome brick buildings, thatched cottages and traditional shop fronts. The Granary stands at the heart of village life and is a lively hub for locals and visitors alike.

It originally opened as a cheese shop in 1985, but such was its popularity that it moved up the road to sprawl out, later adopting the old bank next door too. People-watchers will love the window seats at the wide breakfast bar, which looks onto the high street, while sofas invite a comfortable rest if you're road weary.

Food is all freshly prepared and changes with the seasons. Specials rotate regularly so there's always something new to try, such as a Mediterranean platter or duck pâté with sourdough.

The Granary's deli is a few doors up and still has a strong cheese focus but also stocks bread, olives, cured meats, conserves and other deli goodies. That's the car snacks sorted.

Opening hours
Mon-Sat 9am-5pm

The Granary Delicatessen, 16-18 High Street, Watlington OX49 5PY
WWW.GRANARYDELI.CO.UK   01491 613585

Crazy Bear seems an appropriate moniker for a group that encompasses hotels, restaurants, bars, a members' club and farm. Keen to guarantee the provenance of the ingredients in their restaurants, the team bought an 80-acre farm in the heart of Oxfordshire to rear top-notch meat according to traditional methods, and they've added their signature pizzazz to the farm shop that has grown up alongside.

Wicker shopping baskets hang above the deli and butchery counters, from which a steady stream of customers are plied with home-smoked meats, sausage rolls, quiche, cheeses and meat cuts from the farm's own stock. Tables in front practically sag beneath the weight of the free-range eggs, loaves and cakes piled on top.

Head through the sliding door at the back to find the restaurant, which serves the ingredients as the chefs intended in a rustic, wild-west kind of setting: filled sandwiches, burgers, soups, pies and the popular afternoon teas.

Kids will love the play area and animal pens out front, where they can meet goats, pigs, llamas and reindeer while parents keep watch from the veranda.

Opening hours
Tues-Sun 9am-6pm

Crazy Bear Farm Shop, Newells Lane, Stadhampton OX44 7XJ
WWW.CRAZYBEARGROUP.CO.UK/FARM-SHOP/   01865 890714

CAFÉ
What's Cooking

JUNCTION: 6/ 7/ 8A; 9 MINUTES

It's well worth escaping the M40 for the pretty market town of Thame, nestled at the foot of the Chilterns. It has a handsome and lively High Street with cosy pubs, beautiful homeware shops, and a fantastic deli/café, What's Cooking.

The talented chefs take great care in selecting the finest, fresh, local ingredients and it shines through in the flavours of their food. Breakfast and brunch is served all day and offers something for everyone, from homemade granola, buttermilk pancakes and bacon brioche rolls, to crushed avocado, huevos rancheros and shakshuka. For lunch you can grab a quick toastie or choose from a mouth-watering array of filo tarts and colourful salads.

If it's a flying visit, simply enjoy a slice of one of the excellent freshly-baked cakes over a latte: the baristas here really know their craft and the coffee is very good, brewed using beans from a company up the road that shares their ethical ethos.

Parking is available up the road in the town's large, free car park.

Opening hours
Mon-Sat 7.30am-5pm

What's Cooking, 6-8 Cornmarket, Thame OX9 3DX
WWW.WHATSCOOKINGTHAME.CO.UK   01844 212209

CAFÉ

The Milk Shed

JUNCTION: 9; 2 MINUTES

Don't be put off by its location on an industrial estate. The Milk Shed is one of the best cafés in Oxfordshire. One customer said the ice creams alone are worth a visit, and we agree. They're made on site by Lucie and Dan using only natural ingredients: vanilla pods, lumps of fudge, meringues and mashed-up bananas. Try the grown-up banana split if you want a taste of the divine, or douse a ball of vanilla in locally roasted coffee for a supreme affogato pick-me-up.

The rest of the menu is simple and expertly executed with fine ingredients. People rave about the scrambled eggs on toast, club sandwiches, generous salad bowls and cheese and bean toasties. Lucie indulges her love of cooking in preparing the daily specials, such as smoked haddock chowder or pulled lamb salad with freekeh, garlic yoghurt and pomegranate.

You can also stock up at the food shop here – Spanish olive oil, tasty snacks, local jams and biscuits...

Opening hours
Tues-Fri 9am-4pm
Sat-Sun 9am-3.30pm
last food orders an hour before closing time

The Milk Shed, Manor Farm, Northampton Road, Weston on the Green OX25 3QL
WWW.THEMILKSHEDSTORE.CO.UK   01869 351387

The Yurt at Nicholsons

JUNCTION: 10; 11 MINUTES

Follow the winding paths through the leafy garden centre to find the luminous tent that houses Nicholsons' café, keeping your eyes peeled for wildlife (we spotted the green flash of a woodpecker). The enormous Mongolian yurt is a blissful sanctuary from the road: in winter it twinkles with fairy lights; come summer the canvas roof glows above tables decorated with large boughs of greenery. This is the perfect al fresco dining for a British climate.

The food has an ethically driven vegetarian and vegan focus and is reliably delicious. Try mushrooms served on potato rösti for breakfast; pan-fried spiced mackerel with beetroot salsa for lunch, or a confit duck leg with red cabbage purée. A slice of the 'cake of the month' – elderflower, lemon and pistachio in May, blueberry, lime and lemon thyme in August – will set you up for the onward journey.

The coffee is strong and the hot chocolate, made from Mexican cocoa, is mindblowing.

Opening hours
Mon-Sat 9am-4.30pm

The Yurt at Nicholsons, The Park, North Aston OX25 6HL
WWW.THEYURTATNICHOLSONS.CO.UK   01869 340342

A bastion of traditional farming, the fields around Limes Farm supply the shop and tearoom with lovingly grown and reared produce. The family have been tending the land here for 200 years and eschew chemicals in favour of a more organic approach, which more than shows in the flavour of the meat and vegetables. The tearoom and pared-back farm shop are housed in an old medieval barn. The ancient oven was discovered during renovations and stoked back up to bake bread, cakes and tarts daily. There's a warm homeliness to the low beams, terracotta floor tiles and scrubbed wooden tables.

Service from Peter and his team is convivial and welcoming. They transform the farm's field and hedgerow bounty into a toothsome selection of breakfasts, lunches and snacks. Kids will go crazy for the loaded chocolate brownies, which they can burn off with a visit to the animal petting area. Grown ups can leaf through books in the bookshop over a smooth coffee and slice of courgette and avocado cake.

Opening hours
Mon-Sat 9am-5pm
Sun 10am-5pm

Limes Farm, Main Road, Farthinghoe NN13 5PB
WWW.LIMESFARM.COM/SHOP/   01295 711 229

Lighthorne Pavilion Café

JUNCTION: 12; 5 MINUTES

Your shoulders will drop as soon as you arrive at the Pavilion Café, a wood cabin perched at the side of the cricket pitch in the sleepy Warwickshire village of Lighthorne. Run by owner Ben, the café's relaxed informality, friendly welcome and countryside setting are instantly soothing. Staff ferry plates of steaming comfort food to tables and sofas by the wood burner or out to the terrace, where parents can watch kids run around on the green when there's no match on. Bare wood shelves are stacked with books and magazines to encourage you to linger.

People rave about the breakfasts and afternoon teas (especially popular after working up an appetite on the country paths nearby), and cups of tea are best paired with the homemade cakes, perhaps coffee and walnut or black cherry.

There's ample parking, dogs are welcome outside and a little gift shop at the rear stocks locally made crafts and goodies.

Opening hours
Tues-Fri 7.45am-4.15pm
Sat-Sun 8am-4.30pm

Lighthorne Pavilion Café, Chesterton Road, Lighthorne CV35 0AD
07768 195882

Middleton Hall & Gardens

JUNCTION: 2; 10 MINUTES

The glorious Middleton Hall was saved from ruin by a team of volunteers who have slowly restored the moated, timber-framed building over nearly four decades. Today visitors to the 42-acre estate can explore the its 950-year history, visit the formal gardens (including one of the earliest examples of a heated walled garden in the country) and stroll around the adjoining RSPB Middleton Lakes Nature Reserve. Follow its three miles of winding paths and you may spot kingfishers and herons on the wetlands.

Mind and body restored, head to the Tudor courtyard, which plays host to a small shopping village. Lose yourself for a moment in the second-hand bookshop or head to the tearoom for a friendly welcome and tasty food; it's open every day throughout the year. The paninis are held in high regard and the coffee is very smooth, best paired with a slice of their inventive cakes. Kids will love the unicorn hot chocolate. There is a small car parking charge and an admission charge to enter the Hall and Gardens but there is no admission charge for the Courtyard.

Opening hours
Sun-Thurs & second Sat each month 11am-4pm
(31 Mar to 8 Sept)
Please see website for winter opening

Middleton Hall & Gardens, Middleton B78 2AE
WWW.MIDDLETON-HALL.CO.UK   01827 283095

Forage at Coppice

JUNCTION: 9; 8 MINUTES

Marooned in a sea of gorgeous shrubs and surrounded by emerald lawns, Fig and Olive restaurant is a world away from the frenetic M42. You can find it in a former growing shed at Coppice Garden Centre, washed with the soothing sounds of birdsong and scents of the garden.

You won't be disappointed by the food on offer, rustled up from carefully sourced ingredients. Try the halloumi chips with red pepper hash, salmon teriyaki with steamed coconut rice, or a steak from the grill if you're famished. Sandwiches and coffee are also served, and better still, you can take your lunch outside to the terrace on summer's days to eat among the flowers.

Alongside the restaurant is Forage Food Hall selling a cornucopia of delicious produce. The shelves heave with homemade pâtés, Fruits of the Forage jams and cordials (made with fruit foraged from abandoned orchards) alongside a well-stocked deli counter, butchery, bakery and fresh veg barrows.

Opening hours
Mon-Fri 9am-7pm
Sat 9am-5.30pm
Sun 10am-4.30pm

Forage at Coppice, Coppice Lane, Middleton B78 2BU
WWW.COPPICEGC.COM/FORAGE-BUTCHERY-BAKERY-DELI/   0121 308 7197

Becketts Farm Shop

JUNCTION: 3; 2 MINUTES

If you're skirting Birmingham and looking to escape the traffic, this is the place.

Albert Beckett arrived here in Wythall in 1937, moving from Shropshire with a small herd of cows. Three generations have developed the land and business since, and Albert would no doubt be pleasantly surprised to see what his small herd has become.

Not only do the family grow wheat, oil seed rape, peas and protein beans, but the low, gabled farm building is now also host to a modern, agricultural complex: cookery school, bakery, farm shop, newly renovated restaurant and even a conference centre.

The aim is to reconnect people with food and farming and this is clearly reflected in the café menu, which is filled with products from local suppliers. Dine on vegetable hotpot, handmade scotch eggs and the excellent Ploughman's Plank in the airy dining room, or grab a coffee and a bun from the bakery; don't miss the award-winning breakfasts which are served all day, every day (apart from after 11.30am on Sundays).

Opening hours
Mon-Fri 7.30am-6pm (Sat 5pm)
Sun 10am-4pm
(see website for restaruant opening hours)

Becketts Farm Shop, Heath Farm, Alcester Road, Wythall B47 6AJ
WWW.BECKETTSFARM.CO.UK   01564 823402

Gin & Pickles Ltd

JUNCTION: 2; 4 MINUTES

It's the warm reception and personal service that regulars to Gin and Pickles praise so highly. What started as a simple penchant for gin and pickles has turned into a winning deli-café combination that's hugely popular with the locals.

Zöe behind the counter is an ardent supporter of local producers, from the eye-widening cheese selection, to salted caramel brownies and English charcuterie. The menu mainly features finger food, but you're bound to find something to stave off the hunger pangs, whether a slice of blueberry and violet loaf, a lunchtime deli board or a portion of chilli cashews. At weekends almond croissants and custard chocolate twists are served warm from the oven, and kids love the gingerbread dinosaurs. If you like what you taste, fill a basket from the shelves of the deli – great for snacks, holiday groceries and a tipple on arrival (sample one of the range of small batch gins). Coffee can be made to go, but don't forget to bring your cup as disposables have been phased out. If you forget, Keep Cups are available to buy and you can never have too many. Well, almost never.

Opening hours
Tues 10am-5pm
Weds-Thurs, Sat 9am-5pm
Fri 9am-8pm

Gin & Pickles Ltd, 21 The Square, Alvechurch B48 7LA
WWW.GINANDPICKLES.CO.UK   0121 445 6769

A46 **Teddington Stores**

JUNCTION: TEDDINGTON; 1 MINUTE

Former city worker Deborah has waved her magic wand over Teddington Stores, transforming it from a Little Chef into a delightful food hall to champion the good food of her Gloucestershire farming roots. The cut flowers greeting you in the foyer puts your average petrol station bunch to shame. In the food hall beyond, broad oak tables sag under the weight of gargantuan stacks of freshly baked goodies, groceries and treats, including fruit from Hayles Farm, artisan bread, gorgeous local art, tasteful giftware, and a fantastic selection of wine and British chocolates. High-end frozen meals will dupe any in-law into thinking you've cooked it yourself.

The butchery counter is the piece de resistance, selling the finest cuts from local herds. It should be beef for dinner as the ribs and prime cuts here are dry aged in the store's own salt-lined ager and are melt-in-your-mouth delicious. The café at the entrance is where you can sup a Lavazza coffee and savour a light lunch or crumbly pastry at one of a handful of tables (with charging points). Everything is made in the kitchen and uses ingredients from the shelves.

Opening hours
Mon-Fri 8.30am-6.30pm
Sat 9am-6pm
Sun 10am-4pm

Teddington Stores, Teddington Hands, Evesham Road, Teddington GL20 8NE
WWW.TEDDINGTONSTORES.CO.UK   01386 725400

Ellenden Farm Shop

JUNCTION:B439; 6 MINUTES

Chicken scratch happily in the fields alongside, and birds sing merrily from boughs in the orchard: the relaxed atmosphere and bucolic views make Ellenden a princely stop on any journey.

The farm shop was set up initially to promote the Turner family's award winning beef and lamb, as well as veggies, from the 242-acre farm. You can still pick up cuts in the shop, but the range has expanded dramatically to showcase a wide range of local produce: hand-made pies, pressed juices, excellent loaves of bread, quiches, yoghurts and cheeses.

Take a table in the café or on the sunny terrace to breakfast like a king or lunch on tasty home cooking: lamb tikka baguettes, duck egg frittata, chicken soup, all cooked to order. Staff are very friendly and never too busy for a chat.

Dogs are welcome on the terrace and great walks fan out across the Vale of Evesham if you fancy a leg stretch.

Opening hours
Mon-Sun 9am-6pm

Ellenden Farm Shop, Evesham Road, Evesham WR11 8LU
WWW.ELLENDENFARMSHOP.CO.UK   01386 870296

CAFÉ

The Village Café

JUNCTION: B439; 3 MINUTES

The Village Café is a new addition to the Bidford high street, and has been an instant hit with the locals. The café may be new but the ethos is traditional: decent food and friendly service, and it regularly teems with families and individuals making the most of Ingrid's home cooking as well as freshly-baked delights from Pudding Lane Cakes.

The kitchen is teeny so there's little in the way of hot food, but plenty of toasted sandwiches, pies, pastries and flapjacks to tempt you instead. OUtdoor Pig Company bacon and sausage baps are served till noon. The coffee is smooth and rich and the small courtyard garden at the rear will warm you up on sunny days.

Before you hit the road again, have a look for 'Shakespeare's tree' in the heart of the village. It's alleged that Shakespeare slept off a drinking contest under its boughs!

Opening hours
Mon-Fri 9am-4.30pm
Sat 9am-3pm

The Village Café, 15b High Street, Bidford-on-Avon B50 4BQ
WWW.FACEBOOK.COM/PG/BIDFORDVILLAGECAFE   07871 493102

Hillers Farm Shop

JUNCTION: ARROW; 7 MINUTES

Explore the abundant display garden, browse the homewares, stock up in the farm shop or take a moment of quiet in the wildlife hide, you'll be revived by a stop at Hillers. It's well established, run by fourth generation sisters Emma and Sally, and its connection to nearby Ragley Hall Estate and neighbouring growers means produce for the butchery counter and restaurant are super-local - asparagus, salad, beef, lamb pork, chicken, and even game in season.

The restaurant is in a long, low brick building that was once a fruit preserving factory, with a marquee at the back projecting into those lovely show gardens. Generous portions are served from sun-up onwards, from homemade museli and compote to honey roast ham with potatoes and coleslaw, orzo and courgette salad and filled baguettes. The restaurant is always filled with the clink and tinkle of cutlery on crockery, but if you're just passing for a coffee you don't need a table; just slide into one of the slouchy leather sofas.

Kids are well provided for with a large sandpit to dig at the front of the cafe and a miniature railway to ride.

Opening hours
Mon-Sat 8.30am-5.30pm
Sun 9am-5pm
(café times vary)

Hillers Farm Shop, Dunning Heath Farm, Alcester B49 5PD
WWW.HILLERS.CO.UK   01789 773057

From the moment you step through the doors at The Farm, it's clear that this is a brotherhood of foodies. Brush past the beds of the market garden (which supplies the café, naturally(and you'll find rustic wooden shelves and trestle tables groaning with produce from artisan local producers. From local fruit and oils to kimchi (fermented in one of The Farm's own micro-kitchens where peeping is invited), prime steaks and bouquets of home-grown flowers, everything is carefully selected and drawn from Warwickshire and neighbouring counties.

The café is called Nourish and does just that, serving wholesome, flavourful dishes, much of it organic, to pretty tables topped with posies of flowers – try the fish sharing board or one of the sourdough pizzas. There are work stations and a library corner if you can only give the office the slip for so long, and you can pick up a bag of the coffee in the shop if you, like us, enjoy the flavour.

Kids will be in their element between the wonky playouse, welly wanging, goose herding and meeting the pigs, so allow time for a lengthy stop.

Opening hours
Mon-Fri 8.30am-6pm
Sat 9am-6pm
Sun 10am-4pm

The Farm, King's Lane, Snitterfield CV37 0QA
WWW.THEFARMSTRATFORD.COM   01789 731807

Farmer's Fayre

JUNCTION: 15; 14 MINUTES

People rave about the breakfasts and Sunday roasts at Farmer's Fayre, but whether you stop in for an early bacon sandwich or for a slice of cake at tea time, you'll be impressed by the flavours. Lunches include delicious combinations such as soured and scorched mackerel salad with beetroot, red cabbage and watercress, or mushroom, garlic, mozzarella and spinach tart. Many are cooked on the in-store Aga and you can relax over your coffee next to the cosy wood-burning stove.

The airy, family-run farm shop and restaurant is found on the sprawling National Agricultural Exhibition Centre at Stoneleigh Park (don't be put off by the barrier and cheery security guards), underlining its commitment to good local ingredients from nearby farms. If you like what you taste, pick up some of the produce in the adjoining farm shop, which stocks produce from more than 40 local suppliers: chutneys, home-baked cakes, cheese and regional delicacies alongside a range of tempting homeware and antiques.

Opening hours
Mon-Sat 7.30am-5.30pm
Sun 8.30am-4.30pm

Farmer's Fayre, Stoneleigh Park CV8 2LZ
WWW.FARMERSFAYRE.CO.UK   024 7669 2844

Mrs Bee's Potting Shed Café

JUNCTION: A45; 2 MINUTES

Mrs Bee's is a fitting name for a café tucked amid the flowers of Russell's Garden Centre at the outskirts of Coventry. It's run by Becky and her husband Andy, and its modest size belies the hefty punch it packs on the baking front.

The smiling team serve generous hunks of cake (we can personally recommend the Bakewell slice) alongside home-baked bread, cheese scones and sandwiches, with coleslaw and chutney from the kitchen. The surrounds are quirky and wonderful: grab a table in the luminous conservatory to make the most of the blooms nearby, or outside if weather allows.

Kids will love the miniature railway alongside and no one can fail to lap up a moment with the wildlife in peace. If you've got time to spare, check out the Roman fort of Lunt nearby.

Opening hours
Mon-Sat 9.30am-5pm
Sun 10.30am-4.30pm

Mrs Bee's Potting Shed Café, Russell's Garden Centre, 1-3 Mill Hill, Baginton CV8 3AG
WWW.FACEBOOK.COM/PG/MRSBEESPOTTINGSHEDCAFE   07823 489050

Dickies Butchery & Farm Dining

JUNCTION: SAXONDALE; 13 MINUTES

Diversification is key for today's farmers to survive, which has given the UK a wave of wonderful farm shops and accommodation options to enjoy. Rich – aka Dickie – took a slightly different tack when seeking to make a success of the family beef farm, training as a butcher and setting up an artisan butchery in the garage.

He quickly gained a reputation for the best steak in the area and set up tables in tents alongside to cook up breakfast storms. The rest is history, and it's hard not to enthuse about this truly authentic version of farm dining.

The Cow Shed was built from reclaimed materials found on the farm and is warmed by a roaring fire at one end. Service is super friendly and unpretentious, and the atmosphere lively with tables full of people enjoying juicy roasts, enormous breakfasts and aged steaks. It's very popular so book ahead if you don't want to miss out.

Opening hours
Thurs 7-11pm
Fri 10am-3pm,7-11pm (Sat 9am)
Sun 9-11am, 1-4pm

Dickies Butchery & Farm Dining, 45 Barkestone Lane, PlungarNG13 0JA
WWW.DICKIESBUTCHERS.CO.UK   01949 869733

Hooks in the window and a marble counter turned breakfast bar hint at this wonderful coffee shop's former life as a butcher's shop. It's the long-held dream of owner Melanie (who even wrote her final project for a business degree on the subject) and she's created a homely, hip atmosphere that is welcome respite from both the road and the bustling high street just round the corner. Shelves in the corner are filled with trinkets and plants cascade down walls.

Coffee is roasted by Outpost in Nottingham and brewed on the beautiful Italian coffee machine behind the counter. It's served alongside tasty meals and snacks, perhaps banana pancakes for breakfast, spinach, mushrooms and goats' cheese on toast for lunch, or a slice of delicious, three-tiered caramel cake.

There's some pay and display parking just behind, and dogs are welcome.

Opening hours
Mon-Sat 8.30am-5pm
Sun 9am-3pm

Butler's, 7a Union Street, Bingham NG13 8AD
WWW.BUTLERSCOFFEEHOUSE.CO.UK   01949 838866

Doddington Hall & Gardens

JUNCTION: DODDINGTON; 4 MINUTES

Doddington Hall is a grand Tudor pile that was completed in 1600 and has been in the same family ever since. Four centuries of unbroken ownership means it's host to a fantastic collection of art, textiles, porcelain and weaponry and many visitors revel in the exclusive guided tours. Others come to see the impressive gardens, which have retained an Elizabethan layout in parts and have been left to grow wild in others.

The newest string to the estate's bow, relatively speaking, is the small shopping complex in what was previously the stables. The farm shop sells fruit and veg from the kitchen garden as well as showcasing the best of regional producers – craft ale, honey, pretty ceramics and Lincolnshire sausages. Next door is a bike shop, country clothing store, Farrow & Ball studio and the scrumptious café, which counts hunger-quashing breakfasts, sandwiches, fish and chips and spelt, feta and beetroot salad amongst its repertoire.

The car park is in the orchard over the road (be careful; it's fast) and dogs are welcome on the estate's walks and in the coffee shop.

Opening hours
Mon-Sat 9am-4.30pm
Sun 10am-4pm

Doddington Hall & Gardens, Doddington LN6 4RU
WWW.DODDINGTONHALL.COM   01522 812501

CAFÉ

March Hare Kitchen & Deli

JUNCTION: MARKET RASEN; 2 MINUTES

The March Hare, smart behind a charcoal grey shopfront on Market Rasen's high street, is lively with regulars popping in for their morning coffee or a bite to eat.

Chef and owner Trevor took over the March Hare on the back of a crowdfunder campaign, and has ploughed his energy into creating a welcoming neighbourhood hub and an excellent menu. The initial focus was on brunch, in line with the trend washing in across the country from Australia, and the dishes are finely honed – waffles with bacon and egg, pancake stacks and mackerel on toast. Try the gingerbread milkshake for an afternoon treat. Steaks and tapas are served alongside cocktails in the evening, so it's also a strong contender for dinner stops.

Browse the deli for store cupboard ingredients and car treats before you depart. Takeaway coffees are available too.

Opening hours
Mon-Sat 8.30am-5pm
Sun 9am-noon

March Hare Kitchen & Deli, 14 Market Place, Market Rasen LN8 3HL
WWW.FACEBOOK.COM/MARCHHAREKITCHEN/   01673 842076

The Dunn Deal Tearooms

JUNCTION: NETTLETON; 1 MINUTE

With delphiniums and crocosmia filling the lovingly tended borders and cascades of begonias, the Dunn Deal is balm for the soul on a long journey. It's a family affair with Pat at the helm, and she and the team keep busy ensuring that all visitors are well fed and watered. Breakfast might be a Lincolnshire sausage bap, lunch a bowl of homemade soup, pie and mash or springy filled sandwich. Coffee is from Stokes, a Lincolnshire favourite, and cakes are always homemade – fruit loaf, ginger cake or classic Victoria sponge. Cyclists frequently pop in for breakfast or slices of cake – a sure sign that they're getting it right – and the amiable service encourages a procession of regulars.

The building itself – low and red brick – has had an interesting life, going from farm outbuildings and then holiday cottages before settling into its current tea room guise. Inside is spacious and spotlessly clean, and there's plenty of seating outside for fine days.

You're just at the northern end of the Lincolnshire wolds which are laced with footpaths should you fancy a leg stretch.

Opening hours
Mon-Sat 9.30am-4.30pm

The Dunn Deal Tearooms, Normanby Road, Market Rasen LN7 6TB
WWW.FACEBOOK.COM/DUNNDEALTEAROOMS/   01472 488410

The ☞ M3 & A303

Capital to country, the gateway to the South West

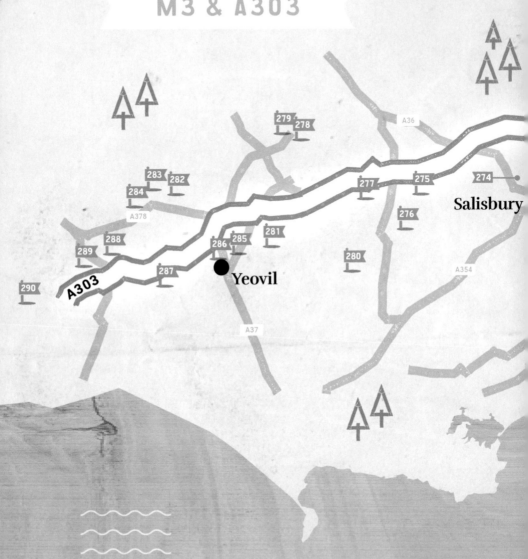

M3 & A303

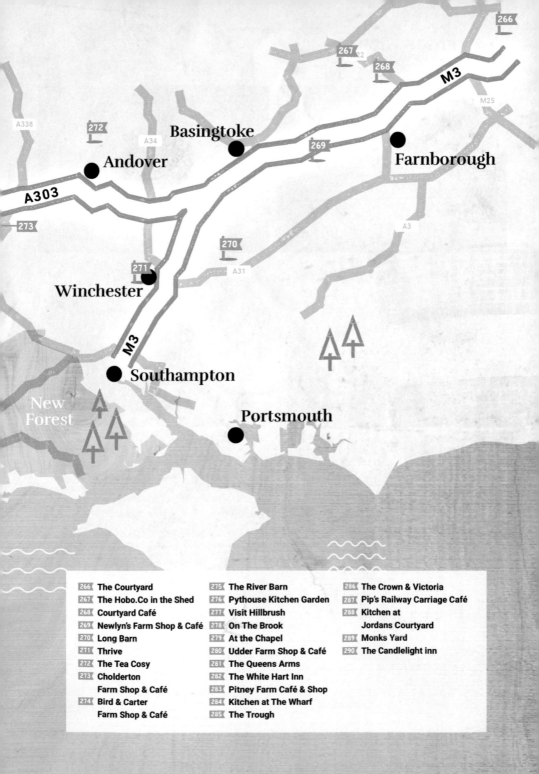

Andover

Basingtoke

Farnborough

Winchester

Southampton

Portsmouth

New
Forest

M3

A303

A338

A34

A3

A31

A25

M25

CAFÉ

The Courtyard

JUNCTION: 5; 10 MINUTES

The Courtyard, just off the high street and thronging with plants inside and out, is chic and relaxing and serves dishes to suit all tastes: mouth-watering breakfasts, daily specials, hot ciabattas, hearty salads and light bites, as well as freshly-baked cakes and sweet treats. The Courtyard burger and salt beef ciabatta are the heroes of the menu and a must for the hungry; try the poached salmon salad with edamame beans and minted yoghurt dressing for a healthier bite. There are plenty of vegetarian, vegan and gluten free options – the gluten-free chocolate and walnut brownies are divine.

There's plenty of seating in the garden for sunny days and well behaved dogs are always welcome too. It's just outside the London Orbital motorway, so a perfect place to pause and soak up village life or take a moment for yourself before heading into the city. Free parking is available just behind, with Ascot and Windsor Great Park nearby if you need to fill your lungs and stretch your legs before your onward journey.

Opening hours
Mon-Fri 8am-5pm
Sat 8am-4pm

The Courtyard, Sunninghill SL5 9NF
WWW.THECOURTYARDSUNNINGHILL.CO.UK   01344 627687

The Hobo.Co in the Shed

JUNCTION: 5; 10 MINUTES

Tucked in a peaceful corner of the award-winning Hortus Loci plant centre, the humble Hobo in the Shed creates some serious magic. Seasonal salads, homemade soups, toasted paninis, delicately flavoured cakes and hearty hot meals emerge from the serving hatch. Expertly made coffee and homemade soft drinks too – lemonade in summer and spiced winter berry juice in winter. Don't miss the courgette, lime and pistachio cake or the famous gluten-free triple chocolate brownies.

Comfy chairs, magazines and hanging seats on the cosy veranda offer an indulgent pause enveloped by blooming boughs and perfumed plants. There's even a bureau nook – complete with WiFi and antique books – should you want to set up office for an hour or so. In cooler months, heaters, blankets and hot water bottles are provided to keep you toasty in the fresh air.

Opening hours
Mon–Sat 9am–5pm
Sun 10am–4pm

The Hobo.Co in the Shed, Hortus Loci, Hound Green, Hook RG27 8LQ
WWW.THEHOBO.CO   07894 150290

Tucked away at the back of an antiques shop in the historic village of Hartley Wintney, the Courtyard Café is a hidden haven serving fresh, high-quality food made with the best local ingredients. A run of bi-fold doors in the garden room crumple back to lead onto a flourishing courtyard where the fountain trickles and birds nest. A gate leads out to the village cricket green where owner Laura recommends taking a turn with restless babes to lull them to sleep.

Grab a newspaper and enjoy a slice of the chef's artful cakes (think ombre, gluten-free blueberry and vanilla cake decorated with fresh flowers) or treat yourself to a healthy breakfast of homemade granola or waffles with berries.

Though the lunch menu changes regularly according to the season, you can expect such delights as parmesan and truffle gnocchi, saffron trout fillet or well-stuffed sandwiches, and wash it down with a civilised glass of wine. A real gourmet stop.

Opening hours
Mon–Sat 9am–5pm
Sun 10am–4pm

Courtyard Café, 63 High Street, Hartley Wintney RG27 8NY
WWW.COURTYARDCAFE.COM   012525 842 616

Newlyn's Farm Shop & Café

JUNCTION: 5; 2 MINUTES

Skirt round a lush field, past the shack selling freshly laid eggs via an honesty box, down a concrete farm track and you'll see the large red-roofed barns of Newlyn's Farm. Friendly Roger the butcher prepares the meat that the family have been producing here (four miles down the road, in fact) for four generations, alongside a heaving deli counter of olives, chicken liver pâté, fresh loaves, Hampshire cheese and fine pressed oils. The spacious farm shop also sells locally grown produce and a covetable range of foodie gifts.

The large, bright café with picture windows leads onto a patio terrace where you can breakfast on home-cured bacon with soft poached egg, or rolled porridge oats with cream, fruit and Hampshire honey washed down with freshly squeezed juice. For lunch, pick from burgers, triple-stacked sandwiches and piggy platters.

Cookery courses show you how to use the farm's produce to best advantage throughout the seasons; if you'd rather someone else do the work, you'll find dinner-party worthy ready meals using the farm's ingredients in the freezer section.

Opening hours
Mon–Fri 8am–6pm
Sat 8am–4pm
Sun 9am–noon

Newlyn's Farm Shop & Café, Lodge Farm, North Warnborough RG29 1HA
WWW.NEWLYNS.COM   01256 704128

FARM SHOP

Long Barn

JUNCTION: 9/10; 12 MINUTES

A wall of the most fantastic scent of lavender greets you as you unfurl yourself from the car at Long Barn. The farm's products are much loved by retailers around the country so you may well have seen them on the shelves before, but this is the mothership.

Owners Richard and Jane founded the lavender-growing company in 2009 because of Richard's passion for the fragrant herb. It has grown from farmer's market stalls to a shop in town to the current rural space, just outside Winchester.

The steep-roofed barn stands on what was once a sheep-herding pen, and contains a wonderland of refined gifts, plants and homewares. The cafe at the centre has a very organic feel, with broad oak beams, hanging plants and small saplings dotted throughou, and food reflects whatever is at its prime in the garden, from Hampshire watercress to rhubarb and butternut squash. There's a beautiful terrace too so on good days take your coffee outside to bathe in the sights and smells of the vibrant garden.

Opening hours
Mon-Sat 9am-5pm
Sun 10am-4pm
(see website for cafe serving times)

Ⓥ Ⓟ

Long Barn, The Old Sheep Fair, Bishops Sutton Road, Alresford SO24 9EJ
WWW.LONGBARN.CO.UK   01962 738684

Thrive

JUNCTION: 11; 4 MINUTES

A modest A-board at the roadside is the only clue that this wonderful neighbourhood café is just off the road. Woven straw lampshades almost float overhead, a soothing space softened with baby pink walls, patterned cushions and houseplants.

Owner Amanda is a yoga teacher and set up Thrive to offer both a space for well-being classes and a place to share her love of vegan and vegetarian food. Tofu-dodgers need not fear though, as flavour is by no means compromised and ingredients are of the highest quality. Toasted mozzarella and pesto sandwiches are served alongside tempting pancake stacks, slices of cake (try the vegan carrot) and bowls of imaginative salads. Pep yourself up for an onward drive with one of the nutrient-packed smoothies or flat whites, though the dirty chai and turmeric latte are also well worth trying. A wholesome but no less indulgent place to pause.

Opening hours
Mon-Sat 9am-4pm
Sun 10am-3pm

Thrive, 95B Olivers Battery Road S, Winchester SO22 4JQ
WWW.THRIVECAFEANDWELLBEING.CO.UK   01962 864999

The Tea Cosy

JUNCTION: A343 ANDOVER; 11 MINUTES

A friendly welcome awaits you in this village tearoom, once you have located it behind the car showroom and convenience store. Retro tables and chairs are painted in bright hues, a sofa area invites the weary to put their feet up. Cheery staff serve tables with a constant stream of light bites, afternoon teas and simple lunches. Seasonal salads, breakfast favourites and selection of sandwiches and paninis, are all on the menu along with homemade milkshakes, made from clotted cream ice cream. There is also a children's menu for smaller guests.

But it is the cakes that have people queuing up here, particularly on a Friday when the 'cake of the week' is revealed. Friday or not, there is always a counter full of creative cakes to tempt you, best washed down with one of the 24 loose leaf teas served in teapots with hand knitted novelty tea cosies. Customers can also indulge in a glass of prosecco or one of The Tea Cosy's specialty, tea-infused gins.

Opening hours
Wed–Sun 9.30am–5pm

The Tea Cosy, The Dene, Hurstbourne Tarrant SP11 0AS
WWW.THETEACOSYHAMPSHIRE.COM   01264 736644

Cholderton Farm Shop & Café

JUNCTION: A338; 1 MINUTE

You'll breakfast like a king at Cholderton Farm Shop & Café, a convenient halfway point between the South West and London. It's a working farm so hens and cockerels scratch around in the yard and tractors park up outside the beautiful flint and red-brick farm shop.

The homely welcome in the café more than makes up for the simple surroundings, not to mention the grade-A bacon butties. Shelves ring the room, laden with essentials – bread, vegetables, chutneys – and the fridges are full of Pieminister pies, local cheese and a range of deli treats that will more than supply you for your destination.

The coffee is barista standard and staff deliver plates of crisp jacket potatoes, amply filled toasties, huge ploughman's and homemade quiches to tables scattered about inside. To get a real taste of the country, take a picnic table in the covered barn outside or a parasoled one on sunny days.

Opening hours
Tues-Sat 9am-4.30pm
Sun 10am-4pm

Cholderton Farm Shop & Café, Cholderton Estate, Tidworth Road, Cholderton SP4 0DR
WWW.CHOLDERTONFARMSHOP.CO.UK   01980 629894

Bird & Carter Farm Shop & Café

JUNCTION: WYLYE; 9 MINUTES

Once a stables, a carpentry workshop and then a percussion school, this long, slate-roofed farm building has had a varied history. Today it's metamorphosed into a super delicatessen and café: brick walls are painted cream, bunches of garlic hang from the rafters and a run of deli counters peddle smoked fish, Wiltshire ham, antipasti and some of the best scotch eggs around. Ask nicely and smiley owner Joff will slice and smear them with mustard. Shelves are loaded with goodies and groceries, from spelt flour to fresh pasta, jars of preserves and crocks of sweeties.

Café seating is found at the far end, a room with a bank of antique drawers, wood-burner and large windows looking out to the paddocks. There are plenty of high chairs and a surplus of toys and books for little ones. The doors are thrown open at breakfast, serving eggs, locally reared bacon and sausages. Sandwiches, quiches and pies are tasty, cakes temptingly moist – such as chocolate Guinness, ginger or lemon meringue.

Opening hours
Mon–Sat 8.30am–5.30pm
Sun 10am–4pm

Bird & Carter Farm Shop & Café, Chilhampton Farm, Warminster Road, Wilton SP2 0AB
WWW.BIRDANDCARTER.CO.UK   01722 744177

RESTAURANT
The River Barn

JUNCTION: FONTHILL BISHOP; 2 MINUTES

Snug and comfy, in a gorgeous riverside setting, the River Barn is a wonderful place to linger between East and West.

A lawn stretches from the handsome stone building down to the murmuring river where you can enjoy a pre-prandial drink beneath a parasol on sunny days, or venture to peaceful spots in the orchard garden to enjoy a slice of cake or pint of cider. Children are encouraged to bowl about on the lawn, or paddle in the river to catch shrimp. Well-trodden walks meander from the door into the Wiltshire countryside where you can work up a healthy appetite, and you can even stay over in one of the gorgeous B&B rooms.

Breakfasts are so good they draw locals daily; bigger brunches are served at the weekend, and the coffee is excellent. Lunch could be a hearty club sandwich or a tasty sirloin steak. Much of the produce is sourced from the gardens of the Fonthill Estate, so couldn't be more local. Perfect.

Opening hours
Tues-Sun 8.30am-5pm
Dinner: Thurs-Sat 6pm-9pm

The River Barn, Fonthill Bishop, Salisbury SP3 5SF
WWW.RIVERBARN.CO.UK   01747 356026

CAFÉ-RESTAURANT

Pythouse Kitchen Garden

JUNCTION: A350; 9 MINUTES

An utterly idyllic spot in Wiltshire where you can malinger from dawn to sundown. The café and restaurant are centred around a sublime, 18th century walled garden where all manner of surprising produce grows, including kiwis, apricots and artichokes.

Inside you'll find a light-flooded conservatory which has a colourful shabby chic style; antique furniture intermingled with scuffed white walls, wood burning stoves, a corrugated iron bar, and bright, upcycled chairs. An old ladder hung above the bar is twisted with willow branches and foliage. In the summer the doors to the garden are thrown up, parasols popped and visitors invited to spill out into the scented calm of the terrace. There's a Wendy House and treasure trail, as well as runabout space, to keep little folk entertained. Slump onto a French day bed next to the fire in winter. Drop in for lunch to enjoy fire pit salmon, courgette and broad beans with cow's curd, pulled shoulder of lamb and homegrown summer tart. Save space for gooseberry fool and lemon verbena posset. Dinner is served on a Friday and Saturday and draws seasonal menu inspiration from what's growing in the beds.

Opening hours
Sun-Thurs 10am-4pm
Fri-Sat 10am-11pm

Pythouse Kitchen Garden, West Hatch, Tisbury SP3 6PA
WWW.PYTHOUSEKITCHENGARDEN.CO.UK   01747 870444

Visit Hillbrush

JUNCTION: MERE (B3092); 1 MINUTE

Not the most obvious of stops but this brush factory – yes, brush factory – is a fantastic place to pull in if you're travelling on the A303. Hillbrush has been making brushes in Mere since 1922 but it only recently opened a visitor centre and fantastic restaurant alongside. The museum is colourful, tactile and surprisingly kid-friendly, and there are plenty of appealing gifts in the shop, from shaving kits to quirky hedgehog door stops. With the factory producing nearly 3,000 different products for export there's every brush you can imagine here.

In the bright, modern restaurant, cakes from local producers tempt you from beneath gleaming glass cloches. Busy tables are served with steaming breakfasts, lunches and afternoon teas, from a selection of delicious burgers, salads and main dishes, including the popular beer battered fish and chunky chips with homemade tartar sauce, as well as special Sunday roast dinners and a bespoke themed evening menu every third Friday of the month. Dogs are welcome on the sunny, south-facing terrace.

Opening hours
Mon-Sat 8am-6pm
Friday 8am-9pm
Sun & Bank Hols 8am-4pm

Visit Hillbrush, Norwood Park, Mere BA12 6FE
WWW.VISIT.HILLBRUSH.COM   01747 440077

CAFÉ

On The Brook

JUNCTION: WINCANTON; 11 MINUTES

The enthusiasm for good food at On The Brook is obvious, from the carefully tended kitchen garden supplying much of the food for the restaurant, to the 'five ways' showcase, which takes one seasonal ingredient and demonstrates five different ways of cooking it. Rhubarb soup, apple leathers and wild garlic seasoning are some of the ingenious dishes that have previously emerged from the kitchen, and the all-day menu is tapas focused to make choosing easier. Homemade cordial and apple juice from the orchards are served alongside excellent coffee.

Despite its bucolic setting in a verdant, sheep-grazed valley, it's only a short walk into the centre of Bruton. Leaflets mark out the footpaths leading from the door, so you can stretch your legs mid-journey and enjoy the countryside. Fill your lungs then park yourself by the woodburner in the unfussy modern restaurant, or bag a table on the terrace to listen to the brook bubbling past while you spot the local wildlife.

If you're travelling with kids, call ahead and they could be treated to a tour of the polytunnel where they can pick their own ingredients.

Opening hours
Mon-Sun 9am-5pm

On The Brook, Coombe Farm, Coombe Street, Bruton BA10 0QP
WWW.ONTHEBROOK.CO.UK   01749 813048

RESTAURANT WITH BEDROOMS

At the Chapel

JUNCTION: LEIGH COMMON; 12 MINUTES

© Tori Hancock

The town set love Bruton, an arty enclave of galleries, bohemian boutiques and antique shops tucked away in Somerset. At the Chapel is a converted 17th-century chapel, transformed with whitewashed, minimalist delicacy into a destination with contemporary bedrooms, restaurant, bar, bakery and winestore. The atmosphere is relaxed but buzzes all day with visitors and you're as well to drop in for a coffee and pastry, warm from the oven, as you are to explore the menu at lunch and dinner. Expect dishes like chargrilled Cornish sardines and ham hock with soft-boiled egg and pizzas (making full use of the bakery's wood-fired oven) at lunch and an enlarged menu at dinner. Puddings could include limoncello Eton mess or salted chocolate fondant, so save space.

Book a table in the calming dining room or spill out onto the south-facing terrace accented with the scent of jasmine. At weekends families arrive en masse to read papers, brunch and sip Bloody Marys after a country walk.

Opening hours
Mon–Sun 8am-9.30pm

At the Chapel, High Street, Bruton BA10 0AE
WWW.ATTHECHAPEL.CO.UK   01749 814070

Udder Farm Shop & Café

JUNCTION: BOURTON; 13 MINUTES

You can do your weekly grocery round in Udder Farm Shop, which has a deli, fishmonger, gift, booze and freezer sections (farm produce, rather than crispy pancakes) and butchery – and that's the point. Farmers Jane and Brian Down opened their vast, modern shop to offer a low-mileage alternative to supermarkets and support British agriculture. Eyes peeled for special treats such as gooseberry vinegar and Cerne Abbas giant shortbread.

Breakfasts are farm-filling (full English, porridge with honey, poached egg on muffins); lunchtime cottage pies and burgers are generous and made with meat reared in the fields over yonder. Home-baked cakes, fluffy meringues and scones will tide you over the afternoon munchies. Children will be absorbed by the outdoor play park where parents can supervise from the patio while admiring views across Blackmore Vale. If you're in a rush you can grab hot drinks, pasties, frittata and slices of quiche to go from the deli.

Opening hours
Mon–Sat 9am–6pm
Sat 8.30am–6pm
Sun 9am–4pm

Udder Farm Shop & Café, Manor Farm, East Stour SP8 5LQ
WWW.THEUDDERFARMSHOP.CO.UK   01747 838899

The Queens Arms

JUNCTION: SPARKFORD; 9 MINUTES

A large blackboard outside advertising film nights and game supper evenings underscores the community feel of this friendly country pub. It's lively and welcoming, with a comfortable, eclectic style, from the boater-wearing bison head to faded rugs flung over flagstones and deep sofas. Muddy paws and sticky fingers are welcome, and rooms are fab should you want to stop the night. The rear courtyard looks over the fields, a good place to soak up the rays or start a walk.

Order a homemade pork pie in the bar and mix with pint-drinking regulars reading leisurely papers and friendly locals catching up on the gossip. Step through to the dining room for delicious, uncomplicated meals – seared wild sea trout, rosary ash goat cheese and roast peach salad, treacle-cured salmon and pineapple salsa or lamb and anchovy butter. Food provenance is 'measured in metres, not miles'; some ingredients come from the pub's own smallholding, some bartered with neighbours in exchange for meals.

Opening hours
Mon–Thurs 7.30am–11pm
Fri–Sat 7.30am–midnight (8am Sat)
Sun 8am–10.30pm

The Queens Arms, Corton Denham DT9 4LR
WWW.THEQUEENSARMS.COM   01963 220317

The White Hart Inn

JUNCTION: PODIMORE; 7 MINUTES

A handsome, 16th-century country pub at the edge of Somerton's octagonal market square, The White Hart is breezy yet cosy with whitewashed walls, stripped floorboards and patchwork tiles, log burners and antler chandeliers. A courtyard garden bursting with olive trees and lavender bushes stands beyond the conservatory dining room.

Broad skylights and sash windows fill the bar with light and in the evening locals often gather for a pint. Shadowy nooks with low-slung lights and chinks of stained glass provide enticing havens for kicking back and unwinding with a paper.

The menu, devised by ex-River Cottage chef Tom Blake, shows seasonal West Country cooking in its best light. Lunch and dinner includes delights such as falafel with baba ganoush, slow-cooked Creedy duck leg, grilled Cornish mackerel and wood-fired pizza. People rave about the breakfasts.

Opening hours
Mon–Sun 9am–11pm

The White Hart Inn, Market Place, Somerton TA11 7LX
WWW.WHITEHARTSOMERTON.COM   01458 272273

Pitney Farm Café & Shop

JUNCTION: PODIMORE; 15 MINUTES

One for the eco-minded, the Pitney Farm Café is one of just a few Soil Association-accredited organic restaurants. Located at the heart of Glebe Farm, a small mixed organic farm, the café serves mostly homegrown food from eggs and veg to home cured bacon and 100% grass-fed beef.

It's a charming wooden hut overlooking the vegetable market garden at the heart of the farm with a focus on sustainably sourced ingredients and everything made from scratch – fresh baked sourdough bread, pasties, cakes; the small, seasonal lunch and brunch menu caters for all. Choose from a homemade sausage roll using pork from their pigs or a hearty vegan lunch with freshly harvested vegetables. Grab a seat on the veranda and breathe in the country air over a cup of tea and a slice of lemon and gooseberry tart made with gluten-free split pea flour shortcrust pastry.

The shelves of the shop are filled with fabulous seasonal and local produce. You'll find home-grown vegetables, homemade sausages, dried, cured Italian-style meats, Mendip Moments ice cream, locally pressed apple juice, handmade chocolates, Somerset cheeses and home-raised organic pork, beef and lamb.

Opening hours
Tues-Sat 9am-4pm (café)
Mon-Sat 9am-5.30pm (farm shop)

(V) (P) (GF)

Pitney Farm Café & Shop, Glebe Farm, Woodbirds Hill Lane, Pitney TA10 9AP
WWW.PITNEYFARMCAFE.CO.UK   07769 173682

CAFÉ

Kitchen at The Wharf

JUNCTION: PODIMORE; 13 MINUTES

Langport belongs to Somerset's trendy renaissance. It's a pretty town with a long history and a raft of independent shops. Kitchen at The Wharf is by the river at the bottom of the high street in an 18th-century old dockside warehouse once used for trading goods from around the world.

This roomy light-filled café with sunny riverside terrace is popular with locals and visitors alike. Bare floorboards, exposed brick and beams with grey painted walls give it an urban vibe and sets off its relaxed friendly feel beautifully. Food is hearty and seasonal: full English breakfasts, homemade quiche, summer salads, sausage and mash as well as homemade pastries and cakes to die for, not to mention their locally-roasted barista coffee.

There's a toy box for kids, treats for well-behaved dogs, a puncture kit and bike racks for cyclists, and they're part of the Positive About Breastfeeding Scheme.

Opening hours
Mon–Sun 9am–4pm

Kitchen at The Wharf, Bow Wharf, Bow Street, Langport TA10 9PN
WWW.KITCHENLANGPORT.CO.UK   01458 254 354

FARM SHOP

The Trough

JUNCTION: ILCHESTER; 7 MINUTES

There's been a stready stream of visitors to the Trough since it opened its doors in early 2018, all wooed by excellent food and tasteful surrounds. As it is just outside Yeovil, in the heart of farming Somerset, the team can take its pick of excellent local suppliers.

The menu is simple but artful – tuna melts, burgers and vegetable tarts – and prices reflect the high-quality ingredients. Busy but friendly staff deliver delicious food, and endless pots of tea served with adorable miniature milk urns. Every detail in the airy but intimate café has been well-thought – through, from the polished-concrete tables to the hand basins in the loos, moulded with the Trough logo.

There's plenty of seating outside with lovely views over the fields where animals peacefully graze, good for soaking up the sunshine on fine days and even better for watching the planes on Yeovilton Air Day. Don't forget to pick up nibbles for your onward journey from the deli fridge in the farm shop.

Opening hours
Tues-Sat 9am-4pm
Sun 9.30am-3.30pm
(Friday event evenings 5pm-11pm)

V P

The Trough, Stone Lane, Yeovil BA21 4NU
WWW.TROUGHFARMSHOP.COM   01935 413027

The Crown & Victoria

JUNCTION: TINTINHULL; 2 MINUTES

The Crown and Victoria is a friendly village pub burrowed in the peaceful Somerset countryside. The broad-smiled welcome is as toasty as the open fires, and there's a large garden filled with flowers, birdsong and picnic benches out front; an orchard with a waste-disposal pig lies just beyond.

Owners Mark and Isabel focus more on the atmosphere and food rather than the interior design (which is well-maintained but charmingly 90s). Food is organic or free range, locally sourced and excellent. As a result, the menu changes regularly, but might include starters of devilled whitebait and chunky tartare or homemade terrine on toasted granary bloomer, perhaps chargrilled pork loin with haricot cassoulet, or wild mushroom wellington for dinner. Roasts on Sundays are generous and very popular, with fish and vegetarian alternatives. For a breath of fresh air after feasting, explore a footpath from the doorstep and the beautiful Tintinhull Garden nearby.

Opening hours
Mon–Sat 9am–3.30pm, 5.30pm–11pm
Sun 9am–4pm

The Crown & Victoria, 14 Farm Street, Tintinhull BA22 8PZ
WWW.THECROWNANDVICTORIA.CO.UK   01935 823 341

Pip's Railway Carriage Café

JUNCTION: SOUTH PETHERTON; 1 MINUTE

You won't find a quirkier place to stop for a bite than an 1880s railway carriage and old double-decker bus. Now transformed into a café, the train carriage with its communal tables is joined by an ivy-strewn marquee to the double-decker bus, which offers sunny table upstairs, cosy corners below and spectacular countryside views. Outside, there are picnic benches for summer months and plenty of grass for little feet to run around on.

Menus change daily depending on what can be harvested from the fields, which means abundant organic salads in summer, and warming comfort foods with a twist in the colder months.

Don't leave without stocking up at the award-winning Trading Post farm shop next door. It offers a cornucopia of local fare and natural whole foods: pickles, smoked fish, eggs, cheese, homegrown veg, organic wine and fresh-cut flowers.

Opening hours
Mon–Sat 9am–4pm
Fris 5pm-8pm (in summer)

Pip's Railway Carriage Café, Lopenhead TA13 5JH
WWW.PIPSRAILWAYCARRIAGE.COM   07729 685412

Kitchen at Jordans Courtyard

JUNCTION: HORTON CROSS; 1 MINUTE

The bistro-style sister of the wonderful Kitchen at the Wharf in Langport, Kitchen at Jordans Courtyard stands conveniently close to the A303 at Horton Cross. Like its counterpart, the food here is wholesome, nourishing and made on site from scratch using seasonal ingredients. A varied menu of old favourites and modern classics include homemade banana bread with cinnamon butter, a wonderful full English and a just-as-good veggie version, homemade sourdough pizza with fennel salami and caramelised onions and salmon gravlax and avocado salad. Puds such as homemade Belgian waffles with ice cream and maple syrup await those with a sweet tooth.

Light spills into the café from a long run of windows and on fine days you can sit at a table on the wide terrace. Jordans Courtyard – an inviting collection of converted hamstone and clapboard barns – is also home to a spa, nail bar and gift shop bursting with Somerset artisan produce, so there's plenty to delay your onward journey if you need a longer break.

Opening hours
Mon-Sun 8.30am-3pm

Kitchen at Jordans Courtyard, Horton Cross Farm, Ilminster TA19 9PY
WWW.JORDANSCOURTYARD.CO.UK   01460 298 608

Monks Yard

JUNCTION: HORTON CROSS; 0 MINUTES

Monks Yard has settled into its swanky new premises very well. Converted cow shed has been swapped for high-ceilinged industrial chic; courtyard for generous gardens – which you're welcome to explore – and ample parking.

One thing that hasn't changed is the unswervingly friendly service, nor the counter loaded with imaginative cakes – apricot and cranberry sponge, perhaps, or coffee amaretto. Ingredients are sourced from the community garden and around Somerset, and transformed into simple but tasty sandwiches, soups and paninis. Breakfasts are brilliant and specials change frequently. Organic, fair-trade coffee is roasted nearby and teas are loose leaf.

Their shop, Nest & Nettle, sells an eminently browseable collection of homeware and lifestyle objets – jewellery, candles, plants and ceramics – so look no further if you need to pick up some gifts.

It's literally metres from the fast food joints and a million miles better.

Opening hours
Mon–Sat 9am–4pm
Sun 10am-4pm

Monks Yard, Horton Manor, Horton Cross TA19 9PY
WWW.MONKSYARD.CO.UK/EAT/   01460 200020

PUB

The Candlelight Inn

JUNCTION: BISHOPSWOOD; 2 MINUTES

Landlords Simon and Mike abandoned their high-flying management jobs in banking to take on the Candlelight Inn on the Devon–Somerset border. It was a gargantuan career leap, but they knew what they were doing. Camped in the stunning Blackdown Hills, it's a beautiful country pub – flint walls, beamed ceilings and inviting fireplaces – just moments away from the A303. The welcome is hospitable and informal and staff clearly enjoy being part of the team. The crowd of locals at the bar in the evenings is proof of the convivial atmosphere.

There's a romance to the dining room, with candles (obviously) on every table and a blazing fireplace. Many ingredients for the impressive plates are sourced from the countryside around and the fresh catch down at Lyme Regis, so you can expect anything from hand-picked crab sandwiches to ham hock terrine and cheddar-stuffed chicken. The range of very local ciders is also very tempting – non-drivers should try them out.

Opening hours
Tues-Thurs noon-2.30pm
Fri 5pm-11pm
Sat noon-11pm (Sun 7pm)

(V) (P)

The Candlelight Inn, Bishopswood, Chard TA20 3RS
WWW.CANDLELIGHT-INN.CO.UK   01460 234476

The
SOUTH COAST
A27, M27, A31, A35, A30, A38

The beautiful south...

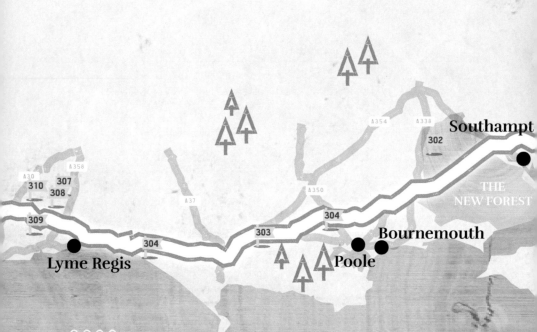

A27 / A31 / A35

Southampt

THE
NEW FOREST

A354   A338

302

A30   A358
310   307
       308

A350

304

309

A37   303   304

304

Lyme Regis

Poole   Bournemouth

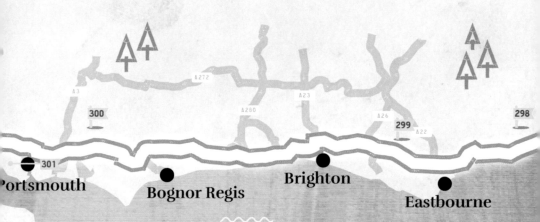

Portsmouth

Bognor Regis

Brighton

Eastbourne

300

301

299

298

△3

△272

△280

△23

△26

△22

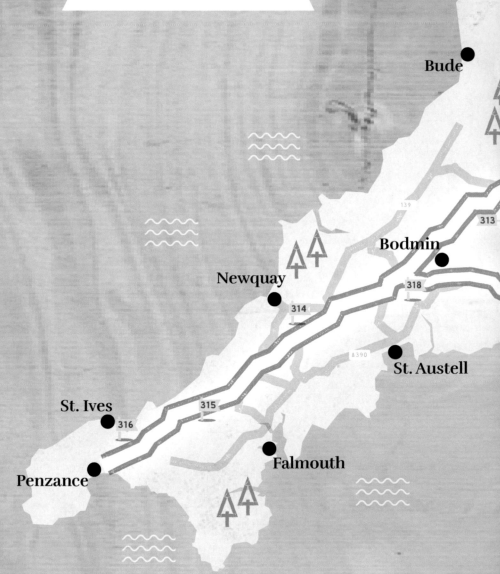

A30 & A38

Bude

Bodmin

Newquay

139

313

318

St. Austell

A390

St. Ives

316

315

Falmouth

Penzance

314

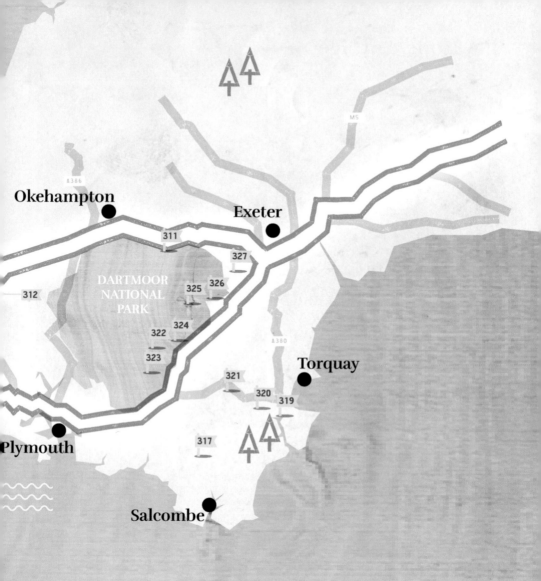

Okehampton

Exeter

311

DARTMOOR
NATIONAL
PARK

327

325   326

312

324

322

323

321

Torquay

320   319

Plymouth

317

Salcombe

311	Hog & Hedge	317	South Devon Chilli Farm	323	Riverford Field Kitchen
312	Strawberry Fields Farm Shop & Restaurant	318	Duchy of Cornwall Nursery	324	Rafikis
313	Tre, Pol & Pen	319	The Curator Café & Kitchen	325	Ullacombe Farm
314	The Plume of Feathers	320	The Hairy Barista	326	Devon Guild of Craftsmen
315	Miss Molly's Tea Rooms	321	The Almond Thief	327	The Seven Stars
316	Scarlet Wines	322	The Seed Wholefood Store and Café		

FARM SHOP

Hope Cottage

JUNCTION: PEVENSEY; 9 MINUTES

Adorably ramshackle and decorated with homemade quilts, you'll feel instantly at ease dropping into Hope Cottage Farm Shop. Gingham-covered tables pepper the room, which is ringed with shelves carrying locally made jams, crafts, free-range eggs, pies and cuts of meat. Pull up a pew to enjoy some of the home baking – famous in these parts, even among the WI – a full breakfast, game casserole or simply a proper pot of tea.

There's seating outside in the gravelled courtyard where you can enjoy the rural views and fluttering bunting; a canopy provides shade on the fiercest summer days (or in the mizzle).

If you've got time to spare, take a moment to wander around the rare plants for sale at Athelas just behind. There are some truly beautiful specimens.

Opening hours
Mon-Sat 9am-5pm (4.30pm in winter)
Sun 10am-4pm

Hope Cottage, Hooe Road, Ninfield, Battle TN33 9EL
WWW.FACEBOOK.COM/HOPECOTTAGEFARMSHOP   01424 892342

The Berwick Inn

JUNCTION: DRUSILLAS ROUNDABOUT; 2 MINUTES

Relaxed and informal, there's a real friendliness to the Berwick Inn, from the duck eggs for sale on the bar to the super-friendly and adaptable staff. The menu calls upon the very best of Sussex ingredients for pub classics (North Sea scampi, steak and ale pie, burger and chips), as well as more culinary alternatives (seared scallops in pancetta, smoked duck breast and pomegranate salad, slow-braised pork belly with bubble and squeak). Breakfast is served from 10am and every bit as good as the afternoon fare.

The garden is a real selling point on hot days, lively with birds and butterflies beyond the vine-entwined pergola on the terrace.

Doors open for coffee and snacks from 7am, out of service to the commuters using the train station next door, so you can find a comfy chair and recharge at pretty much any time of the day.

Opening hours
Mon-Weds 7am-10pm
Thus-Fri 7am-11pm
Sat 9am-11pm (Sun 9pm)

The Berwick Inn, Station Road, Berwick BN26 6SZ
WWW.THEBERWICKINN.CO.UK   01323 870018

Stanstead Park Farm Shop

JUNCTION: DENVILLES; 11 MINUTES

You've got a Kickstarter campaign to thank for Stansted Park Farm Shop. Having ploughed their savings into a successful but smaller farm shop, Fred and Sam raised more than £30,000 from a very loyal following to part fund this fantastic food hub, which includes farm shop, butchery, deli and café.

Much of the food is sourced within 30 miles, so eating here you'll get a real taste of the South Downs. Producer days – where you can meet the people behind the food – are designed to link customers back to the land: ask at the butchery counter to find out how the rare breed cuts have been raised. The deli counter stocks home-pickled and home-cured titbits as well as local charcuterie, cheese and food-to-go.

Brunch and lunch are served in the Kitchen from Wednesday to Sunday, 10am to 3pm, and the chef uses the farm shop as his larder so you can recreate the dishes at home, or at least attempt to. Keep an eye out for the monthly seasonal suppers, when a table is set in the middle of the shop and a feast is served up. Yum.

Opening hours
Mon-Sun 10am-5pm

Stanstead Park Farm Shop, Maze Courtyard, Stansted Park, Rowlands Castle PO9 6DX
WWW.STANSTEDFARMSHOP.CO.UK   023 9241 3576

Salt Café

JUNCTION: 11; 8 MINUTES

This cracking café takes its name from the stunning coastal views it enjoys over the Great Cams Lake end of Portsmouth Harbour, views you can soak up from tables on the waterside terrace and jetty. It's slightly off the beaten track but certainly worth seeking out to watch the boats drifting across the bay.

Staff carry plates of nutritious salads, warm quiches, filled crab rolls, cooked breakfasts and cream-topped hot chocolates to chatty groups inside and out. Coffee is very good and served most often with a slice of one of their cakes: maybe courgette and lime, pistachio and lemon, or apple. Check ahead if you're passing in summer as they occasionally put on Friday pizza nights (which are very good).

It's popular with dog walkers thanks to the recreation ground and coastal path that reaches out to the West, and your four-legged friends are welcome to join you inside.

Opening hours
Mon-Fri 9am-4pm
Sat-Sun 9am-5pm

Salt Cafe, Cranleigh Road, Portchester, Fareham PO16 9DR
WWW.FACEBOOK.COM/SALTCAFE66/   01329 248609

FARM SHOP

Hockey's Farm Shop

JUNCTION: A338; 8 MINUTES

Animal lovers and foodies will love this stop. Not only can you pick up a respectable grocery shop – all of noble provenance – you can also meet the farm creatures: alpacas, donkeys, pigs, sheep, and even chicks in spring. It's a working smallholding and the team are passionate about low intensity methods and supporting other, likeminded producers nearby so you can shop with confidence.

The Farmyard Café is in a charming wooden cabin over the way from the farm shop but plunders the shelves for ingredients (so if you like what you taste, you can attempt it yourself back at home). The bacon and pork has a really unique flavour thanks to the Hockey pigs being allowed to graze in the New Forest over winter. The café counter groans beneath the weight of the cakes and bakes, served next to cooked breakfasts, toasties, veggie burgers and cream teas.

There are plants and a bric-a-brac shop to browse, and of course you're on the edge of the New Forest so there's potential for a glorious forest wander if you're not in a rush.

Opening hours
Mon-Fri 9am-6pm
Sat 8am-6pm
Sun 9am-5pm

Hockey's Farm Shop, South Gorley, Fordingbridge SP6 2PW
WWW.HOCKEYS-FARM.CO.UK   01425 652542

The Potting Shed, Olives Et Al.

JUNCTION: A37; 1 MINUTE

Just seconds from the main road this cosy deli is a proper treat. It's located in the intriguing town of Poundbury, an experimental development built on Duchy of Cornwall land. The architects' aim was to combat post-war suburban sprawl and create a town with real character. They certainly succeeded.

Olives Et Al. sits on the edge of the beautiful central square. The architectural detail of the streets transports you to the continent – as do the contents and decor of the deli and café. The menu is a homage to the Mediterranean, often with a modern twist, such as fig and goats cheese tart served with pomegranate molasses or feta, aubergine and honey pie. The coffee is the 'the best in Poundbury' according to locals and if the smell as you enter is anything to go by, they're right. The deli counter will provide anything you need for a quick pit stop, and you can take away your coffee too.

Parking is plentiful outside on the square

Opening hours
Mon-Fri 8.30am-5pm

Ⓥ Ⓟ

The Potting Shed, Olives Et Al, 81 Poundbury Farm Way, Poundbury DT1 3RT
WWW.OLIVESETAL.CO.UK   01305 216788

FARM SHOP-DELI

The Old Piggery Farm Shop Deli

JUNCTION: LYTCHETT MATRAVERS; 2 MINUTES

The red brick stables and barns of Bere farm had lain empty for a number of years before their transformation into the tranquil Old Piggery complex. Today garden centre, antiques shop, cafe, cookery school and deli combine in a diverting pit stop if you're traversing the South coast.

Stop in the Barn Cafe - relaxed and quirky - for scrumptious cakes (we were powerless to resist the chocolate Malteser cake) and toothsome tidbits: toast and homemade jam or three-egg omelette for breakfast; smoked trout terrine, baked camembert or panini for lunch. Coffee is creamy and teas and hot chocolate from The Guilded Teapot in nearby Dorchester.

You'll need to mind your head as you duck into the farm shop and deli over the yard, but any bumps are rewarded with the cornucopia of produce for your holiday storecupboard: charcuterie made nearby, cheese, olives, Isle of Wight garlic, kombucha tea and proper sausages.

Don't leave without sampling a scoop of the award-winning Purbeck ice cream.

Opening hours
Mon-Sat 10am-5pm
Sun 11am-4pm

The Old Piggery Farm Shop Deli, Bere Farm, Lytchett Matravers, Poole BH16 6ER
01202 621837

Martyrs Inn

JUNCTION: AFFPUDDLE ; 2 MINUTES

At the heart of a rural community, this characterful pub is just a stone's throw from the A35. Tolpuddle is a picturesque village steeped in history. The namesakes of this charming inn – the Tolpuddle Martyrs – were arrested in 1833 for swearing an oath to a 'secret workers' society', which many consider to be the early sketches of a trade union.

Inside it's modern and inviting with comfy chairs, long bars and dining areas surrounding brickwork chimney breasts. There's chatter from locals and friendly staff to greet you. For food, it's pub classics all the way, with a pinch of local influence. The Dorset mushroom risotto, steak and ale pie or Dorset lamb hot-pot won't disappoint. If you need to wear off your meal, take a stroll through the village where references to the martyrs' history can be found in every direction. If you don't fancy that and the weather prevails, there's plenty of seating out the front of the pub, where you can observe the comings and goings of the thatched village.

Opening hours
Sun-Thurs 11am-11pm
Fri-Sat 11am-midnight

Martyrs Inn, 49 Main Road, Tolpuddle, Dorchester DT2 7ES
WWW.THEMARTYRSINN.CO.UK   01305 848249

GARDEN CENTRE

Ivy House Kitchen at Groves Nursery

JUNCTION: CROWN ROUNDABOUT; 2 MINUTES

Gawping koi carp, a glorious array of plants and flowers and a pergola draped with roses and wisteria will immediately lift the traffic-tired spirits at Groves Nurseries before you even reach the radiant Ivy House Kitchen.

The cafe is housed in a purpose-built glass house next to borders that have been designed to inspire budding and accomplished gardeners in their own veggie patches – and the menu to demonstrate novel ways of using their harvest. Chefs serve up creative combinations, perhaps pea and rosemary soup or chicken and nasturtium salad. The jackets are quite literally hot potatoes and one of the most popular items on the menu, while the friendliness of the staff frequently draws praise.

Take yours outside to the terrace to bask in the sun if the weather allows, and if yours is an afternoon stop, head down to West Bay to watch the sun dip below the horizon before heading onwards.

Opening hours
Mon-Sat 8.30am-5pm
Sun 10am-4pm

Ivy House Kitchen at Groves Nursery, Groves Nursery, West Bay Road, Bridport DT6 4BA
01308 807053 / 01308 422654

CAFÉ

River Cottage Kitchen

JUNCTION: A358; 3 MINUTES

Food lovers and organic crusaders will need no introduction to Hugh Fearnley-Whittingstall's River Cottage Kitchen in Axminster. It's just down the road from the famous River Cottage HQ, and three minutes off the A35, the trunk road across the English Riviera.

Hugh spotted an opportunity in the high street's shuttered pub and turned it into a relaxed and welcoming restaurant. Light spills from the ceiling lantern into the rustic but stylish dining room at the back, once the town's dance hall; floorboards are stripped; tables scrubbed and set with fresh flowers and linen napkins. At the front of the restaurant, a well-stocked deli counter is stacked with a host of picnic temptations (show your meal receipt to get 10% off), while locals regularly convene for a natter and languorous coffee.

The food is wholesome and inventive – breakfast, lunch and dinner served with a smile by staff.

Opening hours
Mon-Sat 9am-9pm
Sun 9am-4pm

River Cottage Kitchen, Trinity Square, Axminster EX13 5AN
WWW.RIVERCOTTAGE.NET/RESTAURANTS/AXMINSTER   01297 631715

FARM SHOP

Millers Farm Shop

JUNCTION: KILMINGTON; 0 MINUTES

A family-run farm shop brushing the A35, Millers has a snug café and enough country fayre to fill your larder with flavour. Malcolm and his family have been serving hungry travellers and locals for more than 30 years. The Teapot Café is a charming timber nook, flooded with daylight and instantly inviting. It has a selection of home-made cakes, small treats and light, seasonal dishes. If it's a long journey then a proper full English might be in order or a sausage buttie, all sourced locally, of course, there's freshly ground coffee and traditional Devon cream tea if you just want a pit stop.

The shop is a mine of farming delights – earthy veggies, spring greens, wonky veg that's full of flavour and no plastic in sight. There's also plenty tasty French produce as Malcolm and wife Angela travel to France each week to scour the markets for the country's best food and drink. If you fancy a tipple at the end of your journey, don't leave before browsing the impressive wine selection.

Opening hours
Mon-Sat 7.30am-6pm (9am-5pm café)
Sun 8am-1pm (9am-1pm café – seasonal)

Millers Farm Shop, Gammons Hill, Axminster EX13 7RA
WWW.MILLERSFARMSHOP.CO.UK   01297 35290

Coffee Factory

JUNCTION: SHUTE; 4 MINUTES

An unsuspecting country lane leads you to this truly fortuitous find: a coffee lover's paradise in the middle of the countryside, over the yard from the Lyme Bay Winery. The smell of freshly ground beans guides you in from the forecourt to the artisan coffee roastery where you can catch a glimpse of the roasting in action as you taste the fruits of their labour in the pop-up brew bar, however you take it - from filter to espresso. Proper tea and delicious hot chocolate is on offer for the coffee-averse, and for food there's a selection of delectable cakes and sweet treats from the Exploding Bakery nearby – including apricot flapjacks, carrot cake and salted caramel brownies – that will leave you smiling.

Coffee lovers nationwide have roasted beans despatched from here to their doorstep, such is their renowned quality. Inside, the traditional mechanics are laid bare and the industrial chic offers a clear view of how much care and attention goes into roasting every bean.

There's plenty of parking directly outside and after tasting one of these artisan coffees you're sure to be leaving with a bag of very freshly roasted beans. A truly immersive coffee experience.

Opening hours
Mon-Fri 10am-3.30pm

Coffee Factory, Unit 3 Samurai Buildings, Seaton Junction, Axminster EX13 7PW
THECOFFEEFACTORY.CO.UK   01297 551259

CAFÉ

The Grazing Cow

JUNCTION: OFFWELL; 0 MINUTES

Whether you're stopping for an ice cream on a hot day or a warming hot chocolate by the fire in winter, the Grazing Cow makes for a friendly pit stop in any coast-bound journey. The purpose-built wooden café – which takes its name from Essie, the model cow out front – is light and spacious and decorated in a homely combination of raw wood, blue and white.

Provenance is not just a buzzword in the kitchen and the simple menu – cooked breakfasts, sandwiches, soups, scones and quiches – tastes all the better for being made from local ingredients. Hospitable staff ferry plates of home-cooked food to the tables and carve generous slices of tasty cakes at the counter: homemade Battenberg, blackberry and lemon drizzle, salted caramel. Check the specials boards for hot options such as cottage pie or curry, which change with the seasons.

Dogs are welcome in the seating area outside, where there's also an adventure playground to keep the smalls occupied for a while. If you've got a little time to spare, there are lovely footpaths looping through the Offwell Woods nearby.

Opening hours
Mon-Sat 9am-4pm
Sun 9am-3pm

The Grazing Cow, Offwell, EX14 9RR
WWW.FACEBOOK.COM/THEGRAZINGCOWOFFWELL/   01404 831114

Hog & Hedge

JUNCTION: WHIDDON DOWN; 0 MINUTES

One of the new wave of services, Hog & Hedge is a breath of fresh air. Swing off the A30 on your way to or from Cornwall, and you'll be restored by freshly cooked food and excellent speciality coffee, with views of Dartmoor and the Devonshire fields. Trestle tables stand in the middle of the dining room, heaving with help-yourself cakes and goodies. Traditional rugs are slung over polished concrete floors and scattered with stylishly mismatched tables; there are posh toiletries in the loos and charging points for mobiles and tablets.

Prices are reasonable and food includes full English breakfast, bacon sandwiches, porridge, soups, toasties and ploughman's, all made with the best West Country ingredients. Nothing is fried, so don't expect chips, but everything is delicious.

Children will love the play area with a Wendy house and toys, and there's a dedicated food station for little people, with plastic cups and plates, colouring sheets, a microwave and bottle warmer.

Opening hours
Mon–Sun 7am–7pm
(5pm in winter)

Hog & Hedge, Whiddon Down Services EX20 2QT
WWW.HOGANDHEDGE.CO.UK   01647 213588

FARM SHOP-RESTAURANT-COFFEE BAR

Strawberry Fields Farm Shop & Restaurant

JUNCTION: LIFTON; 1 MINUTE

A stop at Strawberry Fields Farm Shop, at the gateway to Cornwall, makes any traffic jam on the journey to the South West bearable. Restaurant, coffee lounge, farm shop with artisan bakery, deli and butchery – you'll find everything you need to unwind and refuel.

The Mounce family started farming here more than 20 years ago with just a plot of strawberries: now their fields supply almost everything the kitchen needs for the farmhouse menu – meat, eggs, fruit and veg, often muddy from the field. It makes for excellent breakfasts and delicious cream teas, served with clotted cream and the farm's own strawberry jam. 'The scones would have made Mary Berry cry,' reported one customer.

Recreate it yourself at home by raiding the farm shop next door, which is stocked with irresistible goodies from home-reared beef and lamb to home-baked quiches, pies, hams and outrageously good ice cream made with the farm's soft fruit. Parking is plentiful and there is plenty of space for you and your four-legged friends to stretch your legs.

Opening hours
Mon-Sat 8am-6pm (5.30pm winter)
Sun 8am-5.30pm (5pm winter)
See website for full details

Strawberry Fields Farm Shop & Restaurant, Lifton PL16 0DE
WWW.STRAWBERRYFIELDSLIFTON.CO.UK   01566 784605

Tre, Pol & Pen

JUNCTION: LAUNCESTON; 4 MINUTES

Whether feasting in the café, browsing for gifts in the excellent shop or chatting to the butcher about the best cut for dinner, there's something for practically everyone at Tre, Pol & Pen. It's a most modern farm shop – its sharp lines striking against the rural landscape – and the team are fierce advocates of local food. Everything in the store is handpicked to highlight the very best of the producers nearby, from seaweed salami to Ruby Red beef from the herd outside, Cornish cheeses and rose gin.

Grocery shop assured, you can taste some of those flavours over in the Kitchen. Breakfasts are farm-worthy, lunch might be sausage and mash, crayfish and salmon, or spiced falafel salad. Pizzas are served lunch to dinner and are first-rate.

As for the name, it's from an old Cornish rhyme: "By Tre, Pol and Pen, Shall ye know all Cornishmen". The words mean homestead, pool and hill respectively, so very fitting for a hillside farm next to an ancient spring.

Opening hours
Mon-Sat 8am-6pm
Sun 8.30am-5pm

Tre, Pol & Pen, Lezant, Launceston PL15 9NN
TREPOLANDPEN.CO.UK   01566 706527

PUB

The Plume of Feathers

JUNCTION: MITCHELL; 2 MINUTES

Escape the holiday traffic at this belting pit stop, within a minute of the main road. The old A30 runs through the village of Mitchell and the Plume of Feathers, its 16th century inn, melds old-world charm with a spectacular, glass-roofed extension.

Chef (and former MasterChef contestant) Nat Tallents heads up the kitchen. She's renowned for using the best Cornish and seasonal produce, showcasing the vast local larder as well as the pub's own veggie patch and bee hives (you can buy a jar of honey from behind the bar): Cornish lamb with dauphinoise new potatoes, potted venison, locally caught rainbow trout with celeriac and apple remoulade. Even the rhubarb ice cream is sourced from a neighbouring farm.

There's plenty of room in the airy dining room and a lush green lawn stretches up a gentle slope at the rear, perfect if you've struck gold with your holiday weather.

Opening hours
Mon-Sun 7.30am-10pm

The Plume of Feathers, Mitchell, Newquay TR8 5AX
WWW.THEPLUMEMITCHELL.CO.UK   01872 510387

Miss Molly's Tea Rooms

JUNCTION: TOLVADON; 4 MINUTES

An unusual entrance leads through a courtyard full of bric-a-brac and junk shop treasures into a quaint, vintage tea room, where, tucked away in the mine counting house, Miss Molly's serves honest food made in the kitchen from scratch.

The cake is phenomenal, as are the freshly cooked bacon sarnies. Lunch on crusty sandwiches, cheese toasties, jacket potatoes and paninis. Indulge in a caramel flapjack or toasted teacake in the afternoon. Tea is served in delicate vintage cups with finger sandwiches, home-baked cakes, savouries and fruit, and scones with clotted cream – this, after all, is the scone's motherland.

Look out for seasonal, homemade additions (such as elderflower cordial in late spring) and the friendly in-house cat who is prone to commandeering laps. Dogs are welcome in the special dog area, which even has a special 'à la bark' menu of healthy canine treats. Browse the second-hand rooms before you leave to pick up your next upcycling project.

Opening hours
Mon–Sat 9am–5.30pm
Sun 10am–4.30pm

Miss Molly's Tea Rooms, The Old College, Dolcoath Road, Camborne TR14 8RR
WWW.MISSMOLLYSTEAROOM.CO.UK   01209 718196

CAFÉ-DELI

Scarlet Wines

JUNCTION: ST ERTH ROUNDABOUT; 1 MINUTE

An emporium of enticing food and wine, Scarlet Wines makes a fantastic pit stop when Cornwall's crowds get too much. Sitting above the Hayle Estuary (a haven for bird life and good for a stroll), this low stone barn is a popular destination for locals and tourists alike, drawn to the restaurant and amazing deli. You can find delicacies from Cornwall, Italy and Spain: smoked fish from Tregida Smokehouse, apple preserve from the Cornish Bee Farm, Tuscan olive oil, Spanish almond turrón.

The cosy, stove-warmed restaurant is open for breakfast, lunch and dinner. Diners sit at sheepskin-covered benches inside or sunny tables outside and are plied with mouth-watering dishes – cinnamon toast or baked eggs with feta and chorizo for breakfast, warm beetroot salad or fresh seafood for lunch, baked cod with lentils and mezze platters for dinner. There are plenty of options for vegans and the coffee is excellent. Limited parking is available outside and dogs are welcome. Don't leave without browsing the wine shop for an arrival tipple.

Opening hours
Mon-Sun Breakfast 9am-11.30am
Lunch noon-3pm
Dinner 5.30pm-late

Scarlet Wines, The Old Forge, Griggs Quay, Hayle TR27 6JG
WWW.SCARLET-WINES.CO.UK   01736 753696

South Devon Chilli Farm

JUNCTION: A3121; 12 MINUTES

If you're undertaking a long journey to or from the South West, it's worth detouring to experience the gorgeous South Hams countryside. The Chilli Farm is an unusual addition to the landscape here, but a much-loved place to pull in and taste one of the UK's varied and less conventional crops.

Tours of the farm are free and tasters are available in the shop if you want to try some of the creative products before you buy, but even if you're not good with spicy heat you'll find something to tickle your fancy in the cafe, which has beautiful rural views. Brioche bacon rolls are served with chipotle ketchup at breakfast, cream teas with chilli or strawberry jam from 10am and light bites such as sweetcorn fritters and nachos at lunchtime. For a quick pick-me-up, try a slice of homemade cake: perhaps salted chilli chocolate or carrot.

Dogs are welcome on leads, provided they behave, there's a chilli tractor play area and dressing up bag for kids, and you can stretch your legs on one of the walks around the 10-acre site before departing.

Opening hours
Mon-Sun 10am-4pm

South Devon Chilli Farm, Wigford Cross, Loddiswell TQ7 4DX
WWW.SOUTHDEVONCHILLIFARM.CO.UK   01548 550782

GARDEN CENTRE

Duchy of Cornwall Nursery

JUNCTION: TURFDOWN ROAD; 9 MINUTES

A plant lover's paradise. The Duchy of Cornwall Nursery has nested in a former slate quarry, a heavenly sanctum of tumbling flowers and sweeping views over the Fowey valley. Trail through the plants before heading to the café where you can slump into a sofa by the log burner and leaf through gardening books and newspapers at your leisure. Staff are attentive and friendly; breakfasts are made with the freshest ingredients – most from within the county limit – and washed down with free tea and coffee refills.

Enjoy the views to Restormel Castle from the terrace as you lunch on homemade bread, filled sandwiches, salads from the garden or heartier dishes – slow cooked pork belly, venison burgers, lemon sole. Cakes are expertly baked and afternoon teas are proper Cornish, piled with jam and daubed with clotted cream. There's a footpath linking the nursery to the castle if you fancy a leg stretch afterwards and if you can resist the lure of the fabulous garden and gift shop (Italian soaps, local ceramics, traditional toys), you're stronger than us.

Opening hours
Mon-Sat 9am-4.30pm
Suns & Bank Holidays 10am-4.30pm

Duchy of Cornwall Nursery, Cott Road, Lostwithiel PL22 0HW
WWW.DUCHYOFCORNWALLNURSERY.CO.UK   01208 872668

The Curator Café & Kitchen

JUNCTION: BUCKFASTLEIGH; 14 MINUTES

Laid out over two floors, adorned with vintage surfboards, custom cycles, prints and memorabilia for sale, The Curator is the perfect place to start a visit to the unique town of Totnes.

The café sits on the pavement level with outside seating and serves a range of woodroasted coffee beans, speciality teas and a selection of sandwiches and pastries. Focaccia, pizza and other Italian speciality breads and cakes are all prepared in an extension of The Curator just around the corner, Flour & Rice (12 Ticklemore Street).

Above the coffee shop is The Curator Kitchen, a lovely light modern osteria with an open kitchen, serving locally sourced food with Italian flavours. Fresh pasta, small plates and brunch are served all day and evening meals are exceptional. Organic and bio-dynamic wines are imported directly from small vineyards in Italy, on the menu next to local craft beers.

Opening hours
Mon 7.30am-6pm
Tues-Fri 7.30am-9.15pm
Sat 9am-9.15pm (Sun 5pm)

The Curator Café & Kitchen , 2 The Plains, Totnes TQ9 5DR
WWW.ITALIANFOODHEROES.COM   01803 865570

COFFEE SHOP

The Hairy Barista

JUNCTION: A385; 13 MINUTES

It's hard to beat 'The Hairy Barista' as a coffee shop name, and the same goes for the coffee here: Roe and Ruth take their beans seriously. If you're a coffee lover, it's worth diverting on your way to Cornwall to sample the speciality brews at the top of this hill above Totnes.

Food hinges on vegan and organic principles, so you're in the right place if you prefer an oat matcha latte, almond turmeric latte or something from the wide variety of superfood smoothies. The baking may be low in fat and sugar but flavour is never sacrificed – it's finger-licking good and Instagram-pretty too.

It's a bit of a squeeze in the shop, so it's a good job the staff and regulars are so friendly. Order your food to take away or find a quiet corner to enjoy a generously filled sourdough toastie.

Opening hours
Mon-Fri 8am-5pm
Sat 9am-6pm

The Hairy Barista, 69 High Street, Totnes TQ9 5PB
WWW.FACEBOOK.COM/THEHAIRYBARISTA/   01803 867773

The Almond Thief

JUNCTION: SOUTH BRENT; 12 MINUTES

Incongruously located on a small industrial estate, the Almond Thief has earned a fearsome reputation for its quality baked goods. There's no cutting corners here, only traditional techniques and the finest ingredients: watch the bakers at work as you sup a cuppa. The café is starkly minimalist and on-trend, with wooden trestle tables and benches, vintage chairs, polished concrete floors and holly boughs decorating the walls. There's a small play corner for kids.

The menu is small, made from scratch and perfectly formed. Bread features prominently, naturally: perhaps Bob's biodynamic poached eggs on toast served with home-smoked salmon, house granola with raspberry compote and yoghurt, leek and goat's cheese frittata, or red lentil, lemon and ginger soup. Coffee is great and accompanied by princely Semla buns, flakey almond slices and caramelised egg custard tarts.

Don't, whatever you do, forget to pick up a loaf on your way out.

Opening hours
Mon-Sat 9.30am-4pm

The Almond Thief, Unit 3/4 Webber's Yard, Dartington TQ9 6JY
WWW.THEALMONDTHIEF.COM   01803 411290

SHOP-CAFÉ

The Seed Wholefood Store and Café

JUNCTION: BUCKFASTLEIGH; 3 MINUTES

The Seed is a well-established, pioneering and ethical community enterprise company focused on making organic and environmentally conscious foods more affordable, and for that we salute it. Its well-stocked shelves can supply almost anything you could need at your destination, from vegetables grown nearby to organic wholemeal sourdough and bamboo socks.

Dinky and serene, the cafe is at the front among the shelves. Friendly staff serve very good coffee, along with locally-made raw cakes, gluten-free and low-sugar treats like jammy dodgers. The Seed were one of the first 'new wave' waste-free shops, years before it became a national phenomenon.

Better still, profits are ploughed back into the community, so grab a bite here and you're not only enhancing your journey but village life too. Winner.

Opening hours
Mon-Sat 8am-7pm
Sun 10am-4pm

The Seed Wholefood Store and Café, 40 Fore Street, Buckfastleigh TQ11 0AA
WWW.FACEBOOK.COM/OURSEED/   01364 644699

Riverford Field Kitchen

JUNCTION: BUCKFASTLEIGH; 6 MINUTES

The Riverford Field Kitchen is a cornucopia of delights based on the family's organic farm, so you can be assured that the food will be free of any contaminants. There's just one sitting (lunch every day and supper most), tables are shared and the whole restaurant eats at the same time; you must reserve as they only cook for those booked to reduce waste. The food is fresh from the fields, the atmosphere light-hearted and convivial, and the cooking superb. Vegetables are the main focus here, served in all manner of creative guises and varied daily depending on what's in season. Portions are generous and if you've got room, puddings are every bit as delicious as the mains.

Make time, if you can, for a field to fork farm tour. It will certainly work up an appetite for lunch! Check the website for dates. If there's no tour you can wander around the restaurant kitchen garden and polytunnels – there's always plenty to see. People come from far and wide to eat here and it's worth every drop of fuel.

Opening hours
Every day for lunch, most days for supper.
Lunch 12.30pm, Supper 7pm
Booking essential. Check availability online

Riverford Field Kitchen, Wash Farm, Buckfastleigh TQ11 0JU
WWW.THERIVERFORDFIELDKITCHEN.CO.UK   01803 762074

RESTAURANT
Rafikis

JUNCTION: ASHBURTON; 2 MINUTES

Ashburton is a delightful town on the southern slopes of Dartmoor in the heart of the South Devon countryside; its high street could give Totnes a run for its money with a great range of butchers, bakers and artisan producers.

Rafikis is awash with colour, bright and vibrant on the inside and out and the food is as colourful as the décor. All dishes are vegetarian and will leave any carnivore doubting their dietary regime; the Vietnamese Bahn mi (a stuffed spicy baguette) is a particular house favourite. There are specialities you'll struggle to find elsewhere: Canadian pancakes with coconut blossom syrup or the kimchi potato cakes organic eggs and spicy ragu; bold and original food, done to perfection.

For sweeter cravings the counter is awash with daily baked goods, like salted caramel brownies, fresh scones, or a slice of chocolate, banana and walnut cake.

Parking for the town is just yards away, very reasonably priced and a testament the town's dedication to keep things local.

Opening hours
Mon-Weds, Sat 9am-5pm
Fri 9am-11pm
Sun 10am-4pm

Rafikis, 17 West Street, Ashburton, Newton Abbot TQ13 7DT
WWW.RAFIKIS.CO.UK   01364 388865

FARM SHOP-CAFÉ

Ullacombe Farm

JUNCTION: COLDEAST; 8 MINUTES

Carved into the hillside, this quaint farm shop and café will fill your lungs with Dartmoor air. The décor is reminiscent of a log cabin in the mountains, just as cosy but without the jetlag. Outdoor seating is plentiful, accompanied by the rural soundtrack of sheep gently bleating, and there's a secure play area for little guests to run around.

Classics fill the lunch menu and always use locally sourced meats. The homemade 'Barn Burger' reliably pulls in locals and the roasted chilli salmon is a tasty alternative if you fancy something lighter. Cream teas are all homemade and the coffee will revive you. If you're lucky enough to be passing on Sunday, the roasts are something of a local secret and non-drivers can even wash their spuds down with a glass of Prosecco. Stock up on fantastic local produce in the shop and, should you have the time, drive a little further to Haytor just up the road: the famous granite outcrop offers unrivalled views of South Devon.

Opening hours
Mon-Sun 8.30am-5pm

Ullacombe Farm, Haytor Road, Bovey Tracey TQ13 9LL
WWW.ULLACOMBEFARM.CO.UK   01364 661341

CAFÉ·SHOP·GALLERY

Devon Guild of Craftsmen

JUNCTION: BOVEY TRACEY; 4 MINUTES

Craft lovers will revel in a break at the Devon Guild of Craftsmen, which collects together crafts including textiles, jewellery and ceramics in three appealing exhibition spaces. The rooms are filled with the creativity of artists from across the region and in the shop you can find more locally sourced crafts and gifts.

The Terrace Cafe is understandably popular and you'd be forgiven for thinking some of the homemade cakes were exhibits: gooey banoffee, lemon and raspberry decorated with fresh flowers, or cappuccino are just some of the photogenic creations to date. For those wanting a more substantial meal there's breakfasts with veggie options, homemade granola and yoghurt, toasties, daily tarts, falafel burgers and sharing platters among many other options. And of course cream teas; this is Devon after all. If you're with your four-legged friend you are both welcome in the courtyard.

If it's a brisk day outside, warm yourselves by the contemporary fire before getting back in the car; parking is just across the river.

Opening hours
Mon-Sun 10am-5.30pm

Devon Guild of Craftsmen, Riverside Mill, Bovey Tracey TQ13 9AF
WWW.CRAFTS.ORG.UK/CAFE   01626 832223

The Seven Stars

JUNCTION: KENNFORD; 3 MINUTES

You'll wish the Seven Stars was your local. West country ales, cider, gin and award winning food at a reasonable price. Natives chatter at the bar and shoot pool, whilst couples and families fill the dining-room tables. A weekly quiz and even monthly barber haircuts reinforce community links and open-door policy. The interior is quirky-rustic: leather chesterfield next to the log-burner, a table fashioned from an old pub mirror, metro tiles behind the bar and a grandfather clock in the corner. At the back there's a wonderful secret garden with sheltered wooden booths, deck chairs and AstroTurf lawn.

Food is a couple of notches up from pub grub and the menu changes with the seasons with a focus on local and sustainable produce: expect lamb, mussels and vibrant vegetables in summer; venison, duck, mackerel and root vegetables in winter. Pub favourites – sausage and mash, pie of the moment, cod and chips – are available year round. Pizzas are some of the best (and biggest!) in Exeter and are available all day to eat in or takeaway.

Opening hours
Mon 3pm-11pm
Tues-Thurs noon-11pm
Fri-Sat noon–midnight (Sun 10.30pm)

The Seven Stars, Kennford EX6 7TR
WWW.SEVENSTARSKENNFORD.CO.UK   01392 834887

The 👉 M5

Cotswolds, Quantocks Malverns, Mendips & more

M5 NORTH

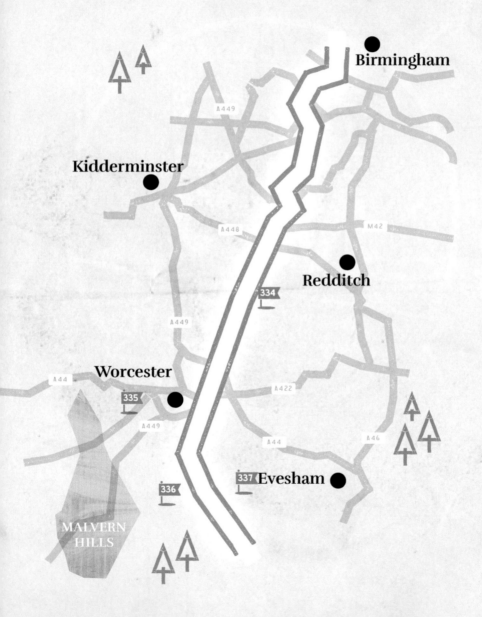

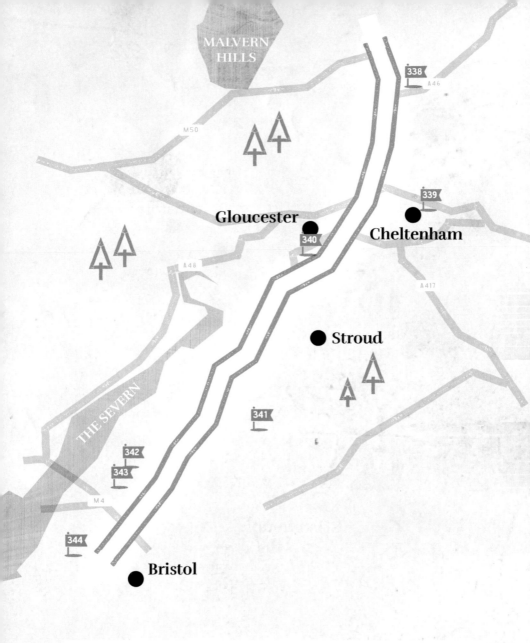

MALVERN HILLS

M50

Gloucester

340

338
A46

339

Cheltenham

A48

A417

THE SEVERN

Stroud

341

342

343

M4

344

Bristol

334 **The Restaurant at Webbs**	
335 **The Fold**	
336 **Clive's Fruit Farm**	
337 **Revills Farm Shop**	
338 **Malt House Emporium**	
339 **Central Cross Café**	
(In the Park)	
340 **Gloucester Services**	
341 **Wotton Farm Shop**	
342 **Hawkes House**	
343 **Papilio at Heritage**	
344 **Morgans Coffee House**	

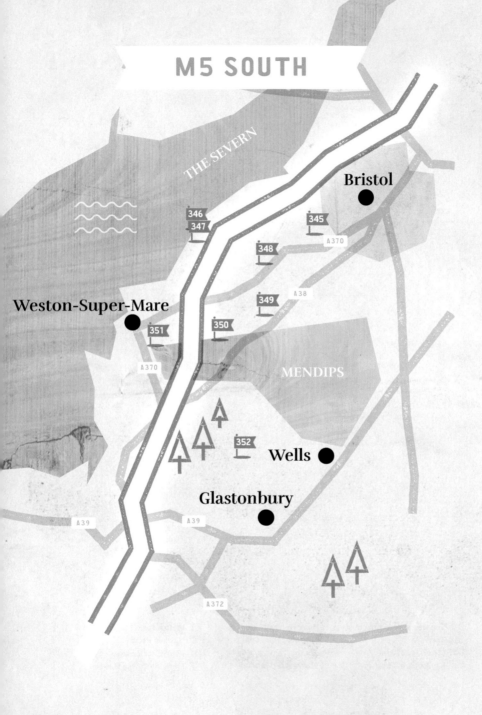

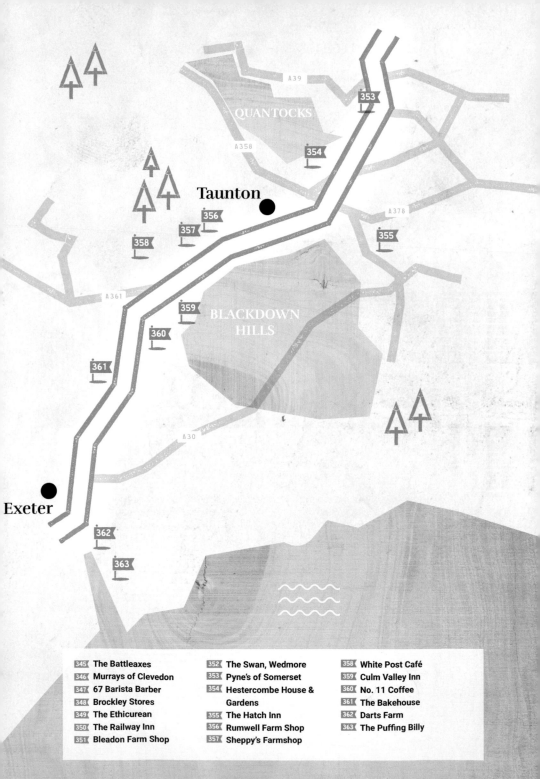

QUANTOCKS

A39

353

A358

354

Taunton

A378

356

357

355

358

A361

359

BLACKDOWN
HILLS

360

361

A30

Exeter

362

363

345	The Battleaxes	352	The Swan, Wedmore	358	White Post Café
346	Murrays of Clevedon	353	Pyne's of Somerset	359	Culm Valley Inn
347	67 Barista Barber	354	Hestercombe House &	360	No. 11 Coffee
348	Brockley Stores		Gardens	361	The Bakehouse
349	The Ethicurean	355	The Hatch Inn	362	Darts Farm
350	The Railway Inn	356	Rumwell Farm Shop	363	The Puffing Billy
351	Bleadon Farm Shop	357	Sheppy's Farmshop		

GARDEN CENTRE

The Restaurant at Webbs

JUNCTION: 5; 4 MINUTES

You'll feel your spirits immediately lift among the peaceful throng of flowers in Webbs' riverside gardens, which are free to visit. Amble through a wisteria walkway, marvel at the colour spectrum garden, let the kids delight in the Hobbit House and learn how vegetables can bring both form and function.

The renovated café seats 400 with more outdoors, plus a picnic area and the kitchen uses Worcestershire ingredients as far as possible – juices from Pershore, traditional farmhouse cheese from Ansteys and luxury ice cream from Bennetts – and serves tasty meals all day. There's a 'grab & go' counter for sandwiches, cakes and hot drinks if you're short of time.

The food hall sells deli delights, including honey and fig cheese, local beers, freshly baked bread, a chocolate library with more than 100 types of chocolate and a gelato bar. Stretch your legs with a riverside walk or, in winter, skate around the temporary ice rink and meet the reindeer.

Opening hours
Mon-Fri 9am-8pm
Sat 9am-6pm
Sun 10.30am-4.30pm

The Restaurant at Webbs, Worcester Road, Droitwich WR9 0DG
WWW.WEBBSDIRECT.CO.UK   01527 860000

The Fold

JUNCTION: 7; 10 MINUTES

The eco-conscious will adore The Fold, a community enterprise on a rambling organic farm in the Worcestershire countryside with the gentle mission of encouraging sustainable living and escaping the commercial norm.

There's a farm shop selling seasonal, organic produce grown on site, an independent wine and spirits specialist, and artisan studios offering gifts, homewares and ethical haircuts. You can even find holistic treatments in the tranquil Therapy Centre, while the first Sunday of every month (apart from Jan/Feb) sees a food and craft market where local businesses sell their wares.

The café serves organic food in an arching 17th-century barn, always using good-quality, local, organic meat. Herbivores are well catered for with an excellent range of vegan and vegetarian soups, tarts, salads and freshly baked traybakes and scones.

There's a fabulous wooden playground for the kids and a nature trail leading down to the river Teme where you can stretch your legs and meet the local wildlife.

Opening hours
Mon–Sat 9am–4.30pm
Sun 10am–4pm

The Fold, Bransford WR6 5JB
WWW.THEFOLD.ORG.UK   01886 833633

FARM SHOP-CAFÉ

Clive's Fruit Farm

JUNCTION: 8; 12 MINUTES

Hemmed in by the Malvern Hills on one side and the river Severn on the other, this pocket of England is perfect for fruit growing. The Clive family have been tending the trees at their fruit farm since 1921, now under the watchful eyes of Jane and Charlie, and their son Rich, and it's well worth swinging off the M5 to find. Once just a small shed and cash drawer, the farm shop and café now fill two long red-brick barns and are supplied by farmers from across the Vale of Evesham. Breakfasts are hearty, lunches liberal and the cakes worthy of a farmhouse kitchen. The shop provides everything you could need for a decent weekly shop or car picnic: the cider, apple and pear juices, grown and pressed here on the farm, are unmissable.

The views over the countryside are sublime and children will love the small play area and feeding the resident pigs, peacocks and hens, especially if you're passing in the morning when they can lend a hand with egg collecting.

Their sister farm shop and café, Clive's of Cropthorne, is well worth a visit if you're travelling closer to Evesham.

Opening hours
Mon-Sat 9am-5pm
Sun 10am-4pm

Clive's Fruit Farm, Upper Hook Road, Upton Upon Severn WR8 0SA
WWW.CLIVESFRUITFARM.CO.UK   01684 592664

Revills Farm Shop

JUNCTION: 8; 12 MINUTES

Isabel Revill set up shop in the old stable 15 years ago with little more than a cash tin and a trestle table selling the farm's asparagus. From this rustic beginning has grown a thriving farm shop and tearoom, now run day to day by her son-in-law Darren and his team. You can still buy Revill's asparagus in season – and their carrots, beetroot, raspberries and baby courgettes – but the shop is also stocked with meat, game, vegetables, cheese and gifts sourced from fellow growers and producers across Worcestershire.

Once you've filled your basket, head to the tearoom to fill your belly. The breakfasts are excellent and the sandwiches, soups, towering cakes and cream teas served for the rest of the day are lovingly made to order. It's all served on charmingly mismatched crockery in a renovated timber-and-brick barn. Newspapers are sold in the shop, if you need any excuse to loiter longer. Or you can stretch your legs before resuming your journey with a stroll along the River Avon.

Opening hours
Mon-Sat 9am-5.30pm (café 5pm)
Sun & Bank Hols 10am-4pm (café 3.30pm)

Revills Farm Shop, Bourne Road, Defford WR8 9BS
WWW.REVILLSFARMSHOP.CO.UK   01386 750466

SHOP-CAFÉ

Malt House Emporium

JUNCTION: 9; 2 MINUTES

Lose yourself in the aisles of the gargantuan Malt House Emporium, a two-storey warehouse on the A46 just off Junction 9 overflowing filled with tantalising homewares, antiques, clothes and gifts. It gathers together 70 traders whose alluring collections – old and new – range from farmhouse tables to upcycled chests of drawers, retro kitchenware, chandeliers and vintage clothes.

Browse the stalls then put your feet up in The Ferns Tea Room at the back. Its long run of floor-to-ceiling windows and the narrow terrace outside have lovely views over the Gloucestershire fields, though you'll have to ignore the fast road in the foreground. Devoted to tea, it has 15 types of loose leaf including the Flora Tea whose petals unfurl in the cup. Excellent barista coffee is also served alongside cakes, cheese scones, sandwiches and delicious homemade quiches.

There's plenty of free parking outside and dogs are welcome inside on leads.

Opening hours
Mon-Sat 10am-5pm
Sun & Bank Hols 10am-4pm

Malt House Emporium, Unit 2, Tewkesbury Retail Park, Northway Gate, Ashchurch GL20 8JP
WWW.MALTHOUSEEMPORIUM.COM   01684 423150

Central Cross Café (In the Park)

JUNCTION: 10; 11 MINUTES

Wide open spaces, lakes to walk around and an enormous adventure playground (complete with rabbits, guinea pigs, chipmunks, duck pond and an aviary); it's well worth zipping off at Cheltenham to drop into Pittville Park. Central Cross Café, an award-winning neighbourhood haunt from 'In the Park', has adopted an old Victorian park pavilion – green and white timbers, ornate fascia boards and blooming floral displays – and sells scrummy fair-trade coffee, hot chocolate, freshly baked cakes, breakfast rolls, pastries, salads and sandwiches.

Free blankets are slung over the outside chairs in winter and you can borrow a picnic blanket in summer. There are newspapers to read and pick-and-mix biscuits for dogs. A smaller Kiosk by the play area sells hot drinks, ice creams, cakes, and lunch boxes for kids; a third, The Boathouse, is nestled by the lower lake and has indoor seating – you can hire a boat out in the summer. The cafés are firmly linked to their green environment so packaging is 100% compostable and cardboard and plastic is recycled. Parking is free for up to four hours.

Opening hours
Mon-Fri 8.30am-4pm
Sat-Sun 9am-4pm

Central Cross Café (In the Park), Central Cross Drive, Cheltenham GL52 2DX
WWW.INTHEPARK.CO.UK   01242 234907

Gloucester Services

JUNCTION: 11A-12; 0 MINUTES

The latest in Westmorland's quiet motorway service revolution, this is a purpose-built Farmshop & Kitchen that blends in with its surroundings: natural stone walls, rugged landscaping and a grass roof over the timber-vaulted main building. A remarkable place.

Step inside the atrium to meet counters heaving with sandwiches, pies, stews, pastries, cakes and the reassuring burr of a barista coffee machine. All the produce is locally sourced – they work with over 130 producers within 30 miles of the services. Enormous scrubbed tree trunks hanging overhead in a unique light underscore the Westmorland family's connection to the land. Seating overlooks a tranquil nature reserve and pond area, plus there's a rustic play area.

The Farmshop flanking the café on either side is impressive: from wild-boar pies on the deli counter to wooden spinning tops, heavenly macarons and enamelware. Forget petrol station flowers: this is the place to get emergency gifts.

Opening hours
Mon–Sun 24 hours

Gloucester Services, Brookthorpe, Gloucester GL4 0DN
WWW.GLOUCESTERSERVICES.COM   01452 813254

Wotton Farm Shop

JUNCTION: 14; 10 MINUTES

You won't regret breaking the journey for this prince among farm shops, outside which fuzzy-headed Bantam chickens scratch around in their pen, like little Cossacks. In spring you can buy an award-winning hanging basket; in summer, punnets of soft fruit from the farm's own fields.

The farm shop is a treasure trove: tayberry jam, Cotswold vegetables, local onion relish, a deli counter filled with pâtés, cooked meats, cheese, scrumptious frozen meals (no one need know) and posies of fresh flowers. The stack of ceramics, garden gifts and country homewares are expertly selected too; you will come away with a bag full of loot.

In the newly built café you can settle down to hillside views and food fresh from the farm kitchen: thick-cut bacon sandwiches, filled baguettes, jacket potatoes, quiches, sandwiches and cream teas. Mouthwatering cakes are carved in generous hunks; try the millionaire's shortbread or coffee and walnut cake.

Opening hours
Mon-Sat 9am-5.30pm
Sun 10am-4pm

Wotton Farm Shop, Bradley Road, Wotton-under-edge GL12 7DT
WWW.WOTTONFARMSHOP.CO.UK   01453 521546

Hawkes House

JUNCTION: 14; 10 MINUTES

An affable café-bar marooned in a 1960s shopping precinct in the thriving market town of Thornbury. Drop in here to enjoy the gentle murmur of gossip and live music, or kick back with the heaps of books and games.

The mottled stone building opened in 1859 as an off-licence and enjoyed a long spell as a pub before its reinvention as a community café. Owners James and Simon have played to its traditional roots, preserving the exposed stone walls, arching beamed ceilings and cosy nooks.

Food is fresh and delicious, the cake cabinet piled high. All-day brunch includes American pancake stacks, one-pan wonders and sourdough sausage sandwiches. The rest of the menu changes seasonally, but might include pork and apricot meatballs with tzatziki or a vegetable burger topped with avocado and baba ganoush. If you're here early, try the breakfast bowl, stuffed with fruit and homemade granola.

Opening hours
Mon–Sun 8.30am–11pm

Hawkes House, St Mary's Street, Thornbury BS35 2AB
WWW.HAWKESHOUSE.CO.UK   01454 417621

Papilio at Heritage

JUNCTION: 15; 9 MINUTES

M5

Spin across the Severn's flood plain to the traditional town of Thornbury with higgledy-piggledy roof lines, cascading floral displays and a castle where Henry VIII once stayed with his queen, Anne Boleyn.

Among the town's cafés and pubs, Papilio at Heritage is one of our favourites. The shop and café were badly damaged by fire in 2015, but have emerged like a phoenix from the flames under the guidance of owner, Tabi, who you'll often find cheerily serving customers.

Wander through the beautifully stocked gift shop to a modern, light-drenched café with views onto a grassy garden where children can safely let off steam. Parents can delve into baskets of toys and books to keep little ones entertained, while grown-ups can pause over the newspapers and magazines with a light lunch or afternoon tea. Borrow a blanket to make the most of the fresh air, even on chillier days.

Opening hours
Mon–Sat 9am–5.30pm

Papilio at Heritage, 24 High Street, Thornbury BS35 2AH
WWW.PAPILIOATHERITAGE.CO.UK   01454 415096

CAFÉ

Morgans Coffee House

JUNCTION: 18; 5 MINUTES

A cosy little hideaway in the arches, Morgans Coffee House is tucked away beneath Kings Weston House, a Grade I-listed mansion and little-known gem at the edge of Bristol. Completed in 1719 it was designed by Sir John Vanbrugh who also sketched Blenheim Palace.

Food is hearty – warming soups, delicious quiches, light bites and fantastic homemade cakes – and the atmosphere cosy. It's a haven for those travelling with dogs and kids. Original flagstones on the floor and colourfully tiled walls mean that dogs are welcome (on leads) to join their owners by the wood burners, and the house is ringed with acres of woodland and gardens, making for respectable leg stretches.

Don't miss the Compass Dial at Penpole Point (an ancient shipping marker used to navigate safely into the Avon) and Lodge gatehouse. A lawn overlooks the Severn and Avonmouth's port and is ideal for games and letting off steam. Parking is free and fairly abundant.

Opening hours
Mon-Fri 9am-4pm
Sat-Sun 9am-4.30pm

Morgans Coffee House, Kings Weston House, Kings Weston Lane BS11 0UR
07954 324043

The Battleaxes

JUNCTION: 19; 9 MINUTES

Cosy country pubs aren't hard to find in Somerset, but The Battleaxes is special for its mock Tudor gables and imposing roadside position. Just south of Bristol its soaring gothic roofline echoes that of its grander neighbour, Tyntesfield; indeed, it was originally the social club for the workers on that estate.

Still a very sociable spot, The Battleaxes' interior is now countryside chic – scrubbed wooden tables, slouchy leather chairs, patterned wallpaper and gilded portraits. It's cavernous too, with plenty of nooks to settle into. Striped deck chairs and white iron tables fill the lawn in summer.

Food is made from local produce: expect imaginative bistro and pub dishes such as ale battered cod and triple cooked chips, wild mushroom and baby spinach cobbler or slow cooked venison with suet pudding and pumpkin purée. Sunday lunches here have long been a neighbourhood mainstay.

Opening hours
Sun-Thurs 8am-9pm
Fri-Sat 8am-10pm

The Battleaxes, Bristol Road, Wraxall BS48 1LQ
WWW.FLATCAPPERS.CO.UK/THE-BATTLEAXES/   01275 857473

RESTAURANT-DELI

Murrays of Clevedon

JUNCTION: 20; 5 MINUTES

Standing proudly on Hill Road and close to Clevedon's graceful Victorian pier (itself worth a visit especially for sunset), Murrays is a food emporium dedicated to the best produce that Britain and Italy can offer. Restaurant, delicatessen, artisan bakery and Italian wine shop rolled into one, it has become as much a community hub as a foodie destination, and John's Italian roots shine through in the cured meats, cheeses, anchovies, olive oil, balsamic vinegars and Amalfi lemons as well as friendly conversation.

The restaurant serves seasonal dishes lovingly made from fresh ingredients: chicken and artichoke rillette terrine, capellini with Cornish crab and fennel, slow braised beef neck. The hummus and freshly baked bread are famous, but whatever you do don't miss the Parma ham and cremini mushroom lasagne.

Parking can be a little tight in town so not one for a whistlestop.

Opening hours
Tues-Sat 9am-5pm (Deli)
Tues-Sat 9am-9pm last orders (Restaurant)

Murrays of Clevedon, 91-93 Hill Road, Clevedon BS21 7PN
WWW.MURRAYSOFCLEVEDON.CO.UK   01275 341222

67 Barista Barber

JUNCTION: 20; 2 MINUTES

It's a unique combination, a barber and a coffee shop, but owner Sue Cooper wanted to set up something a little different in her home town when she retired. As a result, 67 Barista Barber is overflowing with personality, from the retro furniture rescued from reclamation yards to the changing art exhibitions on the walls. Enormous windows framed by the darkest deep blue exterior are perfect for people watching as crowds mill in and out of Hill Road's trendy boutiques. It's a great refuelling stop after a walk along the seafront with its Victorian pier and bandstand.

The laid-back atmosphere means 'queuing was never this easy or enjoyable!' in the words of one customer, and we're inclined to agree. Whether or not you're in the market for a haircut, the coffee is excellent (fair-trade and sourced from Devon roastery, Voyager) and Sue's homemade cakes widely praised. It's dinky but delightful and one of the best spots in town.

Opening hours
Mon, Tues, Wed, Fri 8am-5pm
Thurs 8am-6pm
Sat 8am-3pm

67 Barista Barber, 67 Hill Road, Clevedon BS21 7RR
01275 217740

One of the best local food shops in Somerset, Brockley Stores started life 80 years ago as a roadside stall selling fruit and veg straight form the surrounding fields. Still very much wedded to the same ethos of fresh, local food – 'grown not flown', as they put it – the store is frequented as much by locals as tourists making the trip for the Brockley's delicious range.

Luxuriant bouquets from Kimberley's the Florist sit alongside crates of crisp fruit and vegetables, from peaty potatoes to rosy apples and crimson rhubarb harvested by candlelight, depending on the season. Fresh coffee from local roastery Extract is on sale at the door and the smell of baking wafts over the shop as the ovens are put hard to work creating Brockley Stores' praised goodies, with quiches and pies held in particularly high esteem.

There's a dedicated al fresco picnic area outside for lingering and plenty of gorgeous countryside on the doorstep for a leg-stretch.

Opening hours
Mon-Sat 8am-6pm
Sun 9am-5.30pm

Brockley Stores, Main Road, Brockley BS48 3AT
WWW.BROCKLEYSTORES.CO.UK   01275 462 753

The Ethicurean

JUNCTION: 22; 15 MINUTES

15-minutes' drive from the motorway, the Ethicurean is one of our longest detours but it's worth it. The relaxed restaurant and café is set in the former kitchen garden and tastefully refurbished glasshouse of grand Victorian residence Barley Wood – now separated by the road – with sweeping views towards the fern-mottled Mendips.

Guided by the the natural cycle of the garden, they celebrate the local soil and much of the food on offer is freshly plucked – with a corresponding focus on vegetables – and transformed into an imaginative array of dishes. For those who crave pasture-reared meat and sustainable seafood, there are dishes designed to compliment. Drop in for coffee and cake and you'll be treated to delights such as parsnip, white chocolate and coconut cake from the daily changing menu. Linger for longer and you can lunch on small plates, or dine on more substantial feasts and renowned Sunday lunches (be sure to book in advance). Informal and friendly, there's parking on site and kids are safe to trundle around within the walled gardens. A touch pricey, but well worth it.

Opening hours
Tues-Thurs 11am-11pm
Fri-Sat 10am-11pm
Sun 10am-5pm

The Ethicurean, Long Lane, Wrington BS40 5SA
WWW.THEETHICUREAN.COM   01934 863713

PUB

The Railway Inn

JUNCTION: 21; 10 MINUTES

For that authentic Somerset pub experience, few establishments can rival The Railway, a newly renovated pub that's frequented by M5 travellers (especially those on their way to or from Bristol airport) and immensely popular with locals too.

The garden courtyard is strewn with places to sit and chat, and cosy log burners under impressive timber beams corral guests in on frosty evenings - truly, a pub for all seasons.

The Thatchers Brewery is right next door (you can even see the cider mill from the garden) and the pub takes full advantage. Culinary classics like fish and chips are coated in cider batter, and sharing platters such as the Somerset charcuterie offer savoury nibbles with their very own Cider chutney to top it off.

If it's a flying visit, the coffee is second to none, but the elegant glassed dining area will likely tempt you to book for dinner on your next visit.

Opening hours
Mon-Sat 10am-11pm
Sun 10.30am-10.30pm

The Railway Inn, Station Road, Sandford BS25 5RA
WWW.THERAILWAYINN.COM   01934 611518

Bleadon Farm Shop

JUNCTION: 22; 10 MINUTES

A lovely farm shop and café in an old stone barn across the road from the village croquet green. Zoe is the energetic driving force behind the hub, priding herself on a cheerful atmosphere and hearty, satisfying food. Breakfasts are the toast of the town, sandwiches are freshly made, the coffee is smooth, tea is served in pots and cakes are baked in the kitchen, from classic Victoria sponge to fresh cream buns jewelled with strawberries.

Tables and chairs are set out at the front on sunny days (frequently occupied by cyclists, often a herald of good baking) and there is plenty of space inside when the weather is less kind.

The sandy beaches of Brean and Weston-super-Mare are within easy reach if children and pets need to run and play, and the blustery walk up to the headland at Brean Down is memorable. Pick up some tasty Somerset produce to take on your way from the pint-sized farm shop and post office next door.

Opening hours
Mon–Sat 9am–3pm

Bleadon Farm Shop, Purn Way, Bleadon BS24 0QE
WWW.BLEADONCAFE.CO.UK   01934 814339

PUB

The Swan, Wedmore

JUNCTION: 22; 15 MINUTES

An 18th-century beer house turned coaching inn, The Swan was refurbished by new owners in 2014 to become a much-loved village pub. Locals throng in the open-plan bar with its crackling fires, cosy corners and flagstone floors. In a sunny lounge with overstuffed chairs and a wood-burner you can kick back and tuck into the cake stand and all-day snack menu. Sundays are dedicated to lazy roasts, newspapers and Bloody Marys.

The menu changes regularly, inspired by chef Tom Blake's River Cottage training and fresh ingredients from the market – eggs from Burnham-on-Sea, fish from Bridport, meat from the local butcher's own herd. Loaves of bread are baked here, served with dinner and available to take away too. In summer, chefs make the most of a wood-burning oven and smoker in the lawned garden. Dogs are welcome in the bar area and there are some fabulous walks nearby on the Somerset Levels and around Cheddar Gorge.

Opening hours
Mon–Sun 9am–11pm

The Swan, Wedmore, Cheddar Road, Wedmore BS28 4EQ
WWW.THESWANWEDMORE.COM   01934 710337

Pyne's of Somerset

JUNCTION: 24; 4 MINUTES

Minutes from the motorway, Pyne's is a cracking farm shop and café serving exceptional food – fast. The steady stream of van drivers is testament to the melt-in-your-mouth breakfast rolls, proper pastries and unique roast-dinner-in-a-box. It's all available to take away, along with good coffee, or you can stop for a break at the farmhouse tables.

Sprightly Malcolm Pyne is in charge, together with his wife Julie. One in a long line of butchers, you can't miss him behind the counter sporting his trademark mutton chops whiskers and a bowler hat. There's nothing he doesn't know about the perfect cut and he is uncompromising when it comes to animal welfare, sourcing only from known local farmers. The in-house sausages change frequently and are deservedly described as legendary.

The farm shop showcases some of Somerset's best food, so you can fill your shopping bags from the cheese, fish and meat counters, or load up on locally-blended tea, veg and cider.

Opening hours
Mon-Weds, Fri 7.30am-5.30pm
Thurs 7.30am-6pm (Sat 5pm)
(take-away times vary)

Pyne's of Somerset, Market Way Regional Rural Business Centre, North Petherton TA6 6DF
WWW.PYNETHEBUTCHER.CO.UK   01278 663050

ATTRACTION

Hestercombe House & Gardens

JUNCTION: 25; 14 MINUTES

These magnificent 50 acres of garden, and the house, were a neglected secret for years after the last war. All is now in the benign hands of the Hestercombe Trust.

Stroll through three centuries of design: the Victorian Shrubbery, the Georgian Landscape Garden and the Edwardian Formal Gardens. The Great Cascade is a main feature and you feel your motorway strain subside as you gaze over one of the two great ponds. There is more: a Dutch Garden and Sir Edwin Lutyens' Daisy Steps and impressive Orangery. He also created the Rose Garden and collaborated with Gertrude Jekyll on some of the groundbreaking designs. This is as much a garden for gardeners as for those who just enjoy looking and strolling.

Dine in the refined Column Room, renowned for its traditional and champagne afternoon teas or eat more casually in the charming Stables Café. You can make use of the café without paying to enter the gardens.

Opening hours
Mon–Sun 10am–5pm

Hestercombe House & Gardens, Cheddon Fitzpaine, Taunton TA2 8LG
WWW.HESTERCOMBE.COM   01823 413923

The Hatch Inn

JUNCTION: 25; 7 MINUTES

It is rare to find such a delightful family-owned pub so close to the motorway. You walk in to an immediate sense of welcome. On a cold day the open fire will warm your cockles; on a warm one you can sit outside and admire the scenery of the Blackdown Hills.

An old 18th-century coaching inn, The Hatch has had love and commitment poured into it, the rustic charm nurtured and improved. The welcome is real, the food traditional and delicious, the atmosphere cosy and friendly. If you are in luck there will be something special happening, for the pub is at the centre of things locally.

You may even want to plan your journey to spend the evening and night here. The rooms are perfect and for dinner you might have, for example, rack of lamb, homemade 'proper' pie or fresh fish, which is delivered daily. Breakfast, with local meats and breads, is equally generous, and the Sunday roasts have the best cuts of meat and roast potatoes for miles around. The Hatch is a destination in itself.

Opening hours
Mon 5pm-11pm
Tues-Thurs noon-3pm, 5pm-11pm
Fri-Sat noon-11pm (Sun 5pm)

Ⓥ Ⓟ

The Hatch Inn, Hatch Beauchamp TA3 6SG
WWW.THEHATCHINN.CO.UK   01823 480245

Rumwell Farm Shop

JUNCTION: 26; 5 MINUTES

Like all the best farm shops, Rumwell started life as a small stall selling potatoes and free-range eggs at the farm gate. How times have changed, although it is still family-run.

Today the expansive shop has a well-stocked food hall, butchery, bakery and deli where you can pick up practically anything you want, much of it produced in Somerset. The farm's sausages (which you can sometimes see being made) use meat from home-reared pigs, while the Jam Kitchen is busy year round making jams, chutneys, fudge and Christmas puddings. If you're not sure where to start, just ask one of the smartly dressed staff for recommendations, and if you're conscious about single-use plastics you're welcome to bring your own containers. Try the semi-skimmed and whole milk from the milk vending machine for the ultimate in creamy coffees.

Visitors to the café can enjoy magnificent views of the countryside from its panoramic windows, as well as tasty homemade breakfasts, lunches and afternoon teas. And you can eat outside if weather permits.

There's an impressive playground alongside, with a climbing frame, sand pit and ride-on tractors that should keep little ones entertained.

Opening hours
Mon-Fri 9am-5.30pm
Sat 8.30am-5pm
Sun and Bank Hols 10am-4pm

Rumwell Farm Shop, Wellington Road, Rumwell TA4 1EJ
WWW.RUMWELLFARMSHOP.COM   01823 461599

Sheppy's Farmshop

JUNCTION: 24; 4 MINUTES

The Sheppy family have been pressing apples here for over two hundred years and the orchard is now under the care of David, a sixth generation 'Master of Cider'. Inside, the modern and rustic décor pays homage to the farm's long history of apple growing.

At The Apple Bay restaurant the menu is stacked with all things Somerset, such as in-house butchered sausages with caramelised onion gravy and cider battered fish and chips. If you fancy something lighter, the grilled goats cheese salad won't disappoint. This is artisan cooking at reasonable prices, and you can buy some of the ingredients in the farm shop, which may reel you in with its fresh greens, high quality meats and vast cheese counter.

If you can spare an hour, and have a (selfless) designated driver, hop on a tour of the orchard, see the apples go from branch to barrel and sample the excellent product en route. Take a quick look at the farm museum while the kids have fun in the play area.

Opening hours
Mon-Sat 9am-5.30pm
Sun 10am-4pm

Sheppy's Farmshop, Three Bridges, Bradford-on-Tone TA4 1ER
WWW.SHEPPYSCIDER.COM   01823 461233

CAFÉ

White Post Café

JUNCTION: 26; 12 MINUTES

Music hums gently but otherwise the only sounds here are the rush of wind through the corn and birds twittering in the trees. White Post Cafe is housed in a Scandi-style wood cabin in the middle of the successful plant nursery of the same name. It's a great stop year-round - idyllic views over to the Blackdown Hills on a summer afternoon, and a roaring log fire to settle next to in winter. If the M5 has your nerves jangling there are few better places to unwind.

The menu changes every month or so with the seasons and has a set brunch menu at weekends. Produce is supplied by the wonderful farms and growers of Somerset and stops are perfectly complemented by freshly baked cakes, locally roasted coffee and loose leaf tea. Don't blame us if you're late home.

Opening hours
Tues-Sat 9.30am-5 pm

White Post Café, Langford Budville, Wellington TA21 0RW
WWW.WHITEPOSTCAFE.CO.UK   01823 400322

Culm Valley Inn

JUNCTION: 27; 9 MINUTES

Standing alongside the river Culm, which is spanned by a low, multi-arched, stone bridge and fringed with grassy banks, the Culm Valley Inn feels quintessentially English. Yet the dodo logo and totem pole at the entrance to the car park tell another story.

The low-ceiling country pub combines old-world charm with trendy, left-field accessories. Walls painted a deep, cosy grey accommodate photo galleries, sculpture and taxidermy from antiques dealer and sister company, Stag and Squire. A sunny bay window has become a merry space for large parties; chairs are mismatched, fires open and tables decorated with fresh flowers.

Specials chalked on the board above the fireplace might include venison scotch eggs, spiced cauliflower soup, prawn and mussel curry, or an exotic avocado, peanut and coriander salad. It's still a village pub though, so dogs and kids are welcome and footpaths take you from the door for a turn in the countryside.

Opening hours
Mon-Thurs noon-3pm 5-11pm
Fri-Sun noon-11pm

Culm Valley Inn, The Riverside, Culmstock EX153JJ
WWW.THECULMVALLEYINN.CO.UK   01884 840354

CAFÉ

No. 11 Coffee

JUNCTION: 27; 4 MINUTES

You'll see No.11's handsome shop front – large windows painted a soft shade of sage – standing on Uffculme's village green. Inside, the décor is straightforward and minimalistic, with dark grey church chairs and wooden tables set against white walls. It's a friendly village coffee shop, where the service comes unfailingly with a smile and the coffee is both Fairtrade and excellent. Owner Ian is uncompromising when it comes to food quality, serving delicious cooked breakfasts and then ciabatta (maybe brie and bacon) and fresh soup for lunch. You can fill the gap with homemade cakes, savoury tarts served with crisp salads, filling soups and even an ice cream (the apricot is scrummy) for a sweet bite. Gluten-free diners are well looked after too.

Take time to explore riverside footpaths by the Culm before you head on your way; Coldharbour Mill on the riverbank is one of the UK's oldest woollen mills, part of the UK's industrial revolution in the 18th century.

Opening hours
Mon–Fri 9am–4.30pm
Sat 9am–2.30pm

No. 11 Coffee, The Square, Uffculme EX15 3AA
WWW.NO11COFFEE.CO.UK   01884 842542

The Bakehouse

JUNCTION: 28; 2 MINUTES

Once Cullompton's family grocer as the original signwork still proclaims, the Bakehouse is now a fabulous café and bistro just minutes from the motorway. Painted bright teal with bottle green tiles and a mosaic entrance, it's an eye-catching addition to the High Street. Inside, there's a homely collection of antique furniture with a large serving hub in the centre, buzzing with life and stacked with teetering cakes; the vegan sticky ginger cake is delicious. A corridor at the back opens up into another room where a wood burner crackles against the bare brick walls and broad windows in cooler months. It gives on to a narrow, flower-dressed courtyard for soaking up the sun over a latte.

Breakfast is served until 11.30am. Lunch is a simple and scrummy with soup and salads or homemade burgers or daily specials for a bigger bite. In the evenings, the fairylights glimmer into life and the café becomes a bistro serving dishes such as duck confit, spicy meatballs, antipasti and meze platters; Wednesday is Italian night with pizza, pasta and weekly-changing specials.

Opening hours
Mon-Sat 9am-5pm (café)
Weds-Sat 6pm-10pm (bistro)

The Bakehouse, 3 High Street, Cullompton EX15 1AB
WWW.THEBAKEHOUSECULLOMPTON.CO.UK   01884 35222

Darts Farm

JUNCTION: 30; 5 MINUTES

© Matt Austin

Darts Farm has become a well-known food hub, but the farm is always at the heart of the business. Links to the soil are still strong, and the family's herd of Ruby Red Devon cattle graze on the banks of the nearby river Clyst. The shop makes the most of its location on the Exe estuary, and you can reconnect with nature by visiting the animals, wending your way through the vegetable fields on the farm walk, or wildlife spotting in the hideout overlooking the wetlands.

Inside, every corner of the large shop is filled with goodies, all reared, caught or made locally. The food hall is stacked with various colourful veggies, deli goods and storecupboard essentials, and the butchers have a great reputation. Pick up a ready-prepared beef Wellington for a gourmet meal on arrival at your destination.

Follow your nose and the waft of freshly ground coffee will lead you to the restaurant, with tables inside and out making the most of views. Ingredients come from the food hall and are conjured into delicious meals, perhaps pan-fried sea bass, charcuterie platters or a traditional Devonshire cream team. For food in a hurry, the Fish Shed does great fish and chips.

Opening hours
Mon-Sat 8am-7pm (restaurant 6pm)
Sun 9.30am-4.30pm (restaurant 4pm)

Darts Farm, Topsham EX3 0QH
WWW.DARTSFARM.CO.UK   01392 878200

The Puffing Billy

JUNCTION: 30; 8 MINUTES

The Puffing Billy is a relaxed country pub just beyond the end of the M5 at Topsham. It's more of an eatery than a pub (though that shouldn't stop you popping in to sup a pint at the bar, or grabbing a coffee by the wood burner), so make time stop and sample the seasonal, local dishes in the stylish dining room. The chicken and chorizo terrine with piccalilli is a favourite, along with River Teign mussels, spiced cauliflower and spinach and lentil pie. The Sunday roasts are particularly popular.

Staff are polite and smiley and do their best to keep plates flowing to the often-busy tables.

If you need to take a walk after your meal, the Exe Estuary trail passes right by the door. There's some wonderful wildlife to spot on the riverbanks and marshland.

As for the pub's name, it's shared with the world's oldest surviving steam locomotive, a fantastically elaborate, riveted machine that's well worth looking up for some in-car trivia.

Opening hours
Mon-Sat 11am-11pm
Sun 11am-10.30pm

The Puffing Billy, Station Road, Topsham EX3 0TR
WWW.THEPUFFINGBILLY.CO.UK   01392 877888

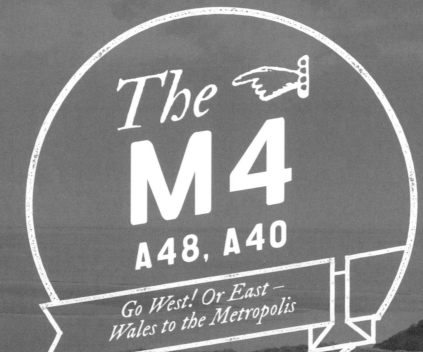

The
M4
A48, A40

Go West! Or East —
Wales to the Metropolis

M4 EAST

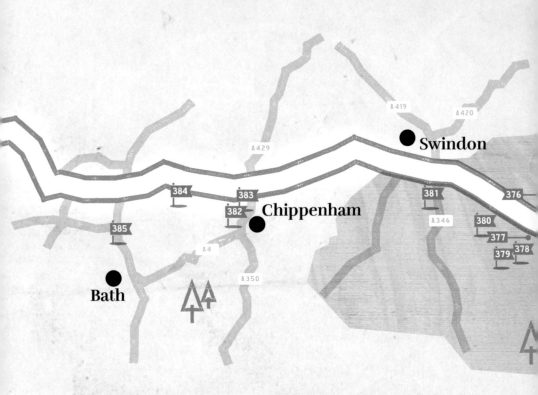

Swindon

Chippenham

Bath

A419
A420
A429
384
383
382
385
381
376
A346
380
377
A4
379 378
A350

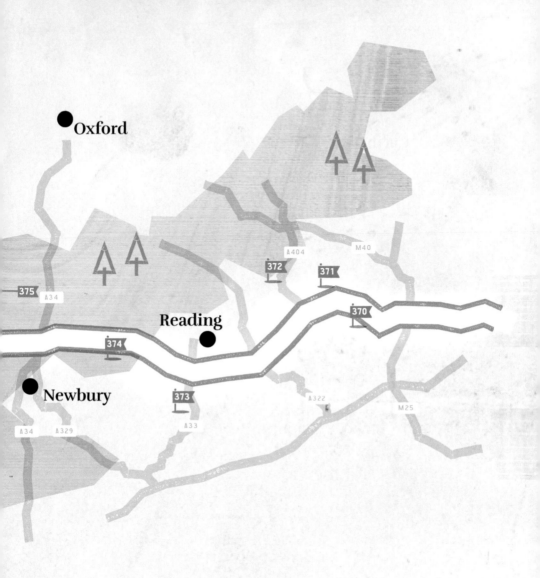

Oxford

Reading

Newbury

370 Crocus at Dorney Court Café
371 The Crown at Bray
372 Stubbings
373 Wellington Farm Shop
374 Cobbs at Englefield
375 Saddleback Farm Shop

376 The Pheasant
377 The Tally Ho
378 The Garden Room Café
     (Libby Blakey Design)
379 Cobbs Farm Shop & Kitchen
380 The Bell at Ramsbury

381 Three Trees
     Farm Shop & Café
382 Allington Farm Shop & Café
383 Folly Row Café
384 Old Stables Coffee Shop
385 The Tollgate

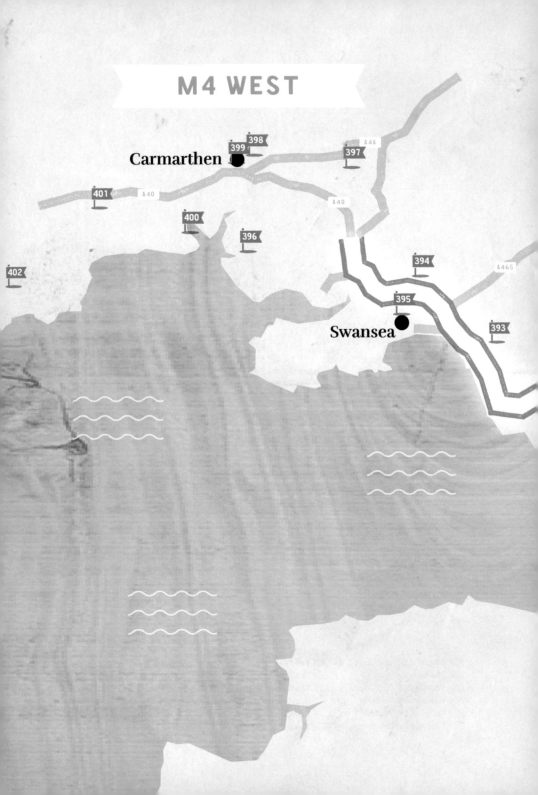

M4 WEST

Carmarthen

Swansea

401 A40 399 398 397 A48 402 400 396 A40 394 A465 395 393

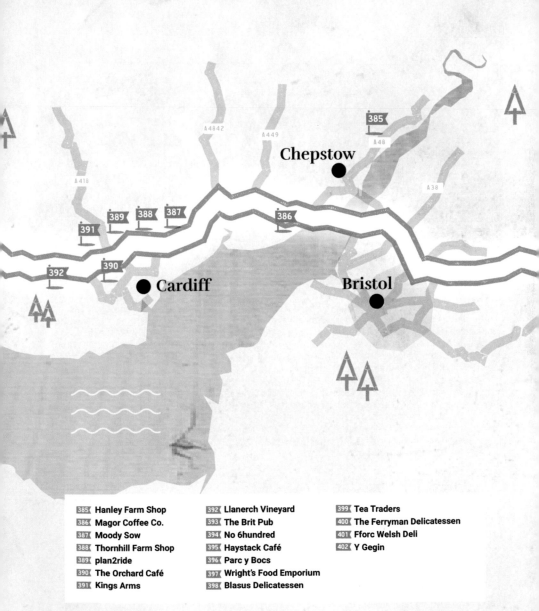

Chepstow

Cardiff

Bristol

385	Hanley Farm Shop	392	Llanerch Vineyard	399	Tea Traders
386	Magor Coffee Co.	393	The Brit Pub	400	The Ferryman Delicatessen
387	Moody Sow	394	No 6hundred	401	Fforc Welsh Deli
388	Thornhill Farm Shop	395	Haystack Café	402	Y Gegin
389	plan2ride	396	Parc y Bocs		
390	The Orchard Café	397	Wright's Food Emporium		
391	Kings Arms	398	Blasus Delicatessen		

Crocus at Dorney Court Café

JUNCTION: 7; 5 MINUTES

This gorgeous walled garden near Eton plays host to a garden centre that transforms the idea of a local garden centre into a celebration of flora and nature, often featuring difficult-to-find plants. As the name suggests, this was once the kitchen garden that supplied the manor house at Dorney with fresh fruit, vegetables and flowers and is even rumoured to be the place where England's first pineapple was grown. For eco-friendly growing supplies, covetable home and garden décor and gifts from around the world, you need look no further than the well-stocked shop.

Basket filled, head for the newly revamped café. It's filled with restful greenery and serves wholesome seasonal produce, delicious cakes and afternoon teas, all made in the kitchen. You'll often rub shoulders with rowers, triathletes and supporters on the hunt for fuel from Dorney Olympic rowing lake nearby. There's plenty of seating in the modern, oak-beamed café but when the sun shines, make the most of the shady garden with its large play area, featuring a Wendy house and a fort for lively little warriors.

Opening hours
Spring & Summer – Mon-Sun 9am-5.30pm (café 5pm)
Autumn & Winter – Mon-Sun 9am-5pm

Crocus at Dorney Court Café, Dorney Court, Windsor SL4 6QP
WWW.CROCUS.CO.UK/DORNEY-COURT   01628 669999

The Crown at Bray

JUNCTION: A308M; 4 MINUTES

Heston Blumenthal's foray into pubs has been a riotous success, combining atmospheric, chic country surroundings with Heston's much-celebrated flair for food. The Crown has an old world feel to it – dark wood bar, brass ornaments, low timbered ceilings and the scent of open fires: rumour has it that Charles II would call in for a drink here while visiting his mistress – but has been flawlessly updated. In summer, you can spill out into the newly landscaped garden, sheltered from any breezes by high brick walls.

Food is excellent – pub food done well. Options might include pastrami and smoked cheese burger, steak with marrowbone sauce, crispy cauliflower cheese or beer-battered fish and chips (sometimes available to take away). Save space for the signature spit roasted pineapple sundae with salted caramel when the BBQ is fired up, or sticky toffee pudding in winter. It's mid-way between Reading and London so a perfect pit stop if you're meeting relatives in the middle, or if you're running early for Heathrow.

Opening hours
Mon-Sat 11.30am-11pm
Sun 11.30am-10.30pm

The Crown at Bray, High Street, Bray SL6 2AH
WWW.THECROWNATBRAY.COM   01628 621936

If you manage to survive (or need to prepare yourself for) the Reading traffic, the lovely Stubbings nursery provides respite.

The café is a recent addition to the established family-run nursery, housed in a new glasshouse which takes full advantage of the 18th-century, Grade-II listed walled garden alongside. Take a table by the window to watch the wildlife in the beautifully tended garden as you fill up on tasty local food, from grilled breakfasts to soups, quiches, jacket potatoes and sandwiches. The freshly made scones are especially recommended. If you're travelling on a Wednesday, Thursday or Friday, book ahead and you can have Afternoon Tea with fresh patisserie treats. Dogs and their owners are welcome on the covered south-facing decking, set with colourful tables and decorated with bunting.

Musically, as well as horticulturally, talented, the family sometimes run a short opera summer season and have also recently hosted productions of Shakespeare and outdoor cinema events. The private grounds of Stubbings House are opened up for charity on a number of weekends – see website for details.

Mon-Sat 8.30am-4.30pm
Sun 9.30am-4pm

Stubbings, Stubbings Estate, Stubbings Lane, Maidenhead SL6 6QL
WWW.STUBBINGSNURSERY.CO.UK   01628 825454

Wellington Farm Shop

JUNCTION: 11; 8 MINUTES

© Milly Fletcher

© Milly Fletcher

© Milly Fletcher

If the kitchen is the heart of the home, the Wellington Farm Shop is the centre of the Wellington Estate, a secret tract of Berkshire with glorious views. The shop sells all the best produce from the area, so you can fill your basket with locally farmed vegetables, honey from the estate's hives, and lamb or Hereford beef from the fields in season. And it's not just food: treat yourself from the range of home, garden and beauty products too.

In the café, wholesome dishes made with the shop's own produce are ferried to rustic wooden tables from breakfast to late lunch (don't miss the award-winning sausages in the Wellington breakfast). Bag a slouchy leather couch and unwind with a slice of cake if the Reading traffic has left you frazzled.

The farm shop is ringed with paddocks – home to rare breed sheep, pigs and cows – and there's a fantastic tree house play area where the children can let off steam.

If you're in a hurry, the takeaway menu is more than a cut above. Look online and call ahead and their hot club sandwich (a firm favourite) could be waiting for you to whisk away.

Opening hours
Mon-Sat 8.30am-5.30pm (café 4.30pm)
Sun 8.30am-4pm (café 3.30pm)

Wellington Farm Shop, Welsh Lane, Heckfield RG27 0LT
WWW.WELLINGTONFARMSHOP.CO.UK   0118 932 6132

FARM SHOP

Cobbs at Englefield

JUNCTION: 12; 2 MINUTES

Cobbs at Englefield is a popular farm shop and delicatessen at the edge of Englefield Estate, between Theale and Pangbourne. A series of converted cow sheds form an incredible spaces with farm shop, delicatessen, traditional butchery counter, florist as well as a café.

This cheerful establishment offers a fantastic array of food from local and British suppliers, including their own home-grown produce, when in season. It sells everything from fresh fruit and veg, eggs, honey and freshly-baked bread to biscuits, smoked fish, pies and juices. The butchery counter sources high-quality meat from farms whose standards of welfare meet their exacting standards; there's a friendly team of master butchers on hand to help you.

The fully licensed café serves food all day: stacked pancakes with streaky bacon and maple syrup for breakfast; home-made soup or quiche for lunch; or spoil yourself with an afternoon tea (perhaps with bubbles?!). If you're with your four-legged friend you are very welcome to dine on the terrace.

Opening hours
Mon-Sat 9am-6pm
Sun 10am-5pm
(Café closed one hour earlier than shop.)

Cobbs at Englefield, Wickcroft Farm, Pangbourne Road, Theale RG7 5EA
WWW.COBBSFARMSHOPS.CO.UK   0118 9304064

Saddleback Farm Shop

JUNCTION: 14; 12 MINUTES

You'll find Saddleback at the edge of the North Wessex Downs, housed in a converted piggery. Farmers Clare and David are enthusiasts of the field-to-fork philosophy and supply the farm shop with as much locally sourced produce as possible.

The café is snug and welcoming and the menu, like the shop, proudly local. Bunting hangs over scrubbed wooden tables and pew benches and from the sunny patio terrace you can enjoy the Berkshire hills rising to a copse on the brow, or watch the combine harvester at work in the fields. Kids can bowl about on the large lawn, visit the chickens and tire themselves out in the play house.

The countryside around is ripe for exploring so if you've got time before heading on, ask staff for a map and explore the nearby footpaths. If you call ahead, the kitchen will prepare you a picnic.

Opening hours
Mon-Sat 9am – 5.30pm
Sun & Bank Hol 9am – 4pm
Café closed 30 mins before shop

Saddleback Farm Shop, California Farm, Brightwalton RG20 7HR
WWW.SADDLEBACKFARMSHOP.CO.UK   01488 638806

PUB

The Pheasant

JUNCTION: 14; 1 MINUTE

A country home tableau – wicker dog basket, newspapers, enormous exotic flower arrangement, milk pail lamp and taxidermy pheasant – greets you as you step through the doors of this countrified, clapboard pub which was once an old sheep drover's inn.

In the seagrass-painted bar you'll find open fires and bookshelves, busts, feathers and knick-knacks, and a cosy nook furnished with trunks and leather furniture – ideal for both a competitive game of Scrabble and kicking back with a newspaper. It's popular with the horse-racing crowd, which you'll notice in the racing TV coverage often buzzing in the background.

Food is excellent and flavoursome; the restaurant suave and animated. Cheese boards and duck spring rolls are offered as bar snacks; Bloody Mary gazpacho is on the menu for starters; Cornish cod with red pepper coulis and chorizo, and Wiltshire sirloin with garlic butter among the mains.

Opening hours
Mon-Sat 11am-11pm
Sun noon-10.30pm

The Pheasant, Ermin Street, Shefford Woodlands RG17 7AA
WWW.THEPHEASANT-INN.CO.UK   01488 648284

The Tally Ho

JUNCTION: 14; 1 MINUTE

A handsome, red-gabled pub on the road to Hungerford. Spirited too, as it was threatened with closure in 2012, forcing a community consortium to gallop to the rescue and reinstate it at the heart of the community. As a result, the atmosphere is now one of mellow conviviality. There's a toy box of books and jigsaws for kids, dog biscuits on the bar for four-legged companions and a couple of shelves in the corner put to use as a teeny shop selling, well whatever happens to need selling: eggs, marrows, honey and trinkets. There also comfortable bedrooms if you plan to break your journey overnight.

Food is classic pub fare, generously portioned and made with tasty local ingredients, including some veg from shareholders' allotments. Expect overfilled baguettes or fish and chips for lunch, which you can enjoy on the sunny terrace. Succulent steak, sweet potato curry and honeyed ham with free-range eggs and chips are on the dinner menu.

Opening hours
Mon-Sun noon-11pm

The Tally Ho, Hungerford Newton RG17 0PP
WWW.THETALLYHOHUNGERFORD.CO.UK   01488 682 312

The Garden Room Café (Libby Blakey Design)

JUNCTION: 14; 6 MINUTES

In a sunny conservatory behind the dove grey shop front and hushed calm of Libby Blakey's interiors shop, you'll find the Garden Room Café. It's is achingly refined, a vision of glass-topped tables, grey wicker chairs, quirky ornaments and hip design books. In the garden Parisienne wire chairs and tables are softened with cushions and tablecloths, the perfect invitation to a coffee and rustle of the newspaper.

This is a spot for elevenses or light bites, so a petit menu offers croissants stuffed with Parma ham and Gruyere, smoked salmon, avocado and mascarpone on rye bread, and a soup of the day. Cakes are impossibly perfect: plump sponges topped with nectarine and mascarpone, or a dense, multi-layered honey cake with salted caramel, walnuts and pecans. The counter is dominated by an enormous Italian coffee machine pumping out rich, dark blends; shelves behind are stacked with loose leaf teas.

Opening hours
Tues-Sat 10am-5pm

The Garden Room Café-, Libby Blakey Design, 3 Bridge Street, Hungerford RG17 0EH
WWW.LIBBYBLAKEYDESIGN.COM 01488 647440

Cobbs Farm Shop & Kitchen

JUNCTION: 14; 7 MINUTES

A bone fide all-rounder, Cobbs Farm Shop has a butcher, fishmonger, delicatessen, florist, cheese counter – even a vineyard. The brightly lit shop has a country chic feel and scours the surrounds for the best local produce – cured meat, pork pies, salads, A-grade cuts of meat, all kinds of veg, and home-grown, Alder Ridge sparkling wine. You could do your weekly shop here and pick up gorgeous gifts at the same time, from handmade soap to ceramics and toys.

The chic café with leafy green plants, wooden tables and cream walls sells delicious breakfasts and lunches that vary from light bites to filling one-pot meals and caters for dietary needs with a seasonally changing menu showcasing homegrown produce.

Family fun is found in the pick-your-own fields, where you can pluck soft fruit in season, and kids will love the play barn, giant games and seasonal events such as pumpkin carving, open-air cinema and bird of prey displays.

Opening hours
Mon-Sat 9am-6pm
Sun 10am-5pm

Cobbs Farm Shop & Kitchen, Bath Road, Hungerford RG17 0SP
WWW.COBBSFARMSHOP.CO.UK   01488 686770

PUB

The Bell at Ramsbury

JUNCTION: 14/15; 13 MINUTES

The succour of this Georgian coaching inn, set at the edge of the Marlborough Downs, is not to be missed. The café, chic in shades of cream and sandstone, serves breakfast (organic sausages, free-range eggs, home-roasted coffee), lunch (toasties, home-cooked ham, egg and chips) and heavenly baking in the afternoon. Seasonal food in the tartan-upholstered restaurant will satisfy more substantial appetites: perhaps pea, lovage and courgette soup to start, mushrooms on toast to follow (don't underestimate these truffle-soaked lovelies) or pork loin with black kale and roast potatoes. Dessert might be a rhubarb and pear crumble with lavender ice cream.

Head chef Jonas notably uses ingredients from Ramsbury Estate, which is nearly all things to all men, with a brewery, distillery, oil press and smokehouse. Trout is cured in beetroot and the estate's vodka, partridge is smoked over beech. Much of the produce is grown in the kitchen garden at Priory Farm and tastes fantastic

Opening hours
Mon-Sat noon-11pm
Sun noon-10pm

The Bell at Ramsbury, The Square, Ramsbury SN8 2PE
WWW.THEBELLRAMSBURY.COM   01672 520230

Three Trees Farm Shop & Café

JUNCTION: 15; 2 MINUTES

Three Trees is a family-run, mixed farm housed on what was once the Chiseldon army camp. Take a pew in the airy café and you can idly watch sheep and cows chew the cud against the backdrop of Liddington Castle.

The coffee is strong and can be boosted with farm-fresh cream. Cakes are varied and home-baked – the cheese scones have a devoted following. Tasty meals and snacks, such as Welsh rarebit, sandwiches, chilli con carne and jacket potatoes, are crafted from ingredients that you can buy in the well-stocked shop. Much of the meat comes from the fields (which makes for unbeatable breakfast sausages), the rest from a community of local Wiltshire producers. You and your dog can eat outside on the decking if weather permits.

Pick up a sirloin for dinner at the onsite butchery, a bag of fudge for the journey, some Cotswold Lavender hand cream or a cheeky tipple of Ramsbury vodka.

Opening hours
Tues-Sat 9.30am-5.30pm (café 4.30pm)
Sun 10am-4pm
See website for opening times over Christmas

Three Trees Farm Shop & Café, The Ridgeway, Chiseldon SN4 0HT
WWW.THREETREESFARM.CO.UK   01793 741436

Allington Farm Shop & Café

JUNCTION: 17; 7 MINUTES

The shop at Allington Bar Farm is cavernous. A wood-clad building at the roadside with sacks of potatoes piled outside the door, it hosts a butchery, delicatessen, locally produced store cupboard essentials and speciality grocery items and a considered range of tasteful cards, gifts including bespoke hampers and toys. The Reynolds family have worked the 700-acre farm for three generations, using low-intensity techniques to raise cereals, potatoes, cattle, pigs and sheep, much of which is available as produce to buy in the shop.

The conservatory café throngs with people enjoying wholesome farm food. Breakfast on sausages and bacon or almond and pumpkin seed granola with fruit and yoghurt; try the chicken chorizo burger, vintage mature Cheddar ploughman's or baked goat cheese, bacon and toasted walnut salad for lunch. Milkshakes are made with real strawberries and cakes and desserts all crafted by their in house pastry chef. On sunny days, take advantage of the decked terrace or picnic in the glorious Wiltshire countryside.

Opening hours
Mon-Sat 9am-6pm (café 4.30pm, 5pm Sat)
Sun 9.30am-5pm (café 4pm)
Bank Hol 10am-4pm (café 3.30pm)

Allington Farm Shop & Café, Allington SN14 6LJ
WWW.ALLINGTONFARMSHOP.CO.UK   01249 658112

Folly Row Café

JUNCTION: 17; 4 MINUTES

Dinky but delightful, Folly Row is cuddled into the high street of Kington St Michael. Panelled walls are painted cream and blue and host local artwork this is a little treasure where stacked crates display vintage teapots, china teacups and various leaf tea and yummy cakes baked on the premises. The gluten free brownies come highly recommended as does their coffee cake.

Their window displays are the talk of the village and their memorable toilet with a baking theme is well worth a visit. Take advantage of the outside seating in the good weather or if sitting indoors, enjoy playing games or knitting while you wait for your food. Dogs on leads are very welcome and can get a treat and a drink on the house!

Opening hours
Weds-Sat 10am-4pm

Folly Row Café, 13 Kington St Michael, Kington St Michael, Chippenham SN14 6JB
WWW.FOLLYROWCAFE.COM   01249 750887

COFFEE SHOP

Old Stables Coffee Shop

JUNCTION: 17; 14 MINUTES

Castle Combe is criminally pretty, which is why it's awash with tour groups and selfie sticks. Don't be deterred; the beautiful sandstone village with appealing gabled houses (notice that TV aerials are banned) and an arched bridge spanning a river is worth the hype.

Few places are more welcoming for a recharge than the Old Stables Coffee Shop, just off the main street. It's a relaxed home from home: stone walls painted cream are hung with bright local art. Loaf around by the log burner, relax on the sofa with a paper or play with Twiglet and Bumble, the often-resident dogs.

Owners Philippa and Yasmin are laid back and hospitable – muddy boots, mucky dogs, sweaty cyclists, even ponies are ushered in. Food is flavourful and most of it comes from within a few miles of the door. Bacon rolls and excellent coffee for breakfast, paninis and freshly made sandwiches for lunch. Tempting cakes are freshly baked each day – maybe a bakewell slice, orange, honey and rosemary loaf or gingerbread muffin.

Opening hours
Tues-Sun 10am-5pm

Old Stables Coffee Shop, The Estate Yard, Castle Combe SN14 7HU
WWW.OLDSTABLESDELI.CO.UK   01249 783872

The Tollgate

JUNCTION: 18; 3 MINUTES

Uplifting views, honest cooking and alpacas, the Tollgate makes a refreshing pause from the motorway. The tea room is housed in a former turnpike, a sturdy building of stone, slate and arched windows, and looks to the sublime Welsh hills.

Settle in a corner next to the wood-burner or in the bright, Victorian conservatory for table service breakfasts of porridge, granola or eggs Benedict, and lunches of halloumi and avocado rarebit, cod and prawn fish cakes or falafel burger. Dainty afternoon teas are available to enjoy on the lawn – where you can also have a game of boules – and cakes are home baked, sticky and delicious. There's a 20% discount for 'cakeaway'. Tea is all loose leaf (speciality blends from Pukka) and coffee perfectly roasted.

Little people can canter around in the gardens, wolf down organic ice creams from Marshfield Ice Cream down the road, or feed carrots to Honey and Bumble, the resident Shetland ponies.

Opening hours
Mon-Fri 9.30am-5pm
Sat-Sun 9.30am-5pm

The Tollgate, Dyrham, Nr Bath SN14 8LF
WWW.THETOLLGATE.CO   01225 891585

Hanley Farm Shop

JUNCTION: 21; 10 MINUTES

Originally a disused 18th century barn and coach house, Hanley Farm Shop stands on the A48 between Chepstow and Lydney, overlooking the beautiful Severn Valley.

Now a farm shop with café, deli and butchery, it has become a culinary showcase for numerous local food and drink producers. Growers on a land share scheme in the field next door supply some of the seasonal vegetables, herbs and micro leaves to the shop. In the butchery, organically reared beef comes direct from the farm and the lamb, pork and chicken sourced from other local farmers, and there's even an on-site florist and golf driving range.

With its exposed oak beams, comfortable sofas, armchairs and a wood burning stove the café is relaxed and homely; food is always freshly prepared. Pies, quiches, sausage rolls and fantastic cakes are all baked in the kitchen. If you're passing in spring, try to catch the Dancing Cow Day when the herd is gleefully released back into the field after a winter indoors.

Opening hours
Mon-Sat 9am – 5pm (4.30pm café)
Sun 10am-4pm (3.30pm café)

Hanley Farm Shop, Tidenham, Chepstow NP16 7NA
WWW.HANLEYFARMSHOP.CO.UK   01291 626642

Magor Coffee Co.

JUNCTION: 23A; 3 MINUTES

Swing off the motorway after crossing the Severn Bridge (and the border) to find sustenance in a stylish, white-hued cafe in the little Monmouthshire village of Magor.

Magor Coffee Co. is a family-run coffee shop serving freshly cooked breakfast and brunch and delicious cakes and Italian pastries. It looks small from the outside, but it's like a tardis on the inside, with plenty of tables and comfy seating. Filament lightbulbs give a warm glow to match the homely welcome. Abbie and her staff smile broadly as they make coffees behind the cake studded, wood-clad serving counter, while husband Gianni – cooks up a storm in the open-plan kitchen.

Enjoy their signature cannoli range, imported especially from Italy, and traditional Welsh baked cakes and pastries sourced from local Welsh suppliers.

Opening hours
Tues-Fri 9am-5pm
Sat 9am-3pm
Sun 9.30am-12.30pm

Magor Coffee Co., 1 Salisbury House, Magor Square, Magor NP26 3HY
WWW.MAGORCOFFEECO.COM   01633 881817

ATTRACTION

Moody Sow

JUNCTION: 28/30 ; 10 MINUTES

Persevere down fiddly but well-signposted roads and you'll find the Moody Sow, a modern farm shop brimming with artisan food. It's housed in a well-lit, contemporary barn with a stream running by and pigs snuffling happily in the woods. Appealing counters are stacked with local cheese, homemade Danishes, Moody Sow jam, honey, fresh bread baked daily on-site, pink lemonade and craft beers ready to loot for finger-licking picnics. Scotch eggs are the speciality; enormous and award-winning. Try the sweet chilli chicken or black pudding.

The butchery is fabulous: pick up melt-in-your-mouth steaks, home-cured bacon, fresh sausages and juicy chops for the BBQ, then reward yourself with a coffee in the small café upstairs.

Animal lovers large and small will adore the farm park next door, part of the same complex, with a huge range of animals to meet and feed (ponies, sheep, goats, chickens, sheep and reindeer) as well as a soft play barn, go-karts and real diggers.

Opening hours
Mon-Sun 10am-5pm

Moody Sow, Cefn Mably Farm Park, Began Road, Old St Mellons CF3 6XL
WWW.MOODYSOW.COM 01633 680034

Thornhill Farm Shop

JUNCTION: 32; 10 MINUTES

A major player in the local food movement, Thornhill has thrived on the growing interest among Cardiff residents to connect with where their food comes from.

The shop is perched on a hill high above the city, at the edge of the family's 80-acre farm where cows and sheep are reared next to an allotment and small orchard which supplies some of the fruit and veg sold; the rest is sourced locally. There is a sterling butchery counter, where friendly staff can happily answer questions about animal welfare and guide you to the right cut. The shelves behind provide almost anything you could want for the store cupboard (as well as some lovely gifts). Cooks in the café turn these ingredients into a selection of crowd-pleasing dishes, from lamb and chorizo pasties to chicken and mushroom pies to light Victoria sponges.

Kids will be in their farming element with the digger play area and animal paddocks to visit, while those looking for a little more peace can grab a latte and marvel at the spectacular views over Cardiff, or get a breath of fresh air with a walk round Parc Cefn Onn woods nearby. It's between junctions so you don't have to retrace your steps to join the motorway again.

Opening hours
Mon-Fri 10am-5pm
Sat 9am-5pm
(cafe times vary)

Thornhill Farm Shop, Capel Gwilym Road, Lisvane, Cardiff CF14 9UB
WWW.THORNHILLFARM.CO.UK   02920 611707

CAFÉ

plan2ride

JUNCTION: 32; 2 MINUTES

Just off the motorway in the shadow of the fairytale Castell Coch, plan2ride is a pit-stop café on the edge of Fforest Fawr, which draws hikers, bikers and walkers to it like moths to a flame. Although born of cycling enthusiasts – they offer advice on local routes and a bike tune-up, and sell cycling-themed gifts and kit – the warm welcome is extended to all. You'd barely know it was once a garage. White walls, grey floors and open beams make it feel airy, and large patio doors from the small café give way to a sun-trap courtyard.

It's primarily a coffee and snack stop. Coffee is smooth, made with South American beans roasted in Caerphilly; teas are varied and smoothies freshly made. Locally baked cakes and pastries are enticing – from pear and chocolate to rhubarb and cinnamon, and rocky road; gluten-free options are readily available.

plan2ride is 100% powered by renewable energy and is committed to reusing or recycling every scrap of waste it produces.

Opening hours
Mon 8am-1pm
Wed-Fri 9am-6pm
Sat 9am-5pm (Sun 4pm)

plan2ride, 51 Merthyr Road, Tongwynlais CF15 7LG
WWW.PLAN2RIDE.CO.UK   029 20 810868

The Orchard Café

JUNCTION: 32; 5 MINUTES

Across the road from a primary school in a quiet, residential neighbourhood on the Cardiff fringe, the Orchard is a relaxed café focused on excellent, freshly made food – right down to the bread and jars of confetti-like fruit tea. Owner Dawn is a welcoming and effervescent host, who will cheerfully sit down in her apron between serving for a chat.

Large floor-to-ceiling windows flood the simply decorated café with light and look onto a wide pavement where tables are set out on fine days. A little courtyard garden at the back not only provides a sunny sanctuary for visitors, it also provides herbs, leaves and produce for the daily changing and earthy menu. Alongside familiar café fare, you might find more substantial dishes, such as ham hock pie and quinoa salad with smoked salmon. Afternoon tea is a new and popular addition, with savouries such as garlic and mushroom bruschetta and roasted vegetables and capers next to the usual sandwich and scone suspects.

Opening hours
Tues-Sat 8.30am-5pm

The Orchard Café, 7 Park Road, Radyr CF15 8DF
029 2084 2129

A lovely old pub in a village wedged in a valley at the edge of Cardiff, the Kings Arms is a 17th-century local with original features, good food and a relaxed atmosphere.

The low-beamed snug with white-painted stone walls and warm lighting has an open fireplace and plenty of cushioned nooks to tuck yourself into. There's a stack of help-yourself board games and a jar of complementary dog treats on the bar for furry visitors.

The menu is modern and flavourful. Lunch on homemade mushroom pâté with toasted sourdough, grilled halloumi with grapefruit and mango salsa, or the much-talked-about fish-finger sandwiches. Dinner might be pan-fried salmon with kale and courgettes, or local sausages with carrot and parsnip mash. The Sunday roast is popular, with a great mushroom nut roast for vegetarians.

The garden area is safe enough to let kids loose and has a large lawn, plus sunny patio with unusual deck games to idle some time away.

Opening hours
Noon-11pm

Kings Arms, Church Road, Pentyrch CF15 9QF
WWW.KINGSARMSPENTYRCH.COM 02920 890202

Llanerch Vineyard

JUNCTION: 34; 3 MINUTES

Wales' oldest vineyard is a delight in 20-acres of woodland, landscaped gardens and, of course, vines, which run down to the Ely valley.

The bar and terrace offers a casual menu: grilled fish of the day, overstuffed ciabatta sandwiches, Middle Eastern mezze. Well-behaved dogs on leads are welcome and rewarded with a dog treat if they wear appropriate puppy eyes. Llanerch Restaurant, housed in the old farmhouse with a sunny conservatory, offers more substantial meals, from pub classics like fish and chips and burgers as well as fine dining options, and the ever-popular afternoon tea.

Explore the beautiful grounds, lakes and precious woodland, rich with flowers and wildlife – eyes peeled for wild orchids, owls, dabchicks, Canada geese and kingfishers. Guided tours of the vineyard run every day from April to October, but must be booked in advance. Wine tasting is included in the price and you can buy some at a small shop on the way out.

Opening hours
Mon-Sun 10am-9pm

Llanerch Vineyard, Hensol CF72 8GG
WWW.LLANERCH-VINEYARD.CO.UK   01443 222716

Roaring fires, flagstone floors, a piano, friendly Welsh welcome and home-cooked food on the doorstep of Afan Forest Park, the Brit is a prince among pubs. Originally built in 1845, it has been eclectically made over with bare stone walls next to illustrated wallpapers, artful knick-knacks, a lamp made from a golden mannequin and Louis XV chairs upholstered in hot pink. Outside, there's a courtyard garden decorated just as quirkily with the River Afan running past.

Sitting a notch above pub grub, the award-winning food includes vegan pies, moules marinère and fresh mushrooms on brioche toast among the thoughtful lunch options, with heartier steaks and line-caught sea bass on the evening menu. Nearly all the food is homemade.

Walkers and cyclists are warmly welcomed and can stay in one of the four bunk rooms upstairs. The stunning Afan Forest, just up the hill, is a lovely spot to unfurl the legs and enjoy some beautiful scenery.

Opening hours
Mon-Weds noon-10pm
Thurs-Sat noon-midnight
Sun 11.30am-10pm

The Brit Pub, London Row, Cwmavon SA12 9AH
WWW.THEBRIT.WALES   01639 680247

No 6hundred

JUNCTION: 45; 2 MINUTES

You'd be forgiven for thinking the blue-framed windows, handsome front door and low ceilings of no6hundred look more like a house than a cafe: owner Donna started the café in the cosy, wood-burner warmed room at the front and has steadily colonised more and more of the house. The bright room at the back overlooking the garden was once her living room.

These days it's a well-liked spot for generous breakfasts, filling lunches (the veggie flatbreads with homemade coleslaw are a favourite) and – the pièce de résistance – tiers of afternoon tea. The cakes are real crowd-pleasers and flavour combinations novel: blueberry and coconut, apple and cinnamon. A series of interconnecting and beautifully decorated rooms – flower twisted pillars and oversized toy soldiers – mean there are plenty of nooks you can grab for a restorative coffee and bite to eat.

A good range of greetings cards and trinkets are scattered about the place to whet your appetite for the gift room upstairs, and the tastefully selected range will be your saviour if you've forgotten to pick up a present.

Opening hours
Mon-Sat 9.30am-6pm
Sun 10am-4pm

No 6hundred, 600 Clydach Road, Ynysforgan, Swansea SA6 5AY
WWW.NO6HUNDRED.COM   07789 075488

Haystack Café

JUNCTION: 46; 7 MINUTES

It's a short spin down the B4489 to reach this neighbourhood café at the edge of Swansea, and worth every drop of fuel.

An enormous painted mural, rustic wooden sign and large window onto the street sets the tone for the quirky, hip interior, where bare brick walls intermingle with vintage trunks, chipboard panels, coffee bean sacks and slouchy Chesterfields. It takes the name Haystack from co-owner Beth's farming connections, and all the wood inside has been reclaimed from the family farm, right down to the tables made from old fence posts.

Coffee is a speciality, expertly made using Coaltown beans roasted down the road in Ammanford. Be tempted by one of the incredible cakes in the stack on the counter (baked in the new bakery upstairs) or order from the menu, made fresh in the kitchen according to family tradition: dippy eggs, full cooked breakfast, bacon caesar salad or a veggie special with homemade hash browns.

There's a large car park alongside and secret garden out the back. Wonderful.

Opening hours
Tues-Fri 8am-5pm
Sat 9am-4pm
Sun 10am-3pm

Haystack Café, 1 Brynhyfryd Square, Swansea SA5 9EB
WWW.HAYSTACKCAFE.COM   01792 417768

FARM SHOP

Parc y Bocs

JUNCTION: A484; 13 MINUTES

The views over the Carmarthenshire countryside from Parc y Bocs' wrap-around terrace really are something. The farm shop, café and play area here have grown from humble beginnings, starting unusually from a successful natural pet food business set up by veterinary surgeon John Burns, with an egg hut and honesty box at the end of the drive.

Today the farm shop stocks a variety of fresh produce, with much of it grown in their own market gardens. Alongside the edible delights, you'll find a selection of homeware and children's treats, and of course specialist pet food.

The café serves farmhouse breakfasts, mac and cheese, soup of the day, burger with triple cooked chips, healthy salads, and delicious cakes, all homemade in the kitchen.

Kids will love meeting the alpacas or running off some steam in the adventure play area, and if you've never been to Kidwelly take some time to explore the castle and estuary footpaths which look over to Laugharne, the village where Dylan Thomas found much of his inspiration.

Opening hours
Mon-Sat 9am-5pm
Sun 10am-4pm

Parc y Bocs, Burns Farm Shop, Carmarthen Road, Kidwelly SA17 5AB
WWW.BURNSFARMSHOP.CO.UK   01554 892 724

CAFÉ

Wright's Food Emporium

JUNCTION: PORTHYRHYD; 7 MINUTES

Wright's Food Emporium sagely adopted the Golden Grove Arms, a former village pub, when it outgrew its previous home in a nearby farm shop. The network of rooms lend themselves perfectly to the holistic foodie concept, with a deli, café, weekend bistro and wine shop catering to almost every whim. Duck-egg blue panelling, mismatched chairs, repurposed bureaux, scrubbed wooden tables and vintage posters create a low-key, relaxed ambience. Munch generous antipasto platters (the charcuterie is second to none) and salads in the bright conservatory, and enjoy the much-celebrated pork belly Cubano in the dining room or in the courtyard garden.

Make the most of the refillable wine and cider (just buy a bottle and top it up from the barrel in the wine shop) or the pie of the day, which you can take away when you buy an enamel dish. Fill your tote bag with delicious homemade focaccia, lumps of Welsh cheese, Wright's signature chilli sauce and organic lavender hand creams.

Opening hours
Mon & Sun 11am-5pm
Wed & Thurs 11am-7pm
Fri & Sat 9am – late (last food orders 9pm)

GF V P ⏀

Wright's Food Emporium, Golden Grove Arms, Llanarthne SA32 8JU
WWW.WRIGHTSFOOD.CO.UK   01558 668929

Blasus Delicatessen

JUNCTION: CARMARTHEN; 1 MINUTE

Blasus means 'tasty' in Welsh, which is the main mission of owners Paul and Delyth. Family-owned and run for over 10 years, it's a Carmarthen institution. The staff are friendly and knowledgeable and are often ready to tempt you with a taste of a magnificent wine or a slice of farmhouse cheese. The cheese counter is exceptional, with good raw-milk examples of Europe's best, and there are lots of delicious Italian wines to accompany them.

Foodies will love the changing menu of takeaway baguettes (sweet chilli crayfish is a winner) with interesting, seasonal fillings. If you're after food for a top picnic you're sorted: chorizo sausage rolls, savoury tarts, charcuterie, antipasti and focaccia and finish with homemade frangipane tarts. And packaging is biodegradable so you can takeaway with a clear conscience. Carmarthen is a warren of narrow streets but the town's St Peters car park is a short walk away.

Opening hours
Mon-Sat 9am-5pm

Blasus Delicatessen, 58 King Street, Carmarthen SA31 1BD
WWW.BLASUSDELI.CO.UK   01267 233811

CAFÉ-TEA SHOP

Tea Traders

JUNCTION: A4242; 2 MINUTES

Carmarthen is a convenient staging post if you're heading to West Wales or on to Ireland via the ferry, and Tea Traders Tea Shop is an ideal place to stop for a tasty snack. It was founded by Paul and Nick who both worked in special needs teaching before deciding to branch out – but true to their roots they offer employment and training opportunities in the cafe to adults with learning difficulties.

Service is friendly and you can choose from a wall of loose-leaf teas. The range is impressive, though we'd recommend the house blend with a slice of one of the excellent cakes.

For authentic souvenirs and Welsh crafts, look no further than the shelves, which are filled with carefully selected objects, from ceramic figures in traditional dress to Welsh language prints. And don't forget to take a peek downstairs, an old bank vault, at the mini art gallery, which hosts a revolving selection of local artists.

The street itself is pedestrianised but there's plenty of parking at John Street car park a short stroll away.

Opening hours
Mon-Fri 9am-5pm
Sat 9am-4.30pm

Tea Traders, 15 Guildhall Square, Carmarthen SA31 1PR
WWW.TEATRADERS.CO.UK   01267 237101

The Ferryman Delicatessen

JUNCTION: ST CLEAR'S ; 6 MINUTES

A delicious little deli above the castle on Laugharne's main high street, the Ferryman is stuffed floor-to-ceiling with tantalising produce from Carmarthenshire and beyond: Perl Las blue cheese from Cardigan, môr seasoning and Welsh ales. Alongside local goodies, there's a strong Spanish theme, from the chorizo jam to alcaparras, treacly honey and el almendro turrón.

Step out the back and there's a dinky dining room where you can sit in and feast on those flavours. Lunch might be a bowl of lamb cawl, cauliflower and lentil pie, seafood chowder or a prawn open sandwich, open largely because it's too stuffed to close. The mixed meat and cheese platters are a smorgasbord of the most delicious charcuterie and pickles owner Tom can lay his hands on. Wrap up with a slice of apricot frangipane or salted caramel brownie.

The coffee is smooth and best paired with a Welsh cake – try the apricot and salted almond. It's a foodie's delight.

Opening hours
Tues-Sat 9am-5pm

The Ferryman Delicatessen , Exeter House, King Street, Laugharne SA33 4SU
WWW.THEFERRYMANDELI.CO.UK   01994 427398

DELI
Fforc Welsh Deli

JUNCTION: B4313; 5 MINUTES

Narberth is a cornucopia of good food, the food capital of the wild West, and one of the newest additions to its already excellent high street is Fforc Welsh Deli.

It's the latest venture from Sam and Martin who have a chicken farm down the road in Laugharne: "it's hard to make money selling eggs so we wanted to open a deli, and it was Narberth or nowhere". They're dedicated to advocating Welsh producers and stock a huge range behind the bright bay window: pickles, gin, chocolate, smoked meats, cheese, jerky, teas, infused oils. Coffee is roasted down the road in Ammanford by Coaltown Coffee, who started their roastery to reinvigorate industry in a former mining town, and is a deliciously smooth credit to them.

Plunder the shelves and pick up a sandwich or deli snack to go along with one of those delicious coffees.

Opening hours
Mon-Thurs 8.30am-6pm
Fri-Sat 8.30am-6pm

Fforc Welsh Deli, 34 High Street, Narberth SA67 7AS
WWW.FACEBOOK.COM/FFORCWELSHDELI-531432030598538/   01834 861994

Y Gegin

JUNCTION: HAVERFORDWEST; 15 MINUTES

Although a slightly creative extension of our 15-minute diversion, if you're heading West along the A40 towards Fishguard and/or the ferry to Ireland, it's well worth taking a detour south for West Wales' hippest food hub.

Of course, Pembrokeshire is no stranger to good food, with Narberth down the road known as something of a gastronomic hub, but Y Gegin (Welsh for kitchen) brings the foodie scene to Pembroke. "We wanted to create an attractive space where people of all ages would come together and explore tastes and dishes from around our county," says co-founder Michelle Evans.

And that they have, adopting the town's former market hall as new home for a growing collective of street food traders. Founding companies Paternoster Farm and Cŵlbox are permanent fixtures, serving their unique charcuterie and seafood respectively, and exciting new companies join them in the food hall to supply tasty dishes at brunch, lunch and dinner. Fantastic.

Opening hours
Fri 5.30-10pm
Sat 10am-10.30pm
Sun 10am-5pm

Y Gegin, Market Hall, Melville Street, Pembroke Dock SA72 6XS
WWW.YGEGIN.COM   07900 244692

WALES & THE BORDERS

From the Severn estuary to the Snowdonia Mountains

WALES & THE BORDERS

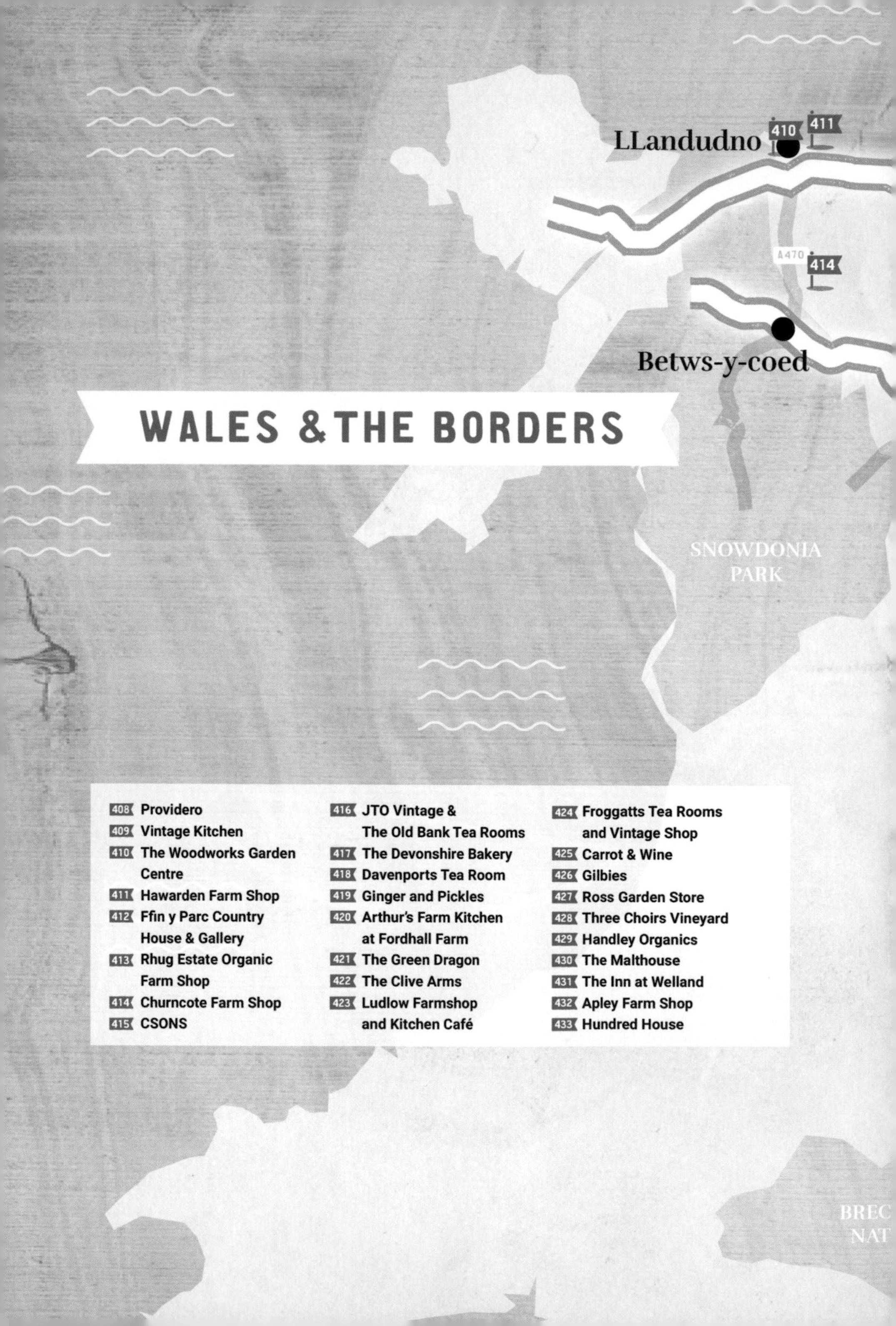

LLandudno 410 411

A470 414

Betws-y-coed

SNOWDONIA
PARK

BREC
NAT

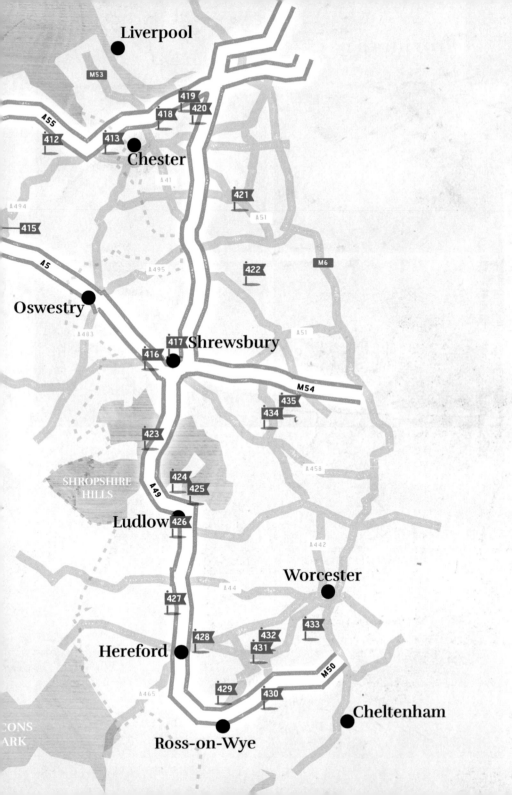

CAFÉ

Providero

JUNCTION: 19; 3 MINUTES

Beginning life in an achingly cool Citroën van, Providero's bricks-and-mortar café sits at the top of a steep hill just off the North Wales Expressway in Llandudno Junction. Blow the cobwebs away with a walk along the harbour bridge to the medieval Conwy castle before heading to Providero to reward yourself with some of the best tea and coffee in Wales.

Smartly dressed on the outside with its grey-painted render and wood cladding, inside you'll find the exposed brick walls and stripped wood floors of a very hip coffee house. Flat whites are exceptional, matched by the Turkish apple tea. Hot chocolate, jams and artisan bread is all locally-made and the delicious cakes are homemade – if you can resist the cakes and traybakes, you're stronger willed than us! Grab a stool at the breakfast bar in the window, sunnily decorated with jam jars of fresh flowers, or find a sofa in the roomy lounge upstairs.

Opening hours
Mon-Fri 8am-5pm
Sat 9am-5pm
Sun 10am-4pm

Providero, 148 Conway Road, Llandudno Junction LL31 9DU
WWW.PROVIDERO.CO.UK   01492 338220

Vintage Kitchen

JUNCTION: 20; 3 MINUTES

It's worth adding the cute seaside village of Rhôs-on-Sea to your itinerary for its charming seafront promenade, lively arts scene and famous puppet theatre.

One of the jewels in the local food scene is the Vintage Kitchen, which started life in a beautiful retro Citroën H van, bringing Leanne's A-grade baking to the masses. You'll have to have iron willpower to resist the sweet treats: caramel cookie brownies, Biscoff cake, or Rolo-topped chocolate and caramel. Finding favour with foodies, the menu has expanded to include healthy, filling lunches too, such as chickpea and tomato salad, mushroom and almond soup, chicken, falafel and hummus wrap or a make-your-own salad box. It's all available to take away (including the excellent coffee; bonus points for bringing your own cup), but if you're lucky you can bag a table behind the curved glass window in the small pristine cafe.

If you want to take one of those delectable cakes home, give Leanne a call in advance and she'll have one waiting for you.

Opening hours
Mon-Fri 8.30am-4pm
Sat 9am-4pm
Sun 10am-4pm

Vintage Kitchen, 43 Penrhyn Avenue, Rhos on Sea, LL28 4PS
WWW.FACEBOOK.COM/PG/VINTAGEKITCHENUK/ 01492 471 208

The Woodworks Garden Centre

JUNCTION: 33B; 10 MINUTES

Woodworks began life as a pallet manufacturing business in a modest timber yard and has now grown into a large, family-run garden centre. It's still true to its wooden roots in both name and services, and visitors can browse the mill warehouse for tempting wooden planters, summer houses, patio sets and barbecue shelters. But the addition of a gift shop, garden emporium, cafe and robust selection of plants makes this a destination in its own right.

Gardening fanatics will be in their element – while they enjoy the plants others can hunker down in the cafe. Furniture is reassuringly chunky and food is wholesome and reasonably priced. Expect generous breakfasts, paninis, jackets, soups, rarebits, scones and decent coffee. There's a covered seating area outside, perfect for a cuppa among the flowers.

Opening hours
Mon-Fri 9am-4pm
Sun 10am-3pm
(garden centre times vary; see website for details)

Ⓥ Ⓟ

The Woodworks Garden Centre, Wrexham Road, Mold CH7 4HE
WWW.WOODWORKSGC.COM   01352 752555

Hawarden Farm Shop

JUNCTION: SAINT DAVIDS PARK INTERCHANGE; 6 MINUTES

The enthusiasm this Flintshire farm shop has for sustainable local produce is catching. Provenance is key: kindly reared meat is sourced from the estate and neighbouring farms, milk is produced over the road and fruit and veg are grown just outside the shop. Local game is stocked in the freezer, and sausages and pies are made on site with meat raised at Hawarden. The Christmas turkeys are particularly sought after – lovingly tended, they have music piped into their barn to keep them calm.

Fill your shopping basket with all manner of countryside treats, from artisan bath oils to indy beer and cast-iron camping pans. Then step through to the airy café to taste the difference that good provenance makes to flavours. Try a black pudding and pork burger for a late breakfast or a farmland platter of local meats and cheeses for lunch. Outside, a huge play fort and a mile-long nature trail will keep kids entertained, and there's PYO fruit in summer and a weekend marketplace twice a month.

Opening hours
Mon-Fri 9am-6pm
Sat 8.30am-5.30pm
Sun 9.30am-4.30pm

Hawarden Farm Shop, Chester Road, Hawarden CH5 3FB
WWW.HAWARDENESTATE.CO.UK   01244 533442

ATTRACTION

Ffin y Parc Country House & Gallery

JUNCTION: A470; 5 MINUTES

The luminous café alone at Ffin y Parc is worth a detour from the A5. The stately manor house sits splendidly in 14 acres of gardens overlooking Snowdonia National Park. Previously used by the council it has been rescued and restored to its former glory by owners Ralph and Roland, who have a passion for 20th-century contemporary art. The gallery has changing exhibitions, including works by the finest Welsh artists, but there's art in every room here.

Mind suitably nourished, head to the café for sustenance. The menu is simple – sandwiches, quiches, salads and daily specials – the coffee great and homemade cakes widely lauded. There are slouchy leather chairs in the adjoining room, warmed by a log burner with the refined feel of a gentlemen's club, where you are invited to sit and ruminate on the paintings over your coffee. In the halcyon days of summer you can settle at one of the tables on the lawn to make the most of those glorious views; if the weather is inclement enjoy the Conwy valley panorama from the large airy conservatory.

Opening hours
Wed-Sat 10am-5pm
Sun 11am-5pm

Ffin y Parc Country House & Gallery, Betws Road, Llanrwst LL26 0PT
WWW.WELSHART.NET   01492 642 070

Rhug Estate Organic Farm Shop

JUNCTION: TYN-Y-CEFN; 0 MINUTES

The sprawling Rhug Estate covers a remarkable 12,500 acres in the rugged Dee Valley. For 20 years it has been a bastion of organic farming and animal welfare, with Lord Newborough at the helm. You might well see his Labrador 'Truffles' roaming around on the scent of a sausage. The dedication to planet and people can be tasted in every bite of the beef, lamb, chicken and game.

If you're on your way to Snowdonia, stop off to enjoy the estate's walks (pick up a map from the shop), play area and treat-yourself, award-winning Bison Grill. Browse the farm shop's local products, from Snowdonia cheeses and Penderyn whisky to Rhug Estate wool duvets.

If you're in a rush, On The Hoof serves fast food a class apart from other takeaways (try the bison burger), while the drive-thru coffee shop is an inspired idea and blows your average café chain out of the water. Drive up to the hatch for farm-grade drinks, sausage rolls, paninis and cakes cheerily served in compostable packaging.

Opening hours
Mon-Thus 8am-5pm
Fri -Sat 8am-5.30pm
Sun 8.30am-5pm

Rhug Estate Organic Farm Shop, Corwen LL21 0EH
RHUG.CO.UK/   01490 413000

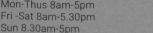

FARM SHOP – CAFÉ

Churncote Farm Shop

JUNCTION: A458; 1 MINUTE

Housed in a redbrick former cowshed, Churncote Farm Shop and Kitchen offers a characterful break from the road and is popular with those travelling to or from mid-Wales.

The shelves are stocked with an impressive selection of produce, from the farm's own beef and lamb to veg, butter, ice cream, cheese and countryside versions of store cupboard essentials, including gluten-free products. Pies and meals from the farm kitchen are available to take home – perfect for the end of your journey. Or if you prefer to cook, talk to the highly knowledgeable butchers behind the counter who are happy to guide customers to the right cut and cooking technique.

The same friendliness extends to the cafe staff over in the Cote Kitchen, an airy modern timber building on the other side of the yard. Replenish your energy with proper home-cooked food – maybe a full English, breakfast roll, something from their range of light bites and main meals or a cup of tea and slice of freshly baked cake.

Opening hours
Mon-Tues 10am-6pm (Sun 3pm)
Weds-Sat 9am-6pm
(cafe times vary – see website)

Churncote Farm Shop, Welshpool Road, Bicton Heath SY3 5EB
WWW.CHURNCOTE.CO.UK   01743 851913 (CAFÉ)/851081 (SHOP)

RESTAURANT

CSONS

JUNCTION: EMSTREY ISLAND; 6 MINUTES

CSONS roosts in the heart of historic Shrewsbury in a 16th-century building that combines Tudor panelling with zingy yellow banquette seating. It's a labour of love for the four brothers behind it, and their excellent food is inspired by their ex-pat experiences. Crafted from local ingredients, the menu changes almost daily depending on the produce available that day.

The English breakfast is served with chorizo and chipotle sauce, granola with house lemon curd. Lunch might be labneh and caponata with flatbread, salted beef or hummus and red pepper sandwiches. Try the cinnamon buns or gluten-free chocolate and quinoa cake with a coffee. Dinner is served from Wednesday to Saturday and is a real flavour adventure (think sesame salmon with kimchi teriyaki) particularly Friday's Mystery Menu.

There's a lovely courtyard garden for soaking up the sun on fine days, and high chairs and colouring pages for little people.

Opening hours
Mon, Tues 9am–3.30pm
Weds-Sat 9am-4pm, 6pm-10pm
Sun 10am-3pm

CSONS, 8 Milk Street Shrewsbury SY1 1SZ
WWW.CSONS-SHREWSBURY.CO.UK   01743 272709

JTO Vintage & The Old Bank Tea Rooms

JUNCTION: 14; 4 MINUTES

Filled with a steady stream of visitors, it's hard to believe that the Old Bank Tea Rooms came about by happy accident. Owner Diane Ormrod planned to relocate her furniture restoration business from Frodsham to a larger space in Helsby's old bank building, including a small space where customers could enjoy tea and cake. But such was its popularity that the furniture was quickly replaced by a full tea room serving crumpets, homemade soup, panini and generous slices of cake baked by women in the village. It is licensed too with a small selection of wine, lager, beer and cider.

Vintage light fittings hang over the counter and tables are dressed with country-chic table cloths; the room rings with chatter. You can find a range of heritage items and gifts for sale on the shelves and dressers. Out back there's a large covered garden decorated with the same thoughtful panache. If you're feeling energetic, earn some extra space for cake with a hike up the iron age hill fort just over the road at Helsby Hill.

Opening hours
Tues-Sat 10am-5pm

JTO Vintage & The Old Bank Tea Rooms, Helsby, Frodsham WA6 0DA
01928 724846

The Devonshire Bakery

© Oliver Perrott

© Oliver Perrott

Nestled on Frodsham's pretty high street the Devonshire Bakery is a welcome break from the M56. Follow your nose to find its vast array of artisan breads (sourdough, rye, ciabatta, spelt, baguette) made on site from recipes honed over five generations.

Pull up a chair at a window table to enjoy a smooth coffee and made-to-order sandwich as you watch the world go by. There's a cosiness to the interior which is hung with bold artwork and in summer tables are set on the pavement. The beef and pork pies are famously good and it's worth picking up a spiced chutney sausage roll or golden-crusted pie for later – our favourite was steak and blue cheese. Don't miss the handmade chocolates at Christmas and Easter too.

There's a pay-and-display car park just round the corner. Make time to browse the Lady Heyes Craft and Antiques centre nearby before you go; the old farm buildings are now host to a run of alluring vintage shops.

Opening hours
Monday, Weds 8.30am-4.30pm
Tuesday, Thurs, Fri 8.30am-5pm
Sat 8.30am-4pm

The Devonshire Bakery, 1 High Street, Frodsham WA6 7AH
WWW.DEVONSHIRE-BAKERY.CO.UK   01928 731234

TEA ROOM

Davenports Tea Room

JUNCTION: WILLOW GREEN; 1 MINUTE

A vintage van parked outside signposts this quintessential English tea room. It sits at the side of the canal in the idyllic Weaver Valley and is adorned with antique furniture, William Morris wallpaper and murals of Alice in Wonderland, making it look like the Mad Hatter's Tea Party.

It's open for breakfast, snacks and light lunches (think sandwiches and ploughman's), but the afternoon teas are the real speciality, and need to be pre-booked. Cakes are homebaked by ladies in nearby villages and china cups will be pre-warmed. The array of teas is bewildering, from English Breakfast to mint choc Rooibos; with over 50 different teas from around the world as well as homegrown British ones, you may need owner Belinda to advise you on the perfect blend.

Roll out onto the gravelled terrace on fine days to listen to the birds singing and admire the donkeys and alpacas. The tea room is popular and can get very busy, so if you're set on the Davenports experience it's a good idea to call ahead and book.

Opening hours
Wed-Sat 10am-5pm
Sun-Mon 10am-4pm
Last orders for light lunches/afternoon tea 3pm

Davenports Tea Room, Bridge Farm, Warrington Road, Bartington CW8 4QU
WWW.DAVENPORTSTEAROOM.CO.UK   01606 853241

Ginger and Pickles

JUNCTION: A534; 13 MINUTES

As a proud member of the Tea Guild, Ginger and Pickles (remember the Beatrix Potter tale?) is firmly focused on tea of the very best kind. When owner Andy set up in the old office of the Nantwich Chronicle newspaper his mind was set on creating a tea room where people could drop by and relax.

It's defined by excellent food and local produce, served on blue-and-white Burleigh china. Breakfast on hearty fry ups or halloumi stacks, lunch on quiches and generous salads, or drop by for tea and cake. There's a dinky courtyard garden to enjoy on fine days.

If you're dashing to get to your final destination, picnics are available to order via the website. But it's well worth stopping for longer to have a look round the town with its medieval timbered buildings and enthusiastic floral displays.

Opening hours
Mon-Sat 9am-5pm
Sun 10am-4pm

Ginger and Pickles, 3a Mill Street, Nantwich CW5 5ST
WWW.GINGERANDPICKLES.CO.UK   01270 610329

FARM SHOP-CAFÉ

Arthur's Farm Kitchen at Fordhall Farm

JUNCTION: B5065; 15 MINUTES

Camped in the Tern Valley, Fordhall Farm is a beacon of organic farming, taking the bold step of eschewing chemicals more than 65 years ago. These days the community-owned farm showcases its light environmental touch in its strikingly renovated Old Dairy building, which houses its shop and dog-friendly organic café.

The slate floors, log burner and sturdy wooden tables give the café a farmhouse kitchen warmth. Fill your bellies with sumptuous plates of grass-fed beef, lamb and Gloucester Old Spot pork – the farm's pigs feast on the by-products of Joules' brewery down the road – all served with locally sourced and organic, where possible, vegetables. Or buy a feast in the farm shop and take it out front to enjoy in the picnic area.

Before you go, take the kids off to make dens in the woodland and climb on the rope trails, or give the kids and dogs some exercise on one of three farm trails (you may need wellies!).

Opening hours
Tues-Fri 9.30am-4.00pm
Sat 9.30am-4.30pm
Sun & Bank Hols 10am-4pm

Arthur's Farm Kitchen, Fordhall Organic Farm, Market Drayton TF9 3PS
WWW.FORDHALLFARM.COM   01630 638696

The Green Dragon

JUNCTION: LITTLE STRETTON; 1 MINUTE

A49

The Green Dragon bustles with customers day round, a sure sign that Jay brothers Adam and Jonathan at the helm are getting it right.

It stands at the roadside in the border town of Little Stretton. Whitewashed and climbing with ivy on the outside, inside it's smart and well-kept without losing the village pub vibe: terracotta floor tiles, horse brass by the fire and dried hops above the bar. Polite, smiling staff deliver a regular stream of excellent plates to tables. Mushroom and paprika stroganoff, duck breast with black pudding, and steak and blue cheese melt are just some of the flavourful dishes you can expect, and there's a dedicated menu for vegans.

In good weather, you can sit in the shade of a parasol in the garden, where kids can keep themselves out of mischief on the sturdy climbing frame. If you've time before you head on your way, hike up to the top of Long Mynd for uplifting views over Shropshire. Breathtaking.

Opening hours
Mon-Sun 11.30am-11.30pm

The Green Dragon, Little Streeton SY6 6RE
WWW.GREENDRAGONLITTLESTRETTON.CO.UK   01694 722925

PUB
The Clive Arms

JUNCTION: LUDLOW; 2 MINUTES

A Georgian coaching inn at the edge of Ludlow, the Clive reopened in 2019 after a radical refurbishment. There's a relaxed warmth to the sunny yellow chairs and low-level lighting, and – ever the country inn – hats and walking sticks are available to borrow.

It's part of the Oakly Park Estate, owned by the Earl of Plymouth, which uses its own farm and those nearby as its larder. Beef, lamb and Gloucester Old Spot pork come from the Oakly Park, as do the dairy products, game, pickles and honey, while the kitchen garden supplies fruit and vegetables. The low food miles really come through in the sensational flavours, and that's saying something in this foodie capital.

The open-plan dining room is beautifully decorated with books and paintings from the Earl's collection and custom-made lamp stands from the Marches Pottery.

The Ludlow Farm Shop next door, sister to the pub, has an excellent range of goodies so it's worth stocking up before your onward journey.

Opening hours
Mon-Sat 11am -11pm
Sun noon-10.30pm

The Clive Arms, Bromfield, Ludlow SY8 2JR
WWW.THECLIVE.CO.UK   01584 856565

Ludlow Farmshop and Kitchen Café

JUNCTION: BROMFIELD; 0 MINUTES

A49

Set on the edge of the Earl of Plymouth's estate and supplied by its farms and fields, the Ludlow Farmshop (formerly Food Centre) is a microcosm of the foodie hub that is Ludlow. They are passionate about local food here and more than half of what they sell is grown, reared or made on the farm, including rare-breed Gloucester Old Spot pork, wild venison and cheese and ice cream made from the farm's own milk.

Park up and head to the café for delicious dishes which use as much of the farm's produce as possible, from hand-churned butter to freshly baked pastries. Breakfast on the house granola with the farm's yoghurt and honey; salads, burgers and well-filled sandwiches are on the lunchtime menu.

Raid the food hall for farm-made cheese and jams, freshly roasted coffee and snacks, then take a moment to soak up the scenery in the free picnic area. There's a respectable play area (with ice cream cabin in summer) where kids can monkey around and tire themselves out ready for a car nap. Winner.

Opening hours
Mon-Sat 9am-5.30pm
Sun 10am-5pm
Kitchen 8am-5pm

Ludlow Farmshop and Kitchen Café, Bromfield, Ludlow SY8 2JR
WWW.LUDLOWFARMSHOP.CO.UK   01584 856000

TEA ROOM

Froggatts Tea Rooms and Vintage Shop

JUNCTION: ASHFORD BOWDLER; 1 MINUTE

It's hard not to love Froggatts Tea Rooms and Vintage Shop, and those who follow the sign from the road on a whim are invariably delighted. Standing at the side of the farm track, overlooking fields of sunflowers, this former farm shop is now an adorable café packed with upcycled furniture – either to buy or to sit at while you have a bite to eat. Sally Froggatt and Helen Cooper love all things vintage and have painted, embellished, reupholstered and restored a wonderfully eclectic range of items. They too are responsible for many of the home-made cakes, scones, jams and pickles on sale alongside appealing retro homewares, tins of chalk paint and home-reared rare breed pork.

It's an eclectic mix, just like the family's Featherknowle Farm, which has added fishing ponds and a caravan park to its portfolio after centuries of rearing livestock. Eyes peeled for the new glamping cabins, soon to be unveiled. A light lunch on the tea room's covered terrace watching bees drift among blooming pots of flowers is pure bliss.

Opening hours
Weds-Sat 9am-4pm

Froggatts Tea Rooms and Vintage Shop, Meadowside, Ashford Bowdler SY8 4AQ
WWW.FROGGATTS.ORG.UK   07837 644896

Carrot & Wine

JUNCTION: MUCH BIRCH; 2 MINUTES

For a small shop Carrot & Wine packs one hell of a punch. One of a group of three stores across Hereford, it's a tremendous reimagination of the traditional village shop and supplies everything you could need from a local store, emphasising low food miles and nearby producers. This is the food revolution in full swing.

The shelves provide everything you need for the store cupboard, with decent organic, vegan and gluten-free ranges. Bottles can be refilled with wine shipped directly from France, vegetables are loose in crates and the deli counter stocks delicious olives, scotch eggs and cheeses. Croissants are delivered daily, the coffee is rich and bars of Hereford chocolate are a tempting pick-me-up. Staff are friendly and can be relied on to tip you off on the best products.

It's near the upper part of the gorgeous Wye valley (looped walks start from Hoarwithy, about 9 minutes' drive away), so consider a restorative riverside walk while you're out of the car.

Opening hours
Mon-Sun 7am-9pm

Ⓥ Ⓟ ↻ GF

Carrot & Wine, Wormelow HR2 8FD
01981 540126

CAFÉ
Gilbies

JUNCTION: HEREFORD; 3 MINUTES

Gilbies is frequently described as a hidden gem, tucked behind the main street in the leafy cathedral town of Hereford. The half-timbered house stands on a light-strung, sheltered courtyard in the shadow of the church spire.

Hereford's fortunes grew from its rich agricultural land (famous for cider and cattle) and remains bountiful to this day, evidenced in the excellent produce in the market. The surfeit of good ingredients has brought with it a renaissance of the food scene, and Gilbies is one of the pioneers. Owners Rob and Hayley returned from Bristol to take the helm in 2016 and brought with them their experience of the urban foodie scene. The result is a relaxed, friendly hang out and a true taste of the region.

Fill up on classic dishes such as cod and chips, thick-cut pork chops, Herefordshire steak and filled jacket potatoes, or allow yourself to be seduced by the tapas menu: chorizo croquettes, Catalan broad beans and crispy pork belly.

Cake lovers won't be disappointed – slices of maple-syrup glazed banana bread, toasted tea cakes and other treats are served alongside decent coffee.

Opening hours
Tues-Thurs 11am-11pm
Fri-Sat 11am-midnight
Sun 11am-6pm

Gilbies, 4 St Peters Close, Commercial Street, Hereford HR1 2DL
WWW.GILBIES.CO.UK   01432 277 863

Ross Garden Store

JUNCTION: WILTON ROUNDABOUT; 5 MINUTES

Isambard Brunel could scarcely have imagined that his Engine Shed at the edge of Ross on Wye would one day become a flower-filled garden centre. Tucked away on a small industrial estate, the enormous doors at one end stand as a reminder of its former life. Have a look at the walls inside for the black and white photos of how it once looked.

A sea of flowers and plants fans out to the boundary of the garden centre, while inside the Shed is a cavern of considered gifts and homewares arranged on trestle tables against the stone walls. A clapboard entrance signals the way into the homely café and gives the air of a station waiting room. Old-fashioned home-cooked values reign in the kitchen where everything is made from scratch – the cheese scones and cream teas are held in particularly high regard.

There's an overflow car park over the road if spaces inside the gates are all taken. A wonderful place to pause on the way to or from Wales.

Opening hours
Mon-Sat 9am-5pm
Sun 10am-4.30pm

Ⓥ Ⓟ

Ross Garden Store, The Engine Shed Station Approach, Ashburton Ind. Estate, Ross-on-Wye HR9 7BW
WWW.ROSSGARDENSTORE.COM   01989 568999

It's all about the views at Three Choirs Vineyard, which is frequently likened to the Napa Valley. From the brasserie terrace you're bathed in bird song and transported to the vineyards of hotter climes. Vines spool down the hillside, bordered in the distance by the Malvern Hills, Cotswolds and Black Mountains, which give the vineyard its unique microclimate.

Homely and informal, the brasserie is relaxed and welcoming with beamed ceiling, and colourful chandeliers made of recycled glasses and decanters. As stops go, it's tremendous: different to a pub, more than a café but not as formal as a restaurant. Ease yourself onto a fireside sofa and revive yourself with a rich coffee, or park yourself at a table for food. The charcuterie, featuring wild boar salami from neighbouring Forest of Dean and pressing of duck, fig and quince is sensational as is the local cheese platter; burgers and hearty soups are always on the menu.

Take time to walk the footpaths that lace the vineyard before you go, or take a tour and pick up a bottle in the shop to uncork at your destination.

Opening hours
Tues-Fri noon-2pm, 6.00pm-8pm
Sat-Sun noon-8pm

Three Choirs Vineyard, Newent GL18 1LS
WWW.THREE-CHOIRS-VINEYARDS.CO.UK   01531 890223

Handley Organics

JUNCTION: 2; 8 MINUTES

Owner Caroline started growing vegetables at home for health reasons almost 30 years ago, and quickly began gifting gluts to friends and family. Her enthusiasm for growing food while protecting wildlife and ecosystems grew steadily, and with it a business emerged.

The polytunnel a Hardwick Hill now supplies the shop and nearby pubs and restaurants with natural, nutrient-rich fruit and vegetables. These are stacked on the shelves alongside whole foods, herbs, teas, organic meat and dairy products. You can fill your tote with almost everything you need for the store cupboard.

Head upstairs to the restful cafe to sample delicious organic home cooking. Specials might include quinoa, spring rolls or broccoli and cheddar fritters. Coffee is Fairtrade and delicious, while the Handley cordials are wonderfully refreshing. Heaven for vegetarians and omnivores alike.

Opening hours
Mon-Sat 9am-5pm

Handley Organics, 5 High Street, Ledbury HR8 1DS
WWW.HANDLEYORGANICS.CO.UK   01885 482415

CAFÉ

The Malthouse

JUNCTION: 2; 9 MINUTES

Swathed in Virginia creeper, you'll find the Malthouse tucked away off the lane up to the church in the heart of handsome Ledbury. Its cobbled courtyard is brimming with flowers and perfect for a chilled lemonade on a hot day. Inside is beamed and cosy.

Customers are struck by the friendliness of the self-effacing owners. Food is reliably tasty: the American pancakes with bacon and berries are hard to resist for breakfast; salmon, leek and tarragon tart or tomato and basil soup are perfect for lunch. The coffee is excellent and the dresser is crowded with scones, cakes and bakes under various glass domes to tempt even the most steadfast dieter. We loved the lemon meringue pie and fig frangipani. Even those on a gluten- or dairy-free diet have a choice of treats to indulge in here.

Take a look at the gallery displaying local art upstairs and make time to stroll through the centre of Ledbury to see its famous 'black-framed' Tudor buildings.

Opening hours
Sun-Mon 10am-4pm
Tues-Sat 9am-5pm

GF V

The Malthouse, Church Lane, Ledbury HR8 1DW
01531 634443

The Inn at Welland

JUNCTION: 1; 11 MINUTES

"Where's the Michelin star?" said one diner, and you do have to wonder. The kitchen team (now with a dedicated pastry chef) serve up a proper gastro medley with homemade desserts, ice creams, sorbets and petit fours. Enjoy pan-fried Cornish scallops, pea mint purée, crisp lardons and tomato oil followed by crisp belly pork, garlic mash, pak choi, orange and ginger jus.

David and Gillian are adept hosts, and have created a muted, contemporary interior with limestone tile flooring, bleached sideboard and mismatched tables and chairs. It's a rural setting so the log fires are stoked up on cold days, and the garden outside has fantastic views over the Malvern Hills. One of the terraces has a glass veranda with a wood-burner, so you can continue soaking up the views even on chilly days.

Dishes are on the pricier side – around £15 to £20 for a main – but, given the quality, it's excellent value for money.

Opening hours
Tues-Sat noon-2.30pm 6pm-9.30pm
Sun noon-2.30pm

The Inn at Welland, Drake Street, Welland WR13 6LN
WWW.THEINNATWELLAND.CO.UK   01684 592317

FARM SHOP-CAFÉ

Apley Farm Shop

JUNCTION: 4; 12 MINUTES

Shropshire's rippling hills pass through the beautiful Apley Estate – set in gorgeous countryside bisected by the upper reaches of the Severn. It's not far from the M54 at Telford so a perfect border stop-off on your journey between England and Wales. At the pint-sized Apley Shopping Village old farm buildings arranged around a square courtyard have been returned to use for the farm shop, deli and café, alongside a handful of local businesses. They hum with life from passing visitors dropping in to pick up groceries or have a quick bite. Trestle tables in the shop sag beneath the weight of tasty produce from nearby farms.

The café is housed in the old creamery, where the award-winning Apley cheese was once made. Chefs draw some of the ingredients from the walled garden (returned to service in 2013) and the wider estate. Tasty tarts, freshly baked cakes, unsparing sandwiches, delicious afternoon teas and seasonal soups are served; the roasts on Sunday come highly recommended. The whole family can enjoy Pigg's Playbarn where little ones can let off steam in the soft play area.

Opening hours
Sun-Thurs 9.30am-5pm
Fri-Sat 9.30am-5.30pm
Café closes 30 mins before the shop

Apley Farm Shop, Norton TF11 9EF
WWW.APLEYFARMSHOP.CO.UK   01952 581 002

Hundred House

JUNCTION: 4; 10 MINUTES

The heady, scented gardens set The Hundred House apart, encircling the eclectic Shropshire restaurant with rooms with a secret garden, running streams and around 70 varieties of herb, fruit and vegetable. The Times recently named it as one of their Top 20 cool places for food and gardens, so if you've had enough of the M54, you'll be revived the moment you step out of the car here.

The building's name reveals its rich history, Hundred House being the term for an ancient administrative centre and court of law. The hotel and restaurant are an unusual warren of buildings, from 14th century to Georgian, red brick to thatched. They are quirkily decorated and show their age in parts. In the cosy farmhouse kitchen restaurant – hexagonal floor tiles, dried herbs hanging from the rafters – flavour is king: chef Stuart prioritises home-grown produce and herbs, which are plucked liberally from the garden.

It's worth factoring in a longer stop to savour your meal and explore the Severn Valley, David Austin Rose centre and the famous Ironbridge Gorge nearby.

Opening hours
Mon-Sat 11am-11pm
Sun 11am-10.30pm

Hundred House, Norton TF11 9EE
WWW.HUNDREDHOUSE.CO.UK   01952 580240

The M6

Natural Lakeland glory & industrial landmarks

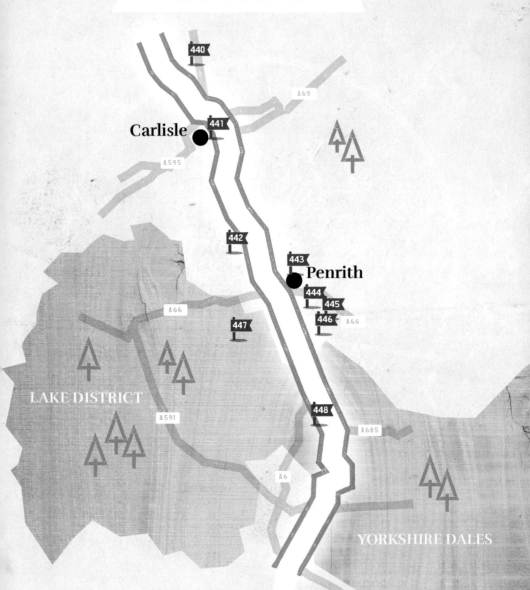

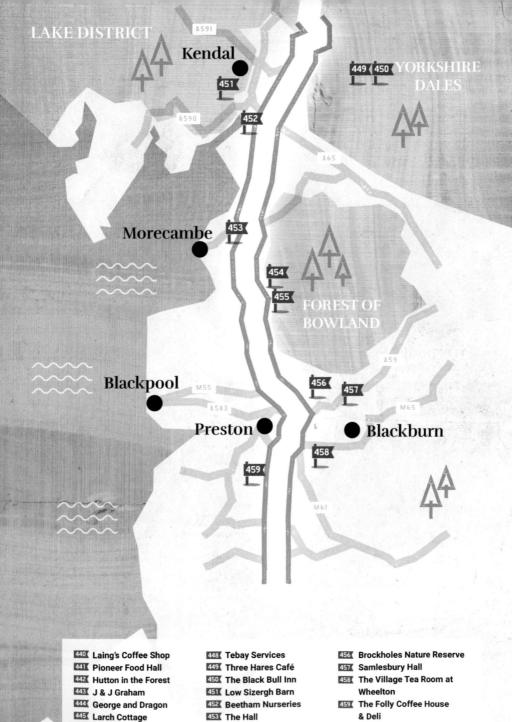

LAKE DISTRICT

A591

Kendal

451

A590

452

449 450 YORKSHIRE
DALES

A65

Morecambe

453

454

455

FOREST OF
BOWLAND

A59

Blackpool

M55

A583

456

457

M65

Preston

Blackburn

458

459

M61

440 Laing's Coffee Shop
441 Pioneer Food Hall
442 Hutton in the Forest
443 J & J Graham
444 George and Dragon
445 Larch Cottage
446 Abbott Lodge Jersey
    Ice Cream
447 Askham Hall Café

448 Tebay Services
449 Three Hares Café
450 The Black Bull Inn
451 Low Sizergh Barn
452 Beetham Nurseries
453 The Hall
454 The Fleece Inn
455 The Applestore Café
    at Wyresdale Park

456 Brockholes Nature Reserve
457 Samlesbury Hall
458 The Village Tea Room at
    Wheelton
459 The Folly Coffee House
    & Deli

M6 SOUTH

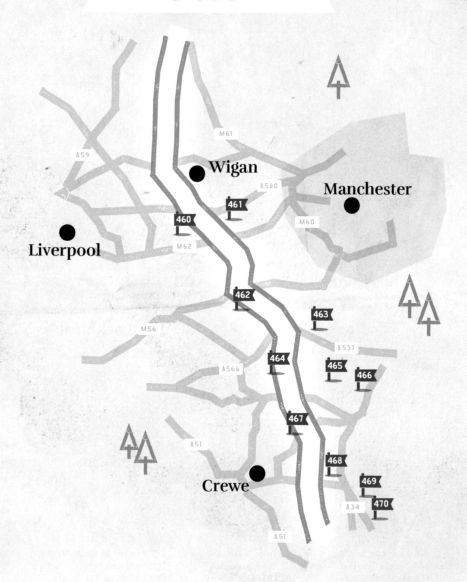

460 Red Bank Farm
461 Kenyon Hall Farm
462 Arley Hall
463 The Lambing Shed
464 The Three Greyhounds Inn
465 Jodrell Bank Discovery
Centre

466 The Old Barn
467 The Wheatsheaf
468 Hall Farm Shop & Café
469 Middleport Pottery
470 Emma Bridgewater
Café & Garden
471 The Fitzherbert Arms

472 Canalside Farm Shop
473 Essington Farm

Laing's Coffee Shop

JUNCTION: 44; 1 MINUTE

If you love glamping, you'll love ogling Laing's gorgeous, hand-crafted shepherd's huts and camping pods. Farmers-turned-timber-artisans, George and Judith Laing started manufacturing wooden buildings in 2001 after a devastating bout of foot-and-mouth hit their farm.

Today their family-run business has flourished. A modern farm shop filled with gifts and produce from the surrounding area stands alongside a roomy coffee shop. The welcome is warm and friendly, the breakfasts hearty, and Judith's cooking comforting. Don't miss out on their in-house jam and biscuits.

In winter months you can snuggle up around the warming wood burner; in summer, spill out onto the sunny terrace. You'll find it hard to crowbar your kids away from the play area: swings, a playhouse and mini tractors provide welcome respite from in-car squabbles. Children's hats, bibs, wipes and sun cream are kindly provided if your bag is buried in the boot.

Opening hours
Mon-Sat 10am-5pm
Sun 10am-4pm

Laing's Coffee Shop, Reiver House, Harker CA6 4DS
01228 672269

Pioneer Food Hall

JUNCTION: 43; 2 MINUTES

Pioneer has only recently flung open the doors to its new food hall and café, and it's already a hit with locals and travellers. It's just off the M6 in the city's Rosehill estate and a haven for foodies.

Mimicking traditional market stalls, the large space stocks Cumbrian food on a supermarket scale, with butchery, deli and bakery counters supplementing the shelves of fresh produce. Choose from local beef, barbecue-ready burgers and their own version of the Cumberland sausage at the butcher's, warm bread, scones or a handmade sausage roll at the bakery. One happy customer called it "the best food store I've ever seen".

There's a Grab & Go counter for sandwiches and salads to take away, but if you've got time, make it a longer stop at the lively 1878 Coffee Lounge upstairs. Head chef Ian sends an endless stream of plates out to booths and tables in the smart café: award-winning Cumberland sausages, sandwiches on in-house bread, and filling breakfasts.

Opening hours
Mon-Sat 7am-6pm (cafe 9am-4pm)
Sun 10am-4pm (cafe 10am-3.30pm)

Pioneer Food Hall, Rosehill Estate, Montgomery Way, Carlisle CA1 2RW
WWW.PIONEERFOODSTORE.CO.UK   01228 422100

Hutton in the Forest

JUNCTION: 41; 3 MINUTES

This magnificent house on the edge of the Lake District is the ancient family home of Lord and Lady Inglewood and is a glorious mixture of architectural and decorative styles. Once a medieval stronghold to protect the Borders (it still has its pele tower), it has been extended into a grand, crenelated mansion. You'll need to pay a small entrance fee to tour the gardens and house but it is well worth it: the extensive grounds are a fittingly magnificent setting for Hutton with the spectacular Walled Garden the jewel in the crown.

The Cloisters Tea Room is free to enter and is a fabulous medieval affair of arched windows, stone floors and walls, beamed ceilings, coats of arms and dark wood furniture. Delicious homemade light lunches are served when the House is open and cakes and scones are baked daily to accompany pots of tea and cafetières of coffee. A huge dresser displays local china ware, preserves, greetings cards and crafts for tasteful souvenirs.

Opening hours
Wed, Thur, Sun & Bank Hol Mon 10.30am-4.30pm (House & Tea room)
Sun-Fri 10am-5pm (Gardens)
(1 April-11 October)

Hutton in the Forest, Penrith CA11 9TH
WWW.HUTTON-IN-THE-FOREST.CO.UK   017684 84449

J & J Graham

JUNCTION: 40; 5 MINUTES

Penrith stands on a route to Scotland that's been strategically important since Roman times and its historic standing shows in the hodge-podge of cobbled lanes, castle ruins, arcades and red stone buildings arranged around a lively square. In the heart stands J & J Graham, an old-fashioned grocers with traditional signage and ornate shop windows still intact.

Established in 1793, these days it's more an artisan deli and perfect for picnics and holiday hampers. The shop is dominated by an enormous counter, a treasure chest of Cumbrian delicacies, and ringed with shelves of groceries. Resist, if you can, the local gingerbread, chutneys, sticky toffee puddings, own-blend teas and chilli sauces, all sourced from the Eden Valley. An in-house bakery provides daily bread, scones, pies, quiches, soup and freshly cooked ham.

If you're here in October, look out for the Winter Droving, an annual festival with a torch-lit procession and rural games.

Opening hours
Mon–Sat 8.30am–5.30pm

J & J Graham, 6-7 Market Square, Penrith CA11 7BS
WWW.JJGRAHAM.CO.UK   01768 862281

PUB

George and Dragon

JUNCTION: 40; 5 MINUTES

Sister to the glamorous Askham Hall hotel and Queens Head pub down the road, the George and Dragon is a classy country inn with gourmet food to match. Long, low and whitewashed, it's been lovingly restored, decorated in period colours and reinstated as a community hub. The run of interconnecting rooms feels intimate with flagstone floors, floorboards, scrubbed tables and walls hung with period photographs. There's a sunny courtyard with chunky benches out front and an enclosed garden beyond where kids and dogs can cheerfully run free – ask behind the bar for suggested walking routes if you're after a longer hike.

Food is foraged, organically home-grown and home-reared, and prepared with finesse. The menu is changed seasonally and may include potted crab, beef and ale cottage pie, venison haunch with bitter chocolate, Askham Hall cured meats with pickles, Lowther honey parfait and cherries, or dark chocolate tart with pistachios. Once you're fed and watered, mingle with the locals in the cosy bar or slump into a sofa next to the smouldering fire.

Opening hours
Mon-Sun noon-2.30pm, 6pm-9pm

George and Dragon, Clifton, Penrith CA10 2ER
WWW.GEORGEANDDRAGONCLIFTON.CO.UK   01768 865381

Larch Cottage

JUNCTION: 40; 10 MINUTES

A labour of love for owner Peter Stott, Larch Cottage is a rambling, theatrical beauty, a maze of Romanesque ruins, sculptures and individual, carefully designed gardens. Pass through a modest entrance at the side of a country lane and it's like stepping onto a stage. An elaborate clock tower stands sentry over a wonderland of winding paths and distinctive gardens.

The restaurant, La Casa Verde, is just as magical, a little chink of Italy with tiled floors, wooden beams and a vine-strung veranda overlooking the pond and gardens. Fresh food is hand-picked from the organic kitchen garden or sourced locally and slanted towards Italian cuisine – marinated olives, tonno e fagioli (marinated fresh tuna loin with mixed Italian beans, capers and rocket), thin-crust pizzas and a daily specials board. Homemade cakes and scones are served all day alongside artisan coffee and tea. Don't forget to visit Red Barn Art Gallery and shop before you leave to discover a hoard of paintings, sculptures, ceramics and handmade jewellery, together with an array of unique and unusual gifts.

Opening hours
Mon–Sun 9am-5pm

Larch Cottage, Larch Cottage Nurseries, Melkinthorpe, Penrith CA10 2DR
WWW.LARCHCOTTAGE.CO.UK   01931 712404

ICE CREAM PARLOUR

Abbott Lodge Jersey Ice Cream

JUNCTION: 40; 9 MINUTES

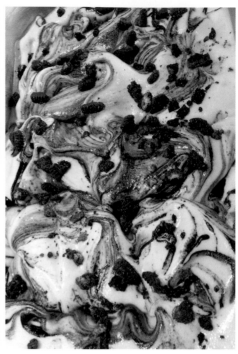

A family-run dairy farm at the edge of the Eden Valley and Lake District, people flock here for the ice cream – all 40 fabulous flavours of it. Choose from Just Jersey classic, mint choc chip, tiramisu, passion fruit, trifle, raspberry pavlova and a host of other delicious concoctions.

The charming, circular café is housed in a former gin case (horse-powered engine house: ask farmers Steve and Claire how it used to help thresh the harvest) and serves good tea and coffee along with traybakes and freshly made waffles; you can watch the milking on cow cam which shows the three robots that work 24-hours a day milking the free-range cows. Kids can burn off the ice cream in the playground at the front, which has a large, wooden play frame, ride on a tractor circuit for under-eights and charge about in oodles of space.

Be sure to visit the adorable calves in the barn alongside the café to meet the next generation of ice cream makers.

Opening hours
Mon–Sun 11am-5pm

Abbott Lodge Jersey Ice Cream, Abbott Lodge, Clifton CA10 2HD
WWW.ABBOTTLODGEJERSEYICECREAM.CO.UK   01931 712720

Askham Hall Café

JUNCTION: 40; 10 MINUTES

Once the Lonsdale family pile, this former manor house at the edge of the Lake District has been turned into an informally elegant hotel by Charlie Lowther, who grew up here.

Tucked away in a Grade II-listed barn in the beautiful gardens, the Kitchen Garden Café has low-beamed ceilings, cobbled floors and white-washed walls – and a counter filled with home-baked cakes and sausage rolls. The food is unmatched (stews, soups, fell lamb with wild garlic risotto) and the kitchen gardens provide much for the table. The oven outside is fired up on busy days for crispy pizzas, which can be enjoyed on benches in the scented orchard if the sun is shining.

Families will love exploring the animal trails, which take in the hall menagerie – shorthorn cattle, boer goats, ducks, chickens and rare-breed piggies. Signs point the way from the village road to the rear car park dedicated to café customers, and if the cafe is shut when you're passing, try one of the sister pubs: the Queen's Head in Askham or George & Dragon, Clifton.

Opening hours
Sun-Fri 10am-5pm (Easter-Oct)
Reduced hours and days in winter.

Askham Hall Café, Askham Hall, Askham, Penrith CA10 2PF
WWW.ASKHAMHALL.CO.UK/GARDENS-AND-CAFE/   01931 712350

Tebay Services

JUNCTION: 38-39; 0 MINUTES

The mothership of good motorway services, Tebay sits amid the pitching, fern-dabbled Cumbrian hills, a paragon of pit stops. In the Kitchen, delicious home-cooked food is heaped upon counters: sausage rolls, shortbreads, sausage and mash, frittata, sweet potato chilli and wedges of cake. Sup your coffee or freshly-squeezed juice by the picture windows and watch the famous Tebay ducks dabbling in the pond, while the kids frolic in the play area in the corner. On sunny days a BBQ is fired up on the terrace.

Before you leave, stock up at the Farmshop a wonderland of Cumbrian produce and covetable gifts: jams made from forest fruit, homemade pies, toffees from Penrith and artisan focaccias; the butchery counter stocks beef and lamb from the family farm. The shop is supplied by over 70 local producers within 30 miles of the services, many exclusive to Tebay. Order ahead and a cool bag will await you on arrival.

At the back, you'll find a hotel where ski-lodge chic intermingles with excellent food, smiley service and more of those wonderful views.

Opening hours
Mon-Sun 24 hours

Tebay Services, Orton, Penrith CA10 3SB
WWW.WESTMORELAND.COM   015396 24511

Three Hares Café

JUNCTION: 37; 10 MINUTES

For delicious, freshly baked goodies, look no further than the Three Hares, run with love by couple James and Nina. Nina is chief baker and her imaginative recipes are influenced by her upbringing in Dusseldorf (expect a range of ryes and sourdoughs), Japanese parents and her time with bakers of the north. Sweet treats might feature red wine and chocolate cake, banana and maple syrup loaf, and overfilled doughnuts.

The tiny shop in charming Sedbergh's old lanes is also a bustling café, often crowded with people savouring coffee and a book, and a large bay at the back looks out onto the fells.

Nearly all bakeries can be relied on for a good breakfast but here they're particularly tasty: crumpets, muesli and fresh fruit with good coffee. Tuck into hearty soups and sandwiches at lunch, perhaps rare roast beef and horseradish mayo, smoked mackerel and watercress or cheddar and pear chutney.

Opening hours
Tues-Sat 9am-5pm

Three Hares Café, 57 Main Street, Sedbergh LA10 5AB
WWW.THREEHARESCAFE.CO.UK   015396 21058

The Black Bull Inn

JUNCTION: 37; 10 MINUTES

When we first met James and Nina they were busy with their excellent cafe and bakery the Three Hares. It proved such a success that they snapped up the forlorn pub down the road and worked their same magic.

Now the Black Bull has been refurbished with easy-going style to create a smart neighbourhood local. The pair is hands-on and passionate about provenance – from Herdwick blankets to locally roasted artisan coffee. Nina bakes the breakfast bread and pastries, they do their own smoking and curing and there's a little kitchen garden at the back. Sample their inventive cooking at a table by the fire in the bar or in the airy restaurant with its floor-to-ceiling windows overlooking the street.

It's a short stroll to all the town's attractions, which include restaurants, antiques, a weekly farmers' market and heaps of book shops. Sedbergh is England's official Book Town, so even the bus shelter has a selection.

Opening hours
Mon-Sun 11am-11pm
(see website for food serving times)

The Black Bull Inn, 44 Main Street, Sedbergh LA10 5BL
WWW.THEBLACKBULLSEDBERGH.CO.UK   015396 20264

Low Sizergh Barn

JUNCTION: 36; 7 MINUTES

Low Sizergh is a paragon of happy animals, organic farming, community growing schemes, environmental stewardship and delectable local food. If only all farms were like this.

A café, farm shop and gift gallery are housed in a 17th-century barn which cuddles round a grassy courtyard where tables are set out in summer. A farm trail loops around the pond, woodland and fields, and includes fairy doors for little ones to spot, so don your wellies and work up an appetite.

The menu in the café is inspired by the farm: vegetable soups, hunks of quiche and farmer's salads on chunky crockery. Thick milkshakes are a sure-fire hit with children. Gallery windows in the café look down into the milking parlour - where else can you watch cows being milked while enjoying a cream tea?

The farm shop shelves are stacked with delicacies – local game, salami, cheeses and regional specialities such as Cumberland sausages and Morecambe Bay shrimp. Freshly baked cakes and shortbread are firm favourites with customers. And you can buy farm-grown organic veg as well as fruit from the orchard. Do try the raw milk from the dispenser – it's unpasteurised and tastes fantastically fresh and creamy.

Opening hours
9am-5.30pm (5pm café)

Low Sizergh Barn, Low Sizergh Farm, Sizergh, Kendal LA8 8AE
WWW.LOWSIZERGHBARN.CO.UK   01539 560426

Beetham Nurseries

JUNCTION: 36; 8 MINUTES

Beetham is a beautiful, Postman Pat-style village of stone houses, narrow lanes, and low walls on the Cumbria-Lancashire border. At its edge you'll find the nurseries, a modern garden centre washed with fresh air and floral scents. The Garden Café is blissful, with massive glass windows and a wide, table-scattered patio to make the most of glorious plants outside.

It's popular with the lunch crowd who stop in for roasted pepper, beetroot and feta sandwiches, crispy jacket potatoes filled with field mushrooms and Swiss cheese, or smoked haddock baked in Mornay sauce. Cakes, hot scones and fudgey brownies are made on-site and are perfect with the freshly ground coffee and Lancashire tea. An artisan food shop alongside sells cheese, deli treats, fresh pies and homemade cakes to take on your way.

Follow the path from the village up to Fairy Steps afterwards, where local legend has it that if you climb to the top without touching the gully sides, the fairies will grant you a wish.

Opening hours
Mon-Sat 9am-5.30pm
Sun 10am-4.30pm

Beetham Nurseries, Pool Darkin Lane, Beetham, Nr Milnthorpe LA7 7AP
WWW.BEETHAMNURSERIES.CO.UK   015395 63010

The Hall

JUNCTION: 34; 10 MINUTES

The flat whites at The Hall, an inauspicious looking 1930's Art Deco parish hall, have been voted the best in the UK. The secret to their success lies next door in the coffee roasters and tea merchants, known as Atkinsons, who have been trading here since 1837. It is steeped in tea and coffee history, with many artefacts, like canisters and scales, still in daily use. The old roaster in the window still puffs out its white smoke heralding every batch of freshly-roasted coffee. The smell alone on entering the shop is worth a visit. Behind the scenes the operation is a hotbed of innovation.

That same blend of heritage and innovation is evident in the café, where the materials palette is all stripped back maple and furniture constructed of upcycled coffee paraphernalia. This is a café run by coffee roasters who really know what they're doing and love to share their passion with their customers. Enjoy cake made daily in-house by The Bakery, sourdough sandwiches and live music on Saturdays. Worth going the extra mile for...

Opening hours
Mon-Fri 8am-6pm
Sat 8.30am-6pm
Sun 10am-5pm

The Hall, 10 China Street, Lancaster LA1 1EX
WWW.THECOFFEEHOPPER.COM   01524 65470

PUB

The Fleece Inn

JUNCTION: 33; 3 MINUTES

Walking and cycling routes abound in the Trough of Bowland, a wonderfully named Area of Outstanding Natural Beauty in Lancashire, and where good tramping lies, good pubs normally follow. Enter the Fleece, built in the 1600s as a farm and now transformed into a lovely local. It has the original exposed beams, stone fireplaces and flagstone floors that you'd expect from a character pub, updated with tartan upholstery, woollen rugs, Laura-Ashley-style blinds and cosy banquette booths. The menu has the same updated-traditional vibe: sausage and mash or vegetable cheese roulade for lunch; and then for dinner, crispy whitebait, seared scallops with crispy pork belly, steak and ale pie and rack of Pilling Marsh lamb with black cherry and rosemary jus.

A pleasant terrace garden features a log cabin for kids. Cementing its place in village life, a small shop to one side of the front door sells groceries (Atkinsons' coffee, Dolphinholme honey, Pennine Way preserves), local artwork and hand-whittled walking sticks.

Opening hours
Mon 4pm-10pm (drinks only)
Tues-Sat noon-11pm
Sun noon-10pm

The Fleece Inn, Dolphinholme, Lancaster LA2 9AQ
WWW.FLEECINN.CO.UK   01524 791233

The Applestore Café at Wyresdale Park

JUNCTION: 33; 11 MINUTES

Greenhouses, it seems, make wonderful cafés. The Applestore fills a beautifully rustic glasshouse – an old vinery. Scarlet rugs thrown over the stone floor, comfortably mismatched tables and turquoise pendant lights have turned it into a gastronomic den with a beautifully landscaped, sunny walled garden. Walk further to a fantastic adventure play area fashioned from fallen trees, stately redwoods and views over to the fells. For a longer leg stretch, the route to Nicky Nook viewpoint is close by; Tipsy the house dog has been known to tag along.

Specials include jacket potatoes with mushrooms in blue cheese, bean and chorizo soup, or a goat's cheese salad with fig chutney. You can normally expect overfilled barmcakes (rolls) served with coleslaw, salad and crisps, cured meat platters or sausage and mash.

Baking is an art form here and there's always a healthy selection to choose from: blackbean chocolate brownies, sultana and blueberry scones, strawberry gateaux. Fabulous.

Opening hours
Mon–Sun 9am-4pm

The Applestore Café Wyresdale Park, Snowhill Lane, Preston PR3 1BA
WWW.WYRESDALEPARK.CO.UK   01524 791011

Brockholes Nature Reserve

JUNCTION: 31; 2 MINUTES

© Bentham Imagery

© David Gaskell

Brockholes is a nature lover's paradise on the site of a (huge) former quarry. The visitor village is one-of-a-kind: strikingly modern and floating on the water. Here you'll find an informative visitor centre, activity room and good value café where you can fill up on simple, home-cooked dishes – full breakfasts, boiled eggs, jacket potatoes with homemade coleslaw, fresh soups and minced beef cobbler – while enjoying panoramic lake views. Pop in to the ice cream parlour for scoops of Lancashire ice cream before exploring the network of well-signposted paths around the expansive 250-acre site and the large adventure playground.

Shop at The Nest where you'll find a good range of gifts and local crafts and you'll be supporting the work of the Lancashire Wildlife Trust too.

The parking charge applies to everyone, regardless of how swift the visit, so it's worth making it a longer break.

Opening hours
Mon-Sun 10am-5pm (Apr-Oct)
Weds-Sun 10am-4pm (Nov-Mar)

(P) (&) (V)
(👪) (📶) (GF) (◊)

Brockholes Nature Reserve, Preston New Road, Samlesbury, Preston PR5 0AG
WWW.BROCKHOLES.ORG   01772 872000

Samlesbury Hall

JUNCTION: 31; 3 MINUTES

The folks at Samlesbury Hall have made a tremendous job of its rescue after the grand house was almost scrapped for timber in the 1920s, restoring the historic home and its impressively ornate, black-and-white exterior to glory. Witch hunts, priest holes, ghost stories – there's plenty of history to explore as well as the blooming gardens. Tours of the house are free and on Sundays are led by gruesome Janey the witch or portly Henry VIII.

Kids will love the fantastic, galleon-themed adventure playground as well as the host of animals – hens, rabbits, goats, sheep and Elvis and Ozzie, the Kunekune pigs. A fabulous restaurant serves simple dishes (the onion soup is highly recommended), afternoon teas and roasts on a Sunday, all made with ingredients from the estate. At Dottie's, claimed to be England's first wafflery, you can feast on sweet and savoury waffles (obviously), Lancashire ice cream and milkshakes. You could make your stop off a longer one and spend the night glamping in one of their fantastic Shepherd's huts (you can even bring the dog!).

Opening hours
Sun–Fri 10am–4pm.
Occasionally closed for weddings – call ahead to check.

Samlesbury Hall, Preston New Road, Samlesbury PR5 0UP
WWW.SAMLESBURYHALL.CO.UK   01254 812010

The Village Tea Room at Wheelton

JUNCTION: 28; 13 MINUTES

The Leeds and Liverpool Canal washes through this former weaving village, bringing with it crowds of narrow boats in the summer; from the top of nearby Heapey's Hill you can see stunning views of the West Pennine Moors and, on a good day, Blackpool Tower. It's worth stretching your legs and exploring Wheelton's Hovis-style sloping streets to make room for the much-fêted afternoon tea at the Village Tea Room. It's served in an individual picnic basket and includes finger sandwiches, fruit scones with cream and paper-wrapped slices of cake. Lighter lunches, such as Welsh rarebit and homemade soup, are also served. And if your eyes are bigger than your stomach you can pop any leftovers in a take-away bag for your onward journey.

The relaxed welcome encourages you to linger. Tables are arranged cosily over three levels, though the best seats in the house are undoubtedly those outside – weather permitting – overlooking the beautiful memorial clock tower. Revel in the tranquility - it's hard to believe you're close to the M6 and only a couple of miles from the M61 (junction 8).

Opening hours
Tues-Sat 9am-4.30pm
Sun 10am-4.30pm

The Village Tea Room at Wheelton, 202 Blackburn Road, Wheelton, Chorley PR6 8EY
WWW.THEVILLAGETEAROOMATWHEELTON.CO.UK   01254 830160

The Folly Coffee House & Deli

JUNCTION: 28; 9 MINUTES

Leyland's Worden Park is a haven of mature woodlands, meadows and playgrounds. The 18th-century outbuildings and parkland of what was once Worden Hall (destroyed by fire in 1941) have been rescued and the old stables have been recently colonised by the wonderful Folly Coffee House and Deli.

It's very much a family affair: sisters Lisa and Paula at the helm, Grandad (a farmer) supplies the veg and Mum and Nan bake magazine-worthy cakes. You can take away a picnic basket to enjoy in the glorious grounds, though many prefer the cosy, almost Victorian-style tea room, where breakfasts of avocado and feta on toast or lunches of black pudding ploughman's are cheerily served.

Dogs are as welcome as people: there's a dedicated shower in the car park for sluicing off furry friends after muddy walks and the Folly also has a doggy deli selling canine treats. The large public car park is a five-minute stroll and staff can provide a permit for the small, adjacent car park in inclement weather.

Opening hours
Mon-Sat 9am-4pm
Sun 10am-4pm

The Folly Coffee House & Deli, Wordern Arts & Crafts Centre, The Avenue, Leyland PR25 1DJ
01772 622707

Red Bank Farm

JUNCTION: 22; 5 MINUTES

A pen of goats bleat for their breakfast outside Red Bank Farm Shop, while Limousin and Angus cows graze in the fields behind. The meat is as fresh as it comes, with much of the produce reared here, and convenient BBQ or breakfast boxes make picking the best cuts easy.

Step through the racing-green doors and you'll find shelves loaded with free-range eggs, flours, preserves, Cheshire honey, dipping crackers and fresh pies to take away. A small but stylish café – painted a charcoal grey with dark wood cladding and cheery festoon lights, and decorated with vintage posters and hessian coffee sacks – serves excellent breakfasts, lunches and coffees.

Breakfast might be bacon on barm cake (bread roll) or smoked salmon and cream cheese on toast; lunch a hot roast beef baguette with caramelised onion gravy or meatball sub, slathered with cheese. In the afternoon, snack on pork pies, sinful gluten-free brownies or chocolate and peanut butter flapjacks.

Opening hours
Weds-Fri 10am-6pm
Sat 10am-5pm
Sun 10am-3pm

Red Bank Farm, Winwick Road, Newton Le Willows WA12 8DU
WWW.FARMSHOPNORTHWEST.CO.UK   01925 292 470

Kenyon Hall Farm

JUNCTION: 22; 1 MINUTE

A working farm on the Cheshire and Lancashire countryside, Kenyon Hall Farm has been tended by the Bulmer family for generations, and the personal touch shows. In the Farm shop you'll find fresh seasonal fruit and veg, home-cooked jams, chutneys and cakes, speciality cheeses and meats, honey from the hives and oven-warm bread – perfect for a gold-standard picnic.

Everything served in the café – soups, stews, sandwiches, salads and cakes – are made fresh in the kitchen using local ingredients. Breakfast is a vision of traditional farmhouse cooking, especially the hearty fry ups with 'proper' sausage, bacon, and free-range eggs served with rich Italian coffee and pots of tea.

In spring, the Plant Centre is in full bloom and a delight to browse. Come summer, the pick-your-own fields open for harvesting strawberries, raspberries, currants and more. The autumn Maize Maze is a must for kids and adults alike; the outdoor play area is great addition and was revamped this year.

Opening hours
Mon–Sun 9am–5pm

Kenyon Hall Farm, Winwick Lane, Croft WA3 7ED
WWW.KENYONHALL.CO.UK   01925 765531

Arley Hall

You'll find this characterful Jacobean-style gem down Cheshire's leafy lanes, in a sea of magnificently tended gardens. The fine stately home (still home to Lord and Lady Ashbrook) and its grand clock tower, intricate carvings, Elizabethan cruck barn and grand state rooms are well worth the entrance fee. Horticulturists will love moseying around the vast, effervescent gardens, celebrated borders and hothouse, while you can tire out the kids and dogs on the woodland walk.

The Gardener's Kitchen is open to all, even those not visiting the house; just get a free sticker from the kindly volunteers at the entrance. Cross the cobbled courtyard and you'll find a vaulted barn strung with lights and proudly decorated with the family heraldry. Specials are chalked up behind the modern counter, which is filled with salads, sandwiches and cakes, many prepared to the 18th-century recipes of Elizabeth Raffald, the Delia of her day who learned her craft here.

Opening hours
Mon-Sun 10am-5pm (11am winter)

Arley Hall, Arley Hall & Gardens, Northwich CW9 6NA
WWW.ARLEYHALLANDGARDENS.COM   01565 777353

The Lambing Shed

JUNCTION: 19; 10 MINUTES

Lambs once took their first tentative steps in this wooden barn. Today, the sheep have gone and the Lambing Shed has become a modern farm shop stocking Cheshire's finest produce. A bank of floor-to-ceiling windows make the former barn sunny and light and the shop is stocked to the brim with delicious products sourced to the philosophy of 'fresh, local and simple'. Head to the deli for hamper-worthy cheese, charcuterie and homemade pies and coleslaw.

From an elegant patio studded with neatly trimmed box hedges and shady tables you can glimpse the 400 acres of Cheshire fields from which the Mitchell family have been producing award-winning meats for decades. The meat is available to buy in the butchery (ask Master Butcher Stewart for advice) or to eat in the deli and café, where you'll find burgers, house-cured bacon and freshly baked sausage rolls; all the lamb and beef comes straight from the farm. For lighter bites, there's Tatton rarebit, quiche of the day or a slab of home-baked cake.

Opening hours
Mon-Sat 9am-5.30pm
Sun 10am-4pm

The Lambing Shed, Moseley Hall Farm, Chelford Road, Knutsford WA16 8RB
WWW.THELAMBINGSHED.COM   01565 631027

PUB

The Three Greyhounds Inn

JUNCTION: 18; 7 MINUTES

A handsome, open-armed pub just minutes from the M6. Inside is snug and easy-going: chairs and benches strewn with royal purple cushions cluster around copper-clad fireplaces; tankards hang from a pot rack. Outside there's a lawned garden where kids can play (till 9.30pm) and a patio terrace where blankets hang thoughtfully on chairs for chillier evenings.

Food is tasty and imaginative, perhaps the legendary homemade chicken, smoked ham, leek and tarragon pie, or the seafood sharing platter with smoked salmon, scampi, smoked mackerel pâté and half a pint of prawns. Round off with a chocolate brownie, delicious Cheshire farm ice cream or the artisan cheese board.

Dogs are so welcome they've even introduced a 'dog beer' (made from meat-based stock) so four-legged friends can drink companionably with their owners. Enjoy a walk afterwards with a lovely loop around Shakerely Mere lake.

Opening hours
Mon-Thurs 10.30am-11pm
Fri & Sat 10.30am-11.30pm
Sun 10.30am-10.30pm

The Three Greyhounds Inn, Holmes Chapel Road, Allostock, Knutsford WA16 9JY
WWW.THETHREEGREYHOUNDSINN.CO.UK   01565 723455

Jodrell Bank Discovery Centre

JUNCTION: 18; 14 MINUTES

© Mike Peel, Jodrell Bank Centre for Astrophysics

Earthlings and would-be astronauts pull in here to be wowed by the enormous, 90m-high Lovell Telescope. Built in 1957 and the world's first steerable radio telescope, the Cheshire landmark is still a working part of Manchester University where scientists probe the cosmos to reveal its secrets. You'll need to buzz to enter and turn your phone off to avoid interference with the radio signals. Educational and interactive displays in the space, star and planet pavilions are fascinating for children and adults alike, teaching the curious about the Big Bang, how the telescope works and mysteries of the observable universe.

Mind filled, turn your attention to tummies in the Planet Pavilion Café, which serves hearty breakfasts and appetising lunches. Cakes, salads, pasties and sandwiches are made on-site every day and can be enjoyed in the airy café or on the terrace. There are 35 acres of tended grounds where you're welcome to stroll and picnic.

Opening hours
Mon–Sun 10am–5pm

Jodrell Bank Discovery Centre, Macclesfield SK11 9DL
WWW.JODRELLBANK.NET   01477 571766

The Old Barn

JUNCTION: 17/18; 15 MINUTES

A dash through leafy Cheshire towards Macclesfield leads to pretty countryside and breakfast or lunch at The Old Barn. Housed in a red-brick stable block, the cycle-friendly café is bright and unfussy with oak beams. Parasolled tables are hemmed in by troughs of lavender and greenery.

The menu is simple but tasty, making good use of the farm produce: cooked breakfasts, sandwiches and deep-filled pies, as well as quiche, pie and soup of the day – perhaps carrot and red lentil soup, or stilton, bacon and mushroom quiche. The counter is loaded with cakes beneath shiny glass domes, with flavours from Ferrero Rocher (sublime) to cherry frangipane. You can pick up groceries from the shelves in the café – milk, bread, meat, eggs, and some of those delicious pastries – so you won't have to go without a cuppa on arrival at your destination.

Next door, the old farm shop has been converted into a game café, so if you've had enough of I Spy, select a board game and pull up a chair!

Opening hours
Wed-Sat & Bank Hol Mon 9.30am-4pm

The Old Barn, Manchester Road, Marton SK11 9HF
WWW.FACEBOOK.COM/THEOLDBARNMARTON   01260 224344

The Wheatsheaf

JUNCTION: 17; 3 MINUTES

The ever-hospitable Pear family, who are also behind the popular (and posh) Pecks restaurant down the road in Congleton, continue to improve the Wheatsheaf. Since taking over the down-at-the-heel hostelry just a few years ago, they have restored its coaching inn glory. Behind heavy front doors, the large Victorian pub – red brick with castellated bays, and gables peeping out of the attic – has been turned into a gleaming gastropub with nine chic bedrooms above.

The dining room has had an art deco facelift: shimmering velvet banquettes, golden pineapples and dusky lighting. Blankets hang considerately on the back of chairs on the terrace, which twinkles with fairy lights. It's opulent but comfortable; you could just as easily drop in for a coffee or a three-course meal. Start the day right with a Wheatsheaf breakfast or fill up properly at lunch and dinner with a well-rounded menu, including dishes such as beef and mushroom pie or pan-fried hake and baby octopus. Round off with a passion fruit and white chocolate cheesecake or an old English trifle.

Opening hours
Sun-Thurs noon-midnight
Fri-Sat noon-1am

The Wheatsheaf, 1 Hightown, Sandbach CW11 1AG
WWW.WHEATSHEAFSANDBACH.CO.UK   01270 762013

Skirt Alsager's mill pond and countryside pub to find the Hall Farm Shop, a friendly family business housed in an old milking parlour at the edge of the farmyard. The shop is known for its butchery, stocking meat from neighbouring farms. It has a good range of homemade sausages, burgers, cuts and ready-to-cook options for cheats (meatballs, chicken carveries in the fresh counter, plenty more in the freezer). The deli is perfect for picnics and pantries. Stock up on cooked meats, a delicious range of cheeses (Caerphilly and leek our favourite), olives, jams, chutneys, fresh bread and sausage rolls. There's also a range of gifts, greeting cards and books.

The café has a warm feel, with tiled floor, chunky wooden furniture and copper pendulum lights hanging over the sage-green counter. Dishes are made to order by the cook, who has a talent for soups, quiches, sandwiches and cakes; cooked breakfasts are a real crowd-pleaser and are served till 2pm.

Opening hours
Tues-Sat 9am-4pm
Sun 10am-3pm

Hall Farm Shop & Café, Alsager Hall Farm, Alsager ST7 2UB
WWW.HALLFARMSHOPALSAGER.CO.UK   01270 876449

Middleport Pottery

JUNCTION: 16; 11 MINUTES

A canalside café true to its industrial roots, Middleport Pottery's Tea room is a gem. Obsolete machine bases have been turned into tables, lightshades fashioned from teapots and a delicate blue mural reflects the Burleigh pottery made here. Only a few years ago the factory was facing closure but it was rescued by the Prince's Regeneration Trust and turned into a wonderful heritage centre that gives a real glimpse of industrial, Victorian England.

Unpretentious homemade food is served on blue and white china, naturally. Rich coffee and various teas are on offer. The Staffordshire oatcakes with bacon and cheese are a firm favourite; cooked breakfasts are generous and lunches simple but filling – toasties, jacket potatoes and paninis. Sit on the outdoor patio and watch the narrowboats glide past.

The museum is well worth a visit and there's a year-round programme of events to entertain kids, from clay craft to a Mad Hatter's Tea Party.

Opening hours
Mon–Sun 10am–4pm

Middleport Pottery, Port Street, Stoke-on-Trent ST6 3PE
WWW.MIDDLEPORTPOTTERY.ORG   01782 499766

Emma Bridgewater Café & Garden

JUNCTION: 15; 10 MINUTES

Cosy and inviting with iron windows, bare brick walls and wooden panelling, the café at the Emma Bridgewater factory is a diamond of a staging post. Colourful walls, industrial accents, steel girders and low hanging lights remind you that this is a working factory. There's even a cream Aga decorated in the same coloured dots that have made Emma Bridgewater a household name.

Coffee is smooth, tea is delicate, and the tasty food is often inspired by Emma's recipes. The menu includes seasonal specials, such as homemade marmalade on toast, quiches, sandwiches, daily soups, yummy cakes and children's lunchboxes. The secret walled garden is a thoughtful, environmentally considerate haven overflowing with colourful blooms.

If you've got time to spare, the experience day is worthwhile: an award-winning factory tour, afternoon tea and a session in the decorating studio.

Dogs are welcome in courtyard area.

Opening hours
Mon– Sat 9.30am–5.30pm
Sun 10am–4pm

Emma Bridgewater Café & Garden, Lichfield Street, Hanley ST1 3EJ
WWW.EMMABRIDGEWATER.CO.UK   01782 201 328

The Fitzherbert Arms

JUNCTION: 15; 8 MINUTES

'The Fitz' as it's known to locals, was spruced up recently, breathing fresh life into a tired old boozer and transforming it into a glamorous gastropub. Large windows give a glimpse of the bar, where chunky furniture, leather wingback chairs, jugs of flowers and open fires cosily intermingle.

In the evening, the dining room has a stately feel, all gleaming gilt, swagged drapes, polished wood, inky tones and twinkling candlelight. Food is home-cooked and wholesome: wild boar sausages with bubble and squeak mash, steak and Swynnerton Stout pie and Fitz Mess, a delicious concoction of meringue, cream and seasonal fruits.

Custom-built furniture in the garden incorporates climbing plants and topiary twisted with fairy lights. The lovely Staffordshire countryside is perfect for a ramble to help you build up an appetite and there are suggested routes on their website.

Opening hours
Mon-Sat 11am-11pm
Sun 11am-10.30pm

The Fitzherbert Arms, Swynnerton, Stone ST15 0RA
WWW.FITZHERBERTARMS.CO.UK   01782 796782

Canalside Farm Shop & Café

JUNCTION: 14; 15 MINUTES

You're as likely to rub shoulders with narrowboaters as landlubbers at this countryside farm shop, thanks to its position right alongside the Trent and Mersey Canal. It's a longstanding fixture here, having been growing, selling, cooking and serving the best of Staffordshire's produce since 1983.

Head directly to the cafe for cooked breakfasts, chicken goujons, pulled pork flatbreads, panini and jacket potatoes. Much of the fruit and veg is grown right here on the farm so the flavours and food miles are pretty unbeatable.

The strawberries here are excellent, and can be picked in season (pumpkins in autumn) or tasted in the jam, doughnuts, and even gin. Punnets are sold in the farm shop, along with almost everything you could need for your destination, whether sausages from the butchery, a warm loaf of bread from the bakery or a tranche of pâté from the deli counter.

It's in the crook of the M6, M6 Toll and M42 so you can cut a corner if you're planning on linking up with any of those roads rather than retrace your steps. The beautiful Cannock Chase is just to the south and a rewarding detour if you want to stretch your legs with a woodland walk.

Opening hours
Mon-Sun 9am-5pm

Canalside Farm Shop & Café, Mill Lane, Great Hayward ST18 0RQ
WWW.CANALSIDEFARM.CO.UK   01889 881747

Essington Farm

JUNCTION: 11; 7 MINUTES

The sprawling Essington Farm has been run by the Simkin family since 1892, selling field-fresh produce year-round (sometimes only hours out of the ground) as well as hosting a pick-your-own field and plant nursery.

Newly renovated, the farm shop and deli is large and stacked with islands of fresh and store-cupboard produce to plunder for a very respectable picnic – award-winning pork pies, fresh juices, slabs of pâté and local honey. The butcher's counter sells free-range pork and Hereford beef reared in the fields outside the window, priding itself on traditional service with a smile. Pick up some speciality sausages, made in-house, for a delicious BBQ treat.

The kitchen staff delight in raiding those shelves for the delicious restaurant food, whether fresh pies, salads, traybakes, soups or roasts with all the trimmings: straight to the fork without even leaving the farm.

Opening hours
Mon–Sun 9am–5pm (4.30pm for restaurant).

Essington Farm, Bognop Road, Essington WV11 2AZ
WWW.ESSINGTONFARM.CO.UK   01902 735724

The INDEX

The INDEX

The INDEX

The INDEX

The INDEX

MAPS Maps are, as you can see, not to scale. They're intended as a guide to show you the approximate location of each place (shown on the map by a flag with the relevant page number), but you'll need a sat nav or smart phone to guide you in: or a detailed road map if you're feeling adventurous.

OPENING TIMES We generally list the times a place is open but, this doesn't always mean the kitchen is open. Do check ahead (we've listed websites and phone numbers) to make sure you won't go hungry.

SYMBOLS Below each entry you'll see a run of symbols indicating what you can expect. They're based on information given to us by owners but things to change, so treat them as a guide rather than gospel.

 Dog friendly: places that accept dogs in some or all inside areas. Be aware that sometimes these areas are restricted and dogs must be on leads. Some have seasonal variations so it's worth checking ahead.

 Child friendly: Specific attractions for kids or places with good play areas.

 Disabled access: People with limited mobility can access the main venue. Some of our venues are old and listed, so won't always be fully accessible.

 WiFi: Free WiFi for visitors.

 Vegetarian or vegan options: A good range of vegetarian options for our meat-free friends, vegan if possible.

 Gluten-fee: One of the most common dietary restrictions these days, so we've highlighted places which can accommodate gluten-free diets and have alternatives on their menus.

 Organic: Food produced with a lighter environmental touch, or with a good number of options made from organic ingredients.

 Parking: Parking available onsite.

 Electric car-charging: Though this is a book centred on the car, it is also devoted to doing things better, so, being firm advocates of the electric car, we've noted any places where you can charge your electro-steed.

 Recycling/sustainability practices: Solar panels, bio fuels, recycled water and sustainable materials; we've marked out the venues going the extra mile towards minimising their impact on the planet.